ANNO DOMINI

THE STORY OF CHRISTIANITY IN THE BRITISH ISLES

ANNO DOMINI

THE STORY OF

CHRISTIANITY

IN THE

BRITISH ISLES

Frances Marrow

Matador
9 Priory Business Park,
Wistow Road, Kibworth Beauchamp,
Leicestershire, LE8 0RX
Tel: 0116 279 2299
Email: books@troubador.co.uk
Web: www.troubador.co.uk/matador
Twitter: @matadorbooks

ISBN 978 1788033 732

British Library Cataloguing in Publication Data.
A catalogue record for this book is available from the British Library.

Printed and Bound in the UK by 4Edge Limited
Typeset in 12pt Minion Pro by Troubador Publishing Ltd, Leicester, UK

Matador is an imprint of Troubador Publishing Ltd

My thanks to my husband
for his general support
and for typing the manuscript

CONTENTS

Soon after its arrival, Christianity has to compete not only with native pagan cults but also with the wide pantheon of Roman gods and sporadic persecution. When the Emperor Constantine decides in favour of Christianity, in the early fourth century, the Church has greater freedom to develop, which occurs largely in the towns.

The departure of the Romans in the early fifth century is closely followed by the arrival of the pagan Anglo-Saxons, but the Church is able to survive throughout the West, particularly in Wales, helped by the new monasticism from Gaul. St Patrick, meanwhile, has taken the faith to Ireland. The Age of the Celtic Saints has been born.

In England, recovery comes through King Alfred and the kingdom of Wessex, while the Danes remain in the north-east. The art of the sculptured high cross reaches its peak in the Celtic countries. The Vikings are gradually Christianised in the tenth century. Dioceses are restored, the parish system develops and monasticism is renewed – a new phase of Anglo-Saxon culture has begun.

The Norman Conquest impacts the Church in every area and brings two Italians to Canterbury as archbishops, via the monastery of Bec in Normandy. Magnificent church building follows. The state struggles to maintain power over the Church and Becket is martyred. New orders of monks and canons are created, together with orders of crusaders and friars.

The fourteenth and fifteenth centuries bring a period of questioning – about the papacy, indulgences and monasticism – most potently, through Wycliffe and the Lollards, also through writers such as Chaucer and Langland. Influences from the Continent add to the ferment: the Renaissance, humanism, the invention of printing, the beginning of Bible translation and, in Germany, Luther acts as the catalyst for the Reformation on the Continent.

In the sixteenth century, Henry VIII's break with Rome begins the Reformation here, confirmed under Edward VI and given liturgical form by Cranmer, then reversed for four years by Queen Mary. Finally, a Protestant settlement under Elizabeth makes attendance at the Church of England obligatory. Roman Catholicism becomes illegal and the number of dissenting groups increases. A different resolution begins to emerge in each of the Celtic countries.

In the seventeenth century, confrontation between the king and parliament leads to the death of Charles I, Civil War and, temporarily, to a Presbyterian national church. When the monarchy is restored in 1660, so too is the Church of England. Dissent is more firmly established: Scotland insists on Presbyterianism, dissent grows stronger in Wales and Ireland remains largely Roman Catholic.

The eighteenth century opens with the Evangelical Revival and the spread of Methodism. The

INTRODUCTION

For almost two thousand years, the Christian faith has been making its impact on the world, and has assumed many faces as each culture finds its own way of expressing it and celebrating it. Even within the small compass of Britain and Ireland, there have been and are different shades of understanding and emphasis, and different modes of expression.

The story of the first thousand years here is set against a background of foreign invasions and aggression between kingdoms, when the advance of Christianity against paganism rested largely on the decisions of kings – if the king was persuaded to adopt it then his people became nominally Christian, at least while he lived. That the British Isles were eventually Christianised at this stage owed much to the monastic movement, which had its origin in the deserts of third-century Egypt.

Our search for evidence of the spread of the Christian faith in the early years takes us to wells and caves that bear witness in some way to Christian activity, to isolated spots where a carved cross tells its own story, and to islands and lonely places where monasteries once flourished. Traces of early building are scant, but other legacies survive, among them beautiful manuscripts such as the Book of

Kells. Early writings fill out the story – of the fifth-century St Patrick; of the monk Gildas, writing probably in Wales in the sixth century; and the more substantial work of the Venerable Bede, a monk of Northumbria, who wrote the remarkable *History of the English Church and People* in the eighth century.

The second millennium tells a very different story. During the course of the Middle Ages the Church became a powerful force, allied to the state and exercising its influence in every area of life. Visual evidence abounds in magnificent medieval buildings. Much art, music and literature was inspired by the Christian faith throughout these centuries, while our laws, our education system and our social institutions became permeated by it. With power came corruption, abuses and disquiet. Reformation followed, with fragmentation in its wake as denominations multiplied. Since then, the discoveries of science and the scrutiny of critical scholarship have challenged the Christian claim and opened up public debate. After the rapid secularisation of the twentieth century, we now live in what is commonly described as the post-Christian era.

Freed from state imposition and social obligation, Christianity is now seen to depend, as it did initially, on the body of committed believers. They bear witness to their faith against a much-changed scenario, where people of other world faiths bear witness to theirs, where sects proliferate and atheism makes its voice clearly heard. Yet interest in spirituality is not lacking and many wait to be persuaded.

I

FROM JERUSALEM TO THE BRITANNIC ISLES

Before the coming of Christianity

To begin to understand the impact Christianity first made in these islands, we need to take into account the way of life of the inhabitants at that time. Their values and beliefs coloured their understanding of the new faith, and, for a while at least, their practice of it.

What kind of people were here when Christianity first came? Successive waves of Celtic tribes had joined earlier inhabitants, bringing with them the culture and religion that they held in common, and their related languages. The latest arrivals, the Belgae, had settled in eastern Kent and Hampshire, and were already partly Romanised.

The area around Salisbury Plain had long been a centre of civilisation. Along with Somerset, Dorset and the Cotswolds, it formed a rich region with a well-organised population gifted in the arts. Around the Humber was a culture of similar origin, but more warlike in character among the tribes of the Brigantes. Other areas were developing more slowly.

There were many defensive hillforts, some reused from an earlier age, which served not only to house people, cattle and workshops but as assembly points for the population. More than three thousand lie scattered throughout England, Wales and Scotland, from Maiden Castle in the south of England to less hospitable places such as Ingleborough in the north, from the forts of Snowdonia to Traprain Law in Lothian. Among the Belgae in the south the use of hillforts was dying out, and the towns of Silchester and Chichester were being created. One wonders what the native inhabitants of the Wrekin in Shropshire would think as they later watched the Roman town of Wroxeter take shape on the plain below, with its large basilica, its forum and its heated baths. In Ireland, there were many ringforts and a few hillforts, some associated with kingship and pagan religion, such as Tara in County Meath, seat of the high king of Ireland, and Emain Macha at Armagh; both were to figure on St Patrick's itinerary.

While most working people were engaged in agriculture, there was some industry. Apart from the iron smelting, which gave the age its name, tin, lead, silver and gold were mined, and there was a flourishing trade with Gaul (roughly present-day France) and with Mediterranean countries. There were also craftsmen and fine metalworkers, to judge from some of the pieces that have survived, including torcs (close-fitting metal necklaces), and fine swords and shields such as the elaborately designed example in bronze and enamel recovered from the Thames at Battersea. Their swirling, exciting designs would reappear in a Christian context later in stone sculptures and in manuscripts.

These weapons and the existence of so many defensive

hillforts bear witness to the very active warrior class in Celtic society – including head-hunters, for whom the severed head was an object of some superstition, which was imbued with other-worldly power, and thought to avert evil and provide protection, to judge from early folk tales. A legacy of the cult survives to our own time in the heads and gargoyles on medieval buildings.

Not all the warriors were men. Boudicca offers an awesome example of a Celtic woman at war. The rebellion that she led against the Romans in AD 60 gives us some idea of the ferocity of the Celtic warriors, who burnt down Colchester, London and other settlements in their path, taking no prisoners. The Roman Tacitus, writing soon after the event, confirms their eagerness to destroy the enemy by cutting throats, hanging, burning or crucifying.

The picture that emerges overall from classical writers, and from early Irish and Welsh literature has two aspects: one of a pastoral people in close communion with nature, and the other of a full-blooded warrior class with a zest for fighting, feasting and storytelling. As they came face to face with the mysteries of life and death, what were their beliefs and how did they express them?

In his book *The Gallic Wars*, Julius Caesar claims that all Celts believed themselves to be descended from one ancestor, the god Dis, father of all, and that they believed in a life after death. Their priests, the druids, were a powerful group in Celtic society and responsible for worship rituals. These were held in the open air in groves and clearings where an oak tree grew. According to Strabo, a first-century geographer, and others, the sacrifices they offered were sometimes human, and human entrails were used to divine the future; we have no means of knowing the extent of such practice. The druids' role was not only that of priest: they also acted as judges and ran schools to hand on their knowledge. As priests, educators and judges, the druids exercised considerable power and, from early in the first century, the Romans sought to suppress them.

But the druids, together with the bards and diviners associated with them, constitute just one element in the Celtic religious scene. In addition to the gods commonly worshipped among Celtic tribes, evidence suggests that the ordinary people had their own localised cults, as they sought to placate and persuade the unknown powers they felt were manifested around them in the natural world – a world that gave a pattern to their year.

Traces of their festivals remain in our own calendar. Samhain on November 1st became All Saints or All Hallows Day, and their belief that spiritual forces were abroad at this time is still perpetuated in Halloween. May 1st, a date that still has some significance for us, was the festival of Beltane (literally the fires of Bel) to honour the sun and celebrate the defeat of darkness, when the cattle were driven out to open grazing and great fires were lit, which is a practice that continued for a long time in folk tradition. On August 1st came Lughnasa, the feast of the Celtic god Lugh or Lugus, a celebration for the fruits of the harvest. This became Lammas-tide, Lammas being literally the "loaf-mass", celebrated throughout the Middle Ages, and surviving in many fairs and carnivals.

Living as close to nature as they did, the Celts appear to have believed that all things natural possessed an in-dwelling spirit to whom they gave a name. So Sinnan gave her name to the River Shannon, Clota to the Clyde and Sabrina to the Severn. Since water spelled fertility, rivers, wells and springs were focal points of their ritual practices. The warm springs at Buxton gave rise to the cult of Arnemetia, while at Bath the cult of Sulis flourished. Wells were especially significant to the people to judge from the quantity of objects found in them, and were later Christianised in an attempt to absorb rather than suppress pagan practices. It made good sense not to antagonise in an age of transition. So, wells came to be used for Christian baptism or as a preaching point, and the local saint replaced the local pagan god associated with the well. The well-dressing practised particularly in Derbyshire is a legacy from our pagan past put into a Christian context, with Biblical themes and receiving the blessing of the Church.

The Celtic horned god with a serpent was later to become a special object of attack by Christians. It appears on the Clonmacnoise Cross in County Offaly and in illuminated manuscripts as a symbol of Satan. Of interest, too, are the groups of three figures, thought to be mother goddesses, and groups of three hooded figures. The number three seems to have been significant to the Celts, as a part of their idea of divinity, which must later have made the concept of the Trinity more accessible. The area around Hadrian's Wall, with its concentration of Roman soldiers and civilians settling close to their camps, was found to be particularly rich in evidence for native cults, as were the areas around Cirencester, Gloucester and Bath.

The Roman invasion under Claudius in AD 43 broke into this Celtic world and, inevitably, evidence for native cults is overlaid with that for Roman cults, since the Romans brought with them their own wide selection of gods and goddesses. Some four hundred inscriptions to them have been found. They brought Emperor-worship too and cults from the east.

Mithraism was an exclusively male cult, which appealed especially to soldiers, with demanding initiation rites. The remains of five temples to Mithras have been discovered, three on Hadrian's Wall. Yet, no doubt, many of the soldiers would have thought it wise to keep on the right side of the local gods too, and, after what may have been initial confusion, Celtic and Roman gods settled down alongside each other. Where there were similarities they merged, as at Bath where the local god Sulis and the Roman Minerva were combined. The Celtic god Maponus was equated with Apollo – an altar stone to Apollo Maponus is built into the crypt of St Andrew's Church at Hexham.

The Roman occupation lasted three and a half centuries, and slowly there emerged a Romano-British culture in which the Celtic gods generally prevailed over the Roman. One feature of this culture was the construction of small temples, often on hilltops on the sites of earlier simple Celtic structures, often a square within a square – an inner shrine, surrounded by a covered walk-way, like the one found within the hillfort at Maiden Castle. Here, individuals could bring offerings or petitions.

While the Romans were tolerant of other religions, their tolerance did not extend to the druids. In AD 60, large numbers of druids were massacred in their stronghold on Anglesey, so Tacitus tells us. It seems their power was broken. The extent to which druidism persisted in the country at large is not known. It is thought that there were still druids on Iona when St Columba arrived there in the sixth century. Their authority and status may well have survived in places. St Columba encountered some during his efforts to convert the Picts, according to his biographer. Certainly, they continued in Ireland, which was untouched by the Roman occupation. To some extent, druidism there merged into Christianity.

The early bearers of Christianity to these islands had

the formidable task of unseating the Celtic and Roman gods from the minds of the people, and turning them from superstitions and sorcery, the dark practices referred to later in the penitentials, and from sacrifices.

What was the alternative they offered? The belief that there is only one God, the Creator of the world, and that He had come to share our life on earth in the then recent times in Palestine, in the historical figure of Jesus Christ. Born a Jew, Jesus lived His early years in obscurity under Roman occupation, but the last two to three years of His short life were spent as an itinerant preacher, teaching the people how they should live in order to be in harmony with God. He also performed many acts of healing. He summarised His teaching in two commands "Love the Lord your God with all your heart and with all your soul and with all your mind and with all your strength" (Mark 12:30) and "Love your neighbour as yourself" (Mark 12:31). This way of life would bring about what He described as the Kingdom of God, or the Kingdom of Heaven.

He cared particularly about those who found themselves on the margins of society and associated with them freely, more concerned with individual human needs than with a strict observance of Jewish law and tradition; this set many of His fellow Jews against Him. He chose twelve men to be His close companions and helpers, known as His disciples, and later His apostles. According to the accounts in the four Gospels of the New Testament, He spoke of God as His Father and of their oneness, and accepted the title of Son of God, which many gave Him, though He often referred to Himself as the Son of Man. To many learned Jews, He assumed an authority they found blasphemous, while His following among the ordinary people increased.

The disturbing challenge that He posed to the

establishment, both religious and secular, exacerbated by the tensions of life in an occupied country, led to His crucifixion as a common criminal when He was about thirty-three years old. This brutal outcome has, in its turn, challenged many in subsequent generations to reflect on that event and even more on its sequel.

For the devastation of His close followers at His death was transformed when they found that His death was not final. According to the New Testament accounts, they encountered Him again on several occasions and talked with Him. His resurrection confirmed their belief that He was, indeed, the Son of God, and His crucifixion a supreme demonstration of the love of God for humanity. This was the source and inspiration of the new faith, and of the Christian Church, which came into being; its main festival a joyful celebration each year of His resurrection, on what became known in the British Isles as Easter Day.

When Jesus finally left His disciples, He commanded them to tell the world what they had seen. He had already promised that the Spirit of God would be with all those who believed, to enable them to live as He had taught and to spread the new faith. This promise was fulfilled at the feast of Pentecost, fifty days after Easter, when His followers experienced the coming of the Spirit of God, or the Holy Spirit. This became the second most important festival of the early Church. Furthermore, Jesus had promised, and His resurrection had shown, that death was not the end and that a personal relationship with God – Father, Son and Holy Spirit – would continue after death. Extraordinary news, intended to renew the world!

With the coming of Christ, the world was presented with a new concept: the supreme power of love in a creation where each individual is important to the Creator – a difficult concept for the Celtic warrior or the Roman soldier. For those struggling simply to live, in harsh and insecure conditions, the message of help for the present and hope for the future would have had much to offer. Among the Celts, the idea of one God had been dimly foreshadowed by their belief in their common ancestor, Dis, father of all, while their deep-seated awe before the world of nature prepared them for the idea of God as the creator and sustainer of the universe. Among the Jews, their holy writings had foretold the coming of a Messiah, an "anointed one" – in Greek "the Christ" – to lead his people. Some Jews saw Jesus as fulfilling this prophecy. In every generation since there have been men and women, from all walks of life, who have responded to the person and teaching of the historical Jesus, who have believed that He was God incarnate – Son of God and Son of Man – and who have found their belief confirmed by experience as they lived out the precepts of the new faith. For Christianity was never an abstract theory, but a way of life – early Christians were known as followers of the Way – a way of life made clear in the life and teaching of Jesus, where love is the guiding principle, love for God expressed in worship and love for others expressed in service; and where the humble, the peacemakers and the merciful are commended. Its significance was universal. The message has sometimes appeared fragile down the years, often diluted, often distorted, but its essence remains.

The Early Days of the Church

Stories to describe the beginnings of Christianity in these islands abound, including one that Jesus himself came to the West Country as a boy with Joseph of Arimathea, who was the man who offered his tomb for the crucified Jesus, and that Joseph later returned and founded the first

Christian church in Britain at Glastonbury. More prosaic minds believe that Christianity was brought by traders and Romans, and had probably arrived by the second century. The early Church Fathers, Tertullian and Origen, writing in the early third century, both claim that Christianity had already reached Britain.

There is an intriguing possibility that a family of Britons was closely involved in the Christian Church in Rome even in the first century. In the New Testament, at the end of his second letter to Timothy, St Paul sends greetings from Pudens, Claudia and Linus. Claudia may well have been the daughter of the British tribal chief Caractacus, who was captured by the Romans and taken as a prisoner with his hostage family to Rome. He was later pardoned. A poem by the contemporary Roman poet Martial refers to a marriage between a Roman centurion, Pudens, and one Claudia, whom he describes as being of British descent. Pudens was martyred for his faith in AD 96. Epiphanius, a fourth-century bishop of Cyprus, claims that it was Claudia's brother, Linus, who succeeded Peter as bishop of Rome.

One tradition claims an apostolic foundation for the British Church. Eusebius, bishop of Caesarea and historian in the late third / early fourth century, claims that "the apostles passed beyond the ocean to the isles called the Britannic Isles", just as St Thomas is credited with having taken Christianity to India. St Augustine, writing to the pope from Britain around the year 600, also refers to the apostolic origin of the British Church.

The earliest native claim concerning the beginning of Christianity here is by Gildas, a British monk, writing in about 540, which states that Christianity was established here before the death of the Emperor Tiberius in 37 AD. There is a tradition that a group of believers fled persecution in Palestine, arrived here around that time and founded a church at Glastonbury. There was an established trade route from Gaul and the Mediterranean via the Severn Estuary to Glastonbury. Certainly, the church at Glastonbury was widely venerated in the early centuries and was known as the Vetusta Ecclesia – the Ancient Church. Perhaps because of the existence of an early church, Irish missionaries established a Celtic monastery there in the sixth century and St David is said to have added a chancel to the east of the ancient clay-and-wattle church. Around the year 620, Paulinus, then bishop of York, who shared in St Augustine's mission, had the ancient church encased with timber and lead to preserve it. Such was its revered status when the Anglo-Saxons settled here that King Ine of Wessex was inspired to build another church adjoining St David's chancel to the east, around the year 800, and gave land and privileges to the monastery. The monk, William of Malmesbury, who wrote a history of Glastonbury Abbey in the twelfth century, knew the ancient church there and described it as "the heavenly sanctuary on earth". Sadly, it was destroyed by fire in 1184.

It is in a thirteenth-century version of this history that the first account known to us appears of Joseph of Arimathea's coming to Glastonbury and founding the ancient church – a claim that is not universally dismissed.

That Christianity may have come to the West Country directly at a very early stage, rather than first to the south-east of Britain, seems credible – all the more so since the Church in the west; in Somerset, Devon and Cornwall; in Wales; north to Strathclyde; as well as in Ireland, developed rather differently in the centuries following.

Glastonbury apart, it was in the south-east that

Christianity was able to infiltrate on a bigger scale, with that region's busy trade routes, and the traffic of Roman soldiers, Roman administrators and Roman families coming to settle here. It may be that some of them had come into contact with Christians in Rome. It is possible, too, that some Christians may have come to Britain fleeing a vicious persecution in the Rhône valley in the year 177.

Wherever the first Christians here came from, whether it was Palestine, Rome or any of the countries around the Mediterranean where the Church had been established, or from Gaul, they would have brought with them their own experience of life and worship within the Church to provide a model for the Christian groups they would help to found.

Under Roman occupation a network of towns had developed, all connected by good roads. It was easier to spread the gospel in towns – this had been St Paul's strategy. This is where the language barrier would have broken down as native Britons acquired a measure of Latin. Latin was not only the language of their conquerors but had become the language of the Church in the West. Probably not many country people became Christians in this town-based culture. Indeed, the Latin word for countryman, *paganus*, acquired the meaning of heathen.

We can reasonably assume that the Christians met in small groups, like the house churches in the New Testament, and that the traditional elements of worship inherited from the Jewish synagogue – the singing of hymns and psalms, with prayers and readings – were part of their experience together. The Gospels, and the letters of St Paul and others had been copied and circulated in Christian communities from an early date for reading and instruction in the faith. Sunday, the Lord's Day, had become the traditional day of worship, when the resurrection of Jesus was celebrated. At the very heart of Sunday worship for the Christian Church everywhere was "the breaking of bread", instituted by Jesus in His Last Supper with His disciples before His crucifixion, to be a memorial of that event. The prayer of thanksgiving over the bread and wine was customary at Jewish meals, but given a new significance by Jesus at this meal.

We have an early description of this service in the writings of Justin Martyr, who was martyred for his faith in 165. While the setting in this case is second-century Rome, the basic framework would have been passed on by early believers wherever they took the faith. The note is one of thanksgiving; a Greek word was already giving a new name to the breaking of bread: the Eucharist. From the beginning, this part of the service, which followed the readings and sermon, was only for committed believers, those who had undergone baptism, with its confession of faith, and its symbolism of being washed clean and starting afresh, or, as Justin Martyr has it, where they are born again and their sins are forgiven. The breaking of bread and baptism were the two sacraments Jesus himself had commanded His followers to observe.

New Testament baptism was usually by immersion in running water, but early documents allow for baptism by pouring water over the head. Lead tanks have been found, which may have been used for baptism. In many places where it is thought there was a Christian church in Roman times, there are traces of a separate structure nearby that may have served as a baptistry. Although baptism seems to have taken place very soon after conversion in the New Testament, in the early centuries of the Church the preparation of candidates for baptism was taken very seriously, and it involved a long period of probation and instruction.

Easter was the great – and only – festival of the early Church, when the resurrection of Jesus was celebrated. It was held, like the first Easter, at the time of the Jewish Passover and was at first known as the Christian Passover or Pasch; subsequently, "Easter", from Eostre, an Anglo-Saxon spring goddess, was adopted here for the Christian festival as it displaced the pagan spring festival. With its message of new life, Easter appropriately became the customary time for baptism, and the period before it a time of preparation, which became our Lent. The festival continued with great rejoicing for seven weeks up to Pentecost, when the coming of the Holy Spirit was celebrated.

Regular meetings of believers were not confined to Sundays. Worship was meant to embrace the whole of life. Private prayer was encouraged several times a day and some of these times became corporate prayer times; the gathering together in the early morning and at the lighting of the lamps were the forerunners of Matins and Evensong in the Church of England. Every Christian was involved in spreading the gospel; this was the priesthood of all believers, for whom their fellowship together was a source of great strength and encouragement. By the time Christianity began to spread here, the threefold ministry of bishop, presbyter and deacon, which developed after the time of the apostles, would have been establishing itself. In the early days, the bishop had pastoral oversight of a congregation, assisted by elders or presbyters, and by deacons, who had a practical role in services and ministered to the poor. As groups proliferated, the bishop would assume charge of an area, the diocese of later church organisation, and would authorise a presbyter to lead a local congregation.

While for much of the time up to the fourth century,

Christianity was tolerated under Roman occupation, there were intermittent periods of persecution. Christians could not acknowledge the Emperor as divine, as they were sometimes required to do by edict. By ignoring the old Roman gods, it was felt that Christians were threatening the well-being of the Roman Empire. The authorities tried to bring Christianity into disrepute, but the lifestyle of Christians was impressive: they cared for the sick and defenceless, they buried the poor, they gave hospitality to travellers, they had clear views of morality, they respected each individual regardless of station, and they were even prepared to die for their faith, which was beginning to permeate many sections of society. It recommended itself to women in regarding men and women as equal before God, and in upholding the sanctity of marriage. Through women it often penetrated the upper classes. There was the possibility of it spreading through the military. So, predictably, from time to time, the state sought to suppress it.

From 209–11, the Emperor Septimius Severus prescribed the death penalty for converts to Christianity. It may have been then or during the middle of the century that Alban of the Roman town of Verulamium was martyred. The story is told of how he had given shelter to a priest, who converted him to Christianity. Alerted to the presence of the priest, soldiers came to take him away, but it was Alban they led away to pay the penalty, dressed in the priest's robes. When stripped of his disguise, Alban refused to recant his new-found faith and Britain acquired its first known Christian martyr, who in time gave the town a new name, St Albans.

After his martyrdom, a shrine was set up in memory of St Alban, which became a place of pilgrimage and worship, probably the most important in southern Britain by the early fifth century. By implication, the story describes the beginning of one of the earliest continuous churches known here. Bede, writing in the early eighth century, tells us that a fine church was built there, where sick people came for healing and where miracles took place. The veneration of martyrs in this country had begun. In one sense, the martyrs took the place of the gods of pagan belief. It was felt that prayers made through the martyrs, who were now closer to God, might prove more effective; their relics were treasured and special celebrations held at the anniversary of a martyr's death – known as his "birthday". The collecting of relics did not meet with approval on all sides; one Vigilantius, a priest from Aquitaine, is on record as seeing them as pagan superstitions, but they seem to have served to give some reality to things unseen and the practice flourished. When the era of martyrdom was over, local saints or holy men were venerated too. Many days became special saints' days and filled out the Church's calendar.

Popular history has chosen to preserve the name of Alban. The sixth-century Gildas also names Aaron and Julius, who were martyred at Caerleon, possibly under a wave of persecution in the middle of the third century. There were, without doubt, many other martyrs whose story has not survived, but the powerful witness of martyrs, and their constancy in the face of death, was counterproductive for the Roman authorities. In any case, an event occurred in 312 which changed the situation radically.

State Approval and Expansion

In 306, on the death of the Roman Emperor Constantius, his son Constantine had declared himself his successor at

York, but he had rivals. One was Maxentius, whom he had to fight at the battle of Milvian Bridge near Rome in 312. Before the battle, Constantine had prayed to the "supreme god" and, according to Eusebius, who was the church historian to whom he later recounted the incident, he saw a cross in the sky, above the sun, together with the words, "Conquer by this". The following night, Christ appeared to him in a dream, he claimed, and commanded him to use the sign in all his battles. Constantine's success in the battle inclined him to believe that the Christian God was the true God. As a result, persecution ceased. He may have seen in Christianity a unifying force – a universal God for an ever-expanding Roman Empire. With Constantine's change of attitude began a relationship between Church and state that has been seen as a mixed blessing, but, at this stage, it undoubtedly enabled a much more rapid spread of the faith. Christianity was not accepted as the state religion until later in the fourth century, but from the time of Constantine Christians were free to acknowledge their faith openly and the Church was allowed to own property. There were other consequences of state approval. Gradually, the number of nominal Christians increased as more and more people conformed to the view of those in authority, diluting the degree of conviction within the Church. The early concept of the bishop as the shepherd of his flock was modified too, as his position assumed a semi-official aspect, with status and power. These were highly significant changes in the story of the Church. In addition, there arose the possibility of interference from emperor or king, for purely secular reasons, as Constantine himself demonstrated when he presided over Church councils and sought to influence their decisions.

Constantine did not abandon his allegiance to the sun

god. For a time, he continued to use the pagan symbol of the Unconquered Sun and he was not baptised until the end of his life, but from the year 313 Christianity was protected. In 321 Constantine made the first day of the week a holiday – "the venerable day of the sun" – preserved in our Sunday. The imagery that the sun inspired found expression in other ways – in church buildings the altar was placed at the east end so that the congregation faced in the direction of the rising sun, to remind them of the light that Christ brought into the world. He had described Himself as the light of the world. Burials, too, were aligned east-west.

Perhaps the Church hoped to reorient pagan thinking about the sun in choosing December 25th to celebrate the birth of Christ. This was a time of great revelry in the Roman calendar, as sun-worshippers celebrated the birth of the sun at the winter solstice. The festival of Christmas was celebrated only from the fourth century, and began to rival the great festival of Easter. Just as Lent had become a period of preparation before Easter, so the season of Advent developed as a time of preparation for Christmas. The use of candles and the present giving of the Roman celebrations were absorbed into the Christian festival in spite of some hesitation on the part of church leaders to incorporate customs with pagan associations into Christian festivals.

In the new climate of official sanction the Church was free to be more visible. British bishops appeared at Church councils abroad. In 314, three bishops, from London, York, and either Lincoln or Colchester, attended a council in Gaul at Arles. In 359, another three British bishops were at a council in Italy at Rimini. With its new freedom and the likely increase in numbers, church buildings would probably have begun to replace house churches at this stage and at the same time the intimacy and full participation of all present – characteristics of house churches that have been appreciated in our own day – would give way to a more formal kind of worship.

Generally the pattern for church building throughout the Roman Empire was the basilica, used for public administration and assembly: a rectangular main hall, divided into three by rows of columns, with a semi-circular shape (the apse) at one end, and a vestibule or narthex at the other. This shape encouraged the separation of clergy and laity: the presbyters and deacons sat around the apse with a seat placed centrally for the bishop. The table for the Eucharist was placed at the front of the apse, sometimes with saints' relics beneath it. The congregation of the baptised occupied the main section, while those who were receiving instruction, the catechumens, and those who were being disciplined, the penitents, had their place beyond them in the narthex.

Such evidence as we have of church buildings here in the Roman period is limited and often inconclusive. Gildas, writing in about 540, refers to churches being rebuilt when persecution ceased and chapels being built to honour martyrs. It is possible that some early church building was in cemeteries outside the town walls. As might be expected, there are many sites in the south-east where it is thought churches existed. The Roman fort at Richborough, the main port of entry at that time, contains the remains of what may have been a Christian church and baptistry. In his *History of the English Church and People*, completed in 731, the Venerable Bede suggests there were many churches built in Kent during the Roman occupation because, when St Augustine's mission began in 597, he says that Ethelbert, then king of Kent, not only allowed churches to be built, but also had some repaired in his kingdom. One of particular interest is the church of St Martin at Canterbury, which played a special part in St Augustine's mission. Some of the chancel of the present building is part of an earlier structure, with its walls of Roman brickwork. How far it extended into the present nave, which is thought to be the work of the seventh or eighth century, is not known. This may be the church that has been in use the longest, and now is part of the same landscape as the great cathedral of Canterbury, itself on the site of a church built by Christians in Roman times and repaired by St Augustine, according to Bede.

Further west, in the excavated Roman town of Silchester in Hampshire, was what is widely considered to have been a Christian church. The site in question occupied a central position and the basilican ground plan dates from the fourth century, when Christianity was in favour. It is unlikely that a pagan temple would have been built in such a prominent position at this stage. The building would have held about sixty people – there was plenty of competition in Silchester in the form of four pagan temples. A similar site was found in Caerwent in South Wales, but the evidence for a church having been there is not conclusive. There are signs that there may have been late-Roman churches in Lincoln and Colchester too. There may well have been churches in all the Roman towns, particularly when Christianity became the state religion, but the practice of reusing sites sacred to previous generations has ensured that they are well hidden under later structures.

A different kind of solution to providing a meeting place for Christians was offered, in one instance at least, by a Roman villa. One or more rooms of the villa at Lullingstone in Kent appear to have been set aside for the use of a

Christian congregation. The wall plaster was painted with frescoes, now in the British Museum, depicting praying figures, standing with arms upraised. Among the figures is the Chi-Rho sign, representing the first two letters of the Greek word for Christ, which to us look like X and P overlapping, along with the alpha and omega – the first and last letters of the Greek alphabet, used to indicate the eternal nature of God; all are symbols commonly used by the early Christians. A similar group was found in 1969 on the wall of a mausoleum unearthed in a Romano-British cemetery at Poundbury in Dorset, thought to be contemporary with the Lullingstone figures. From the Lullingstone villa, one might deduce that the room was used both by the occupants of the villa and by Christians from the area around it, since a second door appears to have been added for additional access. Remains of a church building dating from the early fourth century were found on the estate of another Roman villa at Meonstoke in Hampshire. Part of its well-preserved façade has been removed to the British Museum.

Finds in many villas suggest that Christianity – or at least an awareness of it – was penetrating the wealthier echelons of society. The fine mosaic pavement found in a villa at Hinton St Mary in Dorset, which is now also in the British Museum, has as its centre the Chi-Rho monogram. The head over the symbol is therefore thought to be a representation of Christ, while the figures in the corners may represent the Four Evangelists. The combination of mythological subjects and Christian symbols in Roman pavements may appear curious to our eyes, like the portrayal of Bellerophon killing the Chimera, which is common to Lullingstone and Hinton St Mary. This story may have been assimilated into Christian symbolism as a representation of good overcoming evil, or perhaps it represents a period of transition, when thoughtful people considered it prudent to hedge their bets!

Sometimes, finds of small objects from the fourth century point to the existence of a Christian congregation. The most notable is a collection of Christian silver plate, found at Water Newton in Cambridgeshire in 1975. This was the site of the Roman town of Durobrivae. Many of the objects bear the Chi-Rho sign, and the alpha and omega. Among them are a fine chalice; a large, flat dish; a jug and strainer; several bowls; and eighteen leaf-shaped plaques, like those found in pagan shrines, with messages inscribed on them – an indication that old ways died slowly. We know from the inscriptions that one of the silver bowls was a gift from Publianus "honouring God's holy church"; that Anicilla had fulfilled the vow she promised, and that Innocentia and Vivienta were connected with the congregation (the inscription naming them is incomplete). With the names of these individuals, the Christian community at Durobrivae begins to come to life. The collection may have been buried because Christians still feared a renewal of persecution. There have been many small finds with Christian symbols at various sites: silver spoons are common among them, but also finger rings, bowls and pottery.

For a long time Christian communities would have been small enclaves in a pagan world. There was even a resurgence of pagan beliefs during the fourth century, in spite of imperial edicts forbidding sacrifices to pagan gods and the worship of idols. The most impressive evidence of this resurgence is at Lydney in Gloucestershire, where, in the later part of the fourth century, a temple was built to Nodens, a local Celtic god. The remains suggest it was the scene of a healing cult, with a bath house and guest house in addition to the temple, and a long series of small rooms, which were possibly shops for selling offerings or else a dormitory for those seeking healing.

While much of the evidence for Christianity, both in small finds and in buildings, comes from the south and east, there are many indications that Christianity was also established in the north during the Roman period. We know that York had a bishop in 314, the year of the Church council at Arles. Carlisle, strategically important under Roman occupation, is believed to have had a bishop in the fourth century too. Other bishoprics based on tribal areas around the Forth, in Strathclyde, and in the Tweed basin may have been in place by the end of the fourth century. The British tribes north and south of Hadrian's Wall were Romanised to some extent. Cunedda, a tribal leader based in the area around the Forth, was at least nominally a Christian and there may have been other tribal leaders who were Christian too. When Cunedda went to North Wales in the fifth century to defend the area against attacks from Irish raiders, some of his family and followers stayed there. Their descendants founded churches and so linked the tradition of the Church of northern Britain with that of Wales.

A Christian community in Galloway in the early fifth century offers proof that the Church was moving beyond the bounds of the Roman Empire. This, the first known church in Scotland, was at Whithorn, with a bishop, one Ninian, at its head. It was policy to send bishops only to places where a Christian community already existed. Little is known about Ninian. The earliest written record does not occur until Bede's history of 731, where he is described as a Briton who had been instructed in Rome. He appears to have been influenced by St Martin of Tours, who was an enthusiast for evangelism; he may even have met him. When Ninian came to Whithorn at the end of the fourth century, he built a church of stone. This was unusual among the Britons and became a landmark known as Candida Casa – the white house or in Old English *huit aern* – our Whithorn. At his death around the year 431, he was buried at Whithorn. In those days the burial place of a local saint soon became a place of pilgrimage and Candida Casa continued to attract pilgrims over many centuries. The monastery that grew up there became a seat of learning, which drew students from far and wide, and sent them out as missionaries. Under the ruins of the twelfth-century priory at Whithorn, earlier foundations have been discovered. Today, the museum in a converted cottage near the ruined priory houses a collection of early Christian crosses and stones. Among them is the earliest Christian memorial in Scotland, dating from 450, recording the burial of one Latinus and his daughter; Latinus, at least, may have been a member of Ninian's congregation.

Like many early saints who cherished the notion of spending time apart, Ninian is said to have resorted to a cave on the coast a few miles south of Whithorn: a place of peace and beauty, approached through a glen. Early crosses cut into the rocks bear witness to the pilgrim visitors of subsequent centuries. The spot remains a place of pilgrimage, and a venue for interdenominational services.

Two miles from the cave is the village of Isle of Whithorn and on the headland beyond the harbour stands a ruined thirteenth-century chapel, called St Ninian's. It is perhaps the successor of an earlier church, and would have been well placed for travellers between Ireland and Candida Casa.

There are signs of other Christians in the area. Three inscribed stones are set into the wall of an old church at Kirkmadrine, twenty-five miles from Whithorn; one is inscribed to two "holy and outstanding" bishops, Viventius and Mavorius. Two stones found on the Isle of Man are in the same style. Was this part of Ninian's diocese, only eighteen miles away? Both cases were perhaps the fruits of his labours; St Martin had encouraged evangelism in rural areas. Ninian's activities may have extended north to Strathclyde; one tradition claims he consecrated a burial ground there, which became the site for Glasgow Cathedral.

In Ninian we see something of the great Celtic bishops to come, in whom the zeal to evangelise was balanced by their need for solitude and contemplation. With Ninian the story of the spread of Christianity becomes more personalised. We rely less on hints and clues, and material finds from which to deduce possibilities. Individuals begin to emerge whose lives spell out the progress of the Church as it takes up the challenge of spreading the faith into new terrain.

If all the pieces of evidence for Christianity during the Roman occupation are taken together – the early martyrs, the bishops attending Church councils on mainland Europe, some use of villas for Christian worship, Christian signs in many villas, small finds with Christian symbols, together with an increase in Christian burials from the third to the fourth centuries, with their east-west alignment and the absence of grave goods – all imply that Christianity, now the official religion of the Roman Empire, had spread through much of what became England, and into Wales and the far north – both areas with a strong military presence – and even latterly beyond Hadrian's Wall.

We will never know the true extent of the Church when the Romans withdrew in the early fifth century, nor how deeply it had taken root. Only time would tell whether it would be strong enough to survive in less stable circumstances.

II

THE CHURCH SURVIVES THE DEPARTURE OF THE ROMANS

In the early years of the fifth century, the Roman legions withdrew from Britain. The Roman Empire was under serious threat on the mainland of Europe and, in 410, Rome fell under barbarian attack.

During the latter part of the Roman occupation, all had not been well. Some of the towns were disintegrating and some villas with their estates were not prospering. Since it was in the towns and villas that the Christian Church had established itself, it was almost certainly weakened.

With the departure of the Romans, the native Britons were left not only to govern themselves but also to defend themselves against frequent attacks from the Picts in the north, from Saxons and from Irish raiders, all of whom had posed a serious threat under Roman government. However, one of these threats was to have unexpected repercussions for the Christian Church.

Born somewhere along the west coast, possibly from the same area as Ninian, Patrick, like Ninian, was a son of the Romano-British Church. His connection with Ireland began when he was captured by Irish raiders and taken back to Ireland as a slave. He was then sixteen. A great deal of legend has collected around the person and life of Patrick, but we know his story from his own hand since two of his writings, in Latin, have survived intact, among the earliest British writings to have done so. His *Confessio* is an account of his journey of faith and a defence of his work in Ireland. In it, he describes his family background in western Britain: his father, Calpurnius, a local town councillor and a deacon of the church; and his grandfather, a priest. Yet it was not until his six years as a herdsman slave in Ireland that Patrick came to a personal faith that inspired the rest of his life. He describes his experience of slavery and how he felt God was watching over him, as a father might his son, and how his faith grew. Throughout his life, Patrick felt that he was guided by God.

His story is an extraordinary one, and his resolve to convert the Irish people to Christianity was pursued with a courage and perseverance reminiscent of St Paul's missionary work. It seems that after six years of slavery in Ireland he escaped to a port; a three-day sea crossing was followed by a twenty-eight day trek through uninhabited country, presumably Gaul. The information in his own writings is supplemented by a biography written some two hundred years later by a Leinster priest, Muirchu, using earlier lost sources. Patrick's dates are contested but at this stage of his life, from about 418 to 431, apart from a return visit to his family, it seems he spent some time in Gaul, mostly at Auxerre, where he came to know Germanus, a future bishop of Auxerre. There he would have been exposed to new ideas fermenting in the Church at this time, ideas born of the monastic movement that was to inspire the Church in the West with a new dynamism. The movement had begun in the third century in the deserts of Egypt, where many Eastern Christians had withdrawn to lead a simple, disciplined life; alone, in closer communion with God, apart from the world. In time, there were so many of them that communities were formed alongside those who led a solitary life. In the West the movement was being adapted, firstly under the influence of St Martin of Tours. He believed in a highly disciplined, ascetic way of life too, but he also regarded evangelism as an essential part of monastic life. His example had a powerful impact on the Church in the West.

As bishop of Tours, Martin divided his time between periods of retreat to a cave near Tours, where he founded a monastery of some eighty monks, and periods of active evangelism in the countryside around. This approach marks a new departure: up till then the Church of the Roman Empire had been very much town based. Soon after Martin's death in 397, the influence of the monastic movement was spread further by the founding of a new kind of monastery on an island off the south coast of Gaul called Lérins, now St Honorat, off Cannes. Its purpose was to train scholars and potential bishops. Its founder, Honoratus, and another monk, John Cassian, through his writings, gave monasticism in the West a new direction, with a stress on community living, the important role of the abbot and on learning. One of the chief supporters of Lérins was the Germanus whom Patrick had met at Auxerre. It is thought Patrick may have visited both Rome and Lérins during this time, and his experience on the Continent must have helped prepare him for the major work of his life. He became a deacon and priest, and resolved to return to Ireland.

Patrick was not the first to take the Christian faith there. There was a well-established traffic between Wales and Ireland. Many Irish people had settled on the west coast of Wales, particularly in what is now Pembrokeshire. There may have been comparable traffic between Galloway and the north-east of Ireland. Christianity may have found its way to Ireland through these links, or else it may have come to the south of Ireland from Aquitaine in south-west Gaul or from Spain, both well-established trade routes. It seems there was a sufficiently large number of Christians in the country to warrant a bishop's presence. In 431 Pope Celestine ordained his deacon Palladius as bishop to these Christians. It is thought that Palladius went to the area around Wicklow, where there are Christian foundations commonly associated with him. He may have been helped in his mission by three clergy whose names are recorded – Secundus, Auxilius and Iserninus. Palladius' success was limited and his stay short; according to one tradition he spent the remainder of his life in Scotland. The church of St Palladius at Auchenblae in Aberdeenshire claims that he is buried there.

It was Patrick who replaced Palladius as bishop to the Irish people, possibly with papal approval gained through the influence of Germanus, and approved, with some reservations, by British bishops who were not wholly convinced of the wisdom of the mission or of Patrick's suitability. His education had been interrupted when he was captured, his Latin was not fluent and he appears to have had little interest in theological argument. He always felt himself inferior in this respect to other British bishops, whom he describes as "intellectual clerics".

However, Patrick was motivated by his love for God and for the Irish people, and nothing would hold him back. His mission seems to have been concentrated mostly, but not exclusively, in the north-east of Ireland. His first base was at Saul near Downpatrick. The old church of Saul is on the site of a barn that Dichu, one of Patrick's earliest converts, gave to him for his church. Here he began some thirty years of missionary work. Muirchu, in his biography, gives a graphic account of Patrick's first celebration of Easter, with the lighting of a Paschal fire within sight of Tara, seat of the high king of Ireland, and site of the confrontation that followed between Patrick and the king. This is perhaps a representative account of all Patrick's encounters with pagan local chiefs. He had to gain their permission in order to evangelise, and often met with opposition, and even occasional imprisonment. In his *Confessio*, Patrick writes of the thousands he baptised, from the sons and daughters of royal households to slaves, often paying for the slaves' freedom so that they could follow him. Many priests were ordained to serve the churches he established. Many men and women took monastic vows. At this stage this may have meant an undertaking to lead a strictly disciplined life in quite ordinary circumstances. He went, he tells us, to the most remote districts – often the first to take the faith there, to baptise converts and ordain clergy.

After a decade or more, Patrick was devastated to find himself censured by British bishops, ostensibly for a misdemeanour committed in his youth. His *Confessio* was in part written to defend his work. He refused to return to Britain to answer their summons because he feared his work would be in jeopardy. He chose to depend rather on papal approval. Pope Leo I claimed the Irish Church to be directly dependent on Rome, a significant decision for the future of the Church in Ireland, and so Patrick continued his work.

A letter from Patrick has also survived, written to a king, Coroticus, who ruled a kingdom on the Clyde in the middle of the fifth century. Coroticus's men had raided the Irish coast for plunder and had captured many inhabitants, including some of Patrick's newly baptised converts; some were killed, others sold into slavery. The letter expresses Patrick's horror at the deed. In it we catch a glimpse of the baptised, clothed in white, with the fragrance of the baptismal oil still on their faces as they were captured.

It is to Muirchu's biography that we owe an account of the founding of a church at Armagh after prolonged negotiations between Patrick and the ruler of the kingdom, Daire. Under his successors, Armagh was to be given the primacy of all the sees of Ireland.

At his death, probably in about 462, he left behind an organised Church in the areas he had evangelised, but the Church he established had to relate to the social structure of the country – there were no towns, only tribal kingdoms. There is no record in his own writings or in Muirchu's account that he consecrated bishops, but in the generation following Patrick's death six bishops are recorded in separate kingdoms in the north, most near a royal centre – an adaptation of the Roman town-based system. In the south, four sees were founded by Pope Hilary in the main kingdoms between 461 and 468. It was not until the middle of the sixth century that Ireland as a whole became gripped by Christianity and enthused by the monastic movement that flooded the country.

Nonetheless, Patrick's legacy remains. The hymn, "St Patrick's Breastplate" is traditionally attributed to him, though possibly written some time later. It certainly evokes the kind of person Patrick's writings suggest he was – someone inspired by and totally dependent on Christ, as he faced a pagan culture. The hymn sounds like a counter-claim to a pagan invocation. Each year in July, thousands of people make their pilgrimage to Croagh Patrick in County Mayo in memory of Patrick, as do many to Lough Derg in County Donegal, in a spirit of penitence. His example remains a source of spiritual inspiration.

The Fifth-Century Church in Romanised Britain

As for the Church in Romanised Britain, most of what we know of the early fifth century is concerned with the efforts of the pope to protect the British Church from heresy.

During the century since Constantine's conversion and with the increasing favour shown towards Christianity, the Church had become much more firmly established. Some emperors had helped the cause by ordering the closure of pagan shrines or forbidding the worship of idols. At the same time, the authority of the bishop of Rome, as the successor of St Peter and head of the Church in the capital of the Roman Empire, had increased. His authority grew as he sought to preserve orthodox belief and unity in the Church: any kind of heresy brought the threat of schism and a less-than-united front against paganism.

A Briton called Pelagius had gone to Rome around the year 380 to study and had been appalled by the moral standards of the Christians there. In expressing his views, he had crossed swords with some of the highly respected theologians of his day, most notably with St Augustine of Hippo and his views on original sin and predestination. St Augustine emphasised man's total dependence on the grace of God. While Pelagius did not deny man's need of grace, he maintained the need for self-discipline too, and opposed Augustine's belief in predestination with his own belief in man's freewill, and his freedom to choose to believe and to obey God's laws. To St Augustine this savoured too much of human will and not enough of the grace of God. Pelagius had his supporters, but was, after some controversy, pronounced a heretic. Pelagianism was banned in Gaul around 417, but not in Britain which was no longer part of the Roman Empire.

In so far as the British Church was aware of it, it does not appear to have been regarded as heresy. That was not how the pope viewed the matter: his deacon Palladius persuaded him to send Germanus, bishop of Auxerre, to Britain, along with Lupus, bishop of Troyes, to eradicate Pelagian views. Bede, in his history of the English Church, describes how they preached not only in churches but also in the streets and countryside, and established what they considered true belief in the minds of the people. As a former army commander, Germanus further helped the Britons to wage a successful battle against the Saxons and Picts – possibly at Maes Garmon near Mold. Before the battle Germanus had instructed large numbers of soldiers in the faith and baptised them. He then led them to a victory reminiscent of the battle of Jericho, when the enemy was routed by sudden loud cries of "Alleluia". Germanus returned home, satisfied with his mission. However, the heresy, if such it was – some have disagreed – persisted and Germanus returned for a second visit to try to restore what Rome regarded as the true faith.

Pelagius wrote on many matters other than freewill, though much of what survives of his writings is in fragments. He had strong views on the fair distribution of wealth. In this he was not alone – many leading Christians were concerned about this, recalling the sharing of resources in the very early Church as described in the New Testament Acts of the Apostles.

Pelagius was only one of a number of intellectuals who were going abroad from the British Church at this time. We know of Fastidius who had settled in Sicily and wrote on the Christian life; he held similar views to Pelagius on wealth. Another Briton, Faustus, went to the new monastery at Lérins, and became abbot there and, subsequently, a bishop in Provence.

When the Romans left Britain, an important part of their legacy was an organised Church, but it was limited in area. Some parts of the country were untouched by Christianity, and paganism was still a force to be reckoned with everywhere. But the Church was beginning to reach out beyond the frontiers of the Roman Empire, through the personal commitment of men such as Ninian in the north and Patrick in Ireland. It was also in lively contact with the Church in Gaul, taking its place in the universal Church and making its contribution to the thinking of the time.

Sadly for the British Church of this period, other forces were at work: Britain was facing another invasion, this time by pagan Germanic tribes from the Continent – Angles, Saxons, Jutes and Friesians – bringing their own beliefs and practices. After the Pelagian incident, relations between the Church in that part of Britain which was to become known as England, and the wider Church on the mainland of Europe were broken for about one hundred and fifty years. This was an exceptional state of affairs: for most of Christian history there has been close contact between the two and mutual influence.

There is no contemporary account of what happened in Britain in the fifth century and we have to rely largely on Gildas the monk, writing a century later, probably in South Wales. He describes a period of intense fighting in the middle of the fifth century. The Saxon federates, who had been invited by the British leader Vortigern to settle in the south-east to help ward off enemy attacks, revolted. Larger-scale incursions of Germanic tribes followed. The British upper class was decimated and many survivors emigrated to northern Gaul. Gildas describes their departure by sea, taking with them such books as had not been burnt by the enemy. The signature of one Bishop Mansuetus survives from a council at Tours in 461, where he is described as "Bishop of the British", suggesting the immigrants were recent, and had not yet been absorbed into established dioceses.

It seems so many Britons arrived on the westernmost peninsula of north Gaul that its name changed from Armorica to little Britain – Brittany. How many of these were Britons fleeing from the Saxons, and how many were from Wales and the south-west moving for other reasons, perhaps due to pressure from Irish settlers, is not certain. Place names in Brittany suggest these western Britons formed a substantial proportion of the new arrivals there. About the same time a colony of Britons established themselves in northern Spain, which was sufficiently large to figure in records of Christian councils in the sixth century.

These movements of population must have depleted numbers in the British Church considerably. The remaining Britons renewed their resistance to the invaders and eventually achieved a great victory at the end of the fifth century, traditionally attributed to Arthur. As a result the invaders were confined for a time to the east – a breathing space for the rest of the country and for the Church there. It was only a respite. The movement westwards and northwards by the invaders was renewed, and by 600 they had overrun most of what is now England.

While some of the defending Britons may have moved west and north as the new arrivals encroached ever further, many of those who stayed would have become slaves. Most of the peasant population had not been converted to Christianity; pagan Britons would have merged with pagan invaders and, in time, adopted both their language and their gods – the names of their gods survive in the days of our week: Tiu, Woden, Thor and Frig.

The Survival of the Church in the West: The Age of the Saints

What, we wonder, happened to the Christians? The settlement of the invading tribes was a very long and uneven process. Where they settled heavily that probably spelt disaster to the Church, whether through slavery, death or emigration. Perhaps it was able to survive in places where it was very well established, such as St Albans. The further north and west, the more likely was the survival of the Britons' way of life; the British kingdom of Elmet near Leeds was independent until well into the seventh century. As time passed the process of settlement by the newcomers may, in some places, have become less aggressive and more tolerant of British ways. Their greatest interest was in acquiring land. Some twenty place names with the element "Eccles", from the Latin *ecclesia* – meaning church – suggest the Church may have survived in these places. The form varies from simply Eccles to compound forms including Eccleston and Eccleshall. Most are in the Midlands and the north, places of later settlement by the invaders. How long the Church could have survived elsewhere in these areas we do not know.

What we do know is that the Church was able not only to survive in the west of Britain, but to spread and flourish. Initially, it was especially in Wales that the Church proved resilient, and it is Gildas who provides some explanation. Writing around 540, more than a century after the departure of the Romans, he gives the clear impression that he regards his countrymen in general as Christian, nominally at least. How had this come about?

References by Gildas to bishops, priests and deacons, and to the continued use of Latin as the language of the Church suggest the survival of a Church established under the Romans, perhaps continuing in decayed urban communities. We also know that when the Emperor Maximus was killed in 388, his wife Elen returned to her native North Wales with her many children. The family had been influenced by St Martin of Tours, who had visited the Emperor's court at Trier, and on their return the family founded churches in Wales. We know too that when Cunedda, a Christian tribal leader from southern Scotland, came to North Wales to deal with Irish raiders, some of his descendants settled in Wales in the fifth century and founded churches or *llans*. Originally the word *llan*, the prefix of so many place names in Wales, simply meant a sacred enclosure, bounded by a bank or stone wall, to indicate an area for worship, refuge or where converts could be buried. At a stage when ministry to a scattered population may have consisted only of occasional visits, a preaching cross rather than a building would have sufficed for services, along with a portable altar. Open-air worship was natural to the people.

While the influential families of Maximus and Cunedda were contributing to the expansion of the Church in Wales, the influence of eastern monasticism was growing there. It may have come through the Church's links with Gaul and people such as Germanus, or directly from the eastern Mediterranean through missionaries. By the end of the fifth century, an important monastic school had emerged on the coast in the Vale of Glamorgan at Llantwit Major. The western part of the present church of St Illtud is probably on or near the earlier church. A few stone crosses of the eighth and ninth centuries serve as a reminder of the community that continued until the arrival of the Normans: one bears the name "Illtut" on the back, and another the names of local kings.

While there is a lack of early material from this and other monasteries in South Wales, an account of the life of the Welsh St Samson, born around 480, sheds valuable light on the Church there at that time. Unlike most saints' lives, this was written soon after his lifetime around the year 610 and tells us that Samson was sent to the monastery at Llantwit Major when he was five, and was taught at the feet of Illtud, whom the author describes as the most learned of all the Britons not only in his knowledge of the Old and New Testaments but also in philosophy. Tradition claims that Illtud was a disciple of Germanus, and that many early saints of the Welsh Church were educated at the school at Llantwit Major, Gildas and possibly David among them, as well as Samson.

A few miles away another important monastery grew up at Llancarfan, founded by St Cadoc. Further east in the kingdom of Erging, in present-day Herefordshire, St Dyfrig (or St Dubricius), one of the abbot-bishops of this early period, was establishing a number of monasteries with schools. Both Hentland and Moccas are particularly associated with his work. His name survives in a few church dedications around Hereford and in the place name of St Devereux. Dyfrig spent his later years as a hermit on Bardsey Island, a familiar pattern in the lives of early saints, and died there around 546.

Under Illtud, Cadoc and Dyfrig, a tradition of learning and scholarship had been developing in the eastern part of South Wales. Yet only a few years before Dyfrig's death in 546, his contemporary Gildas paints a very different picture of the Church in Wales generally in the work he called *The Ruin and Conquest of Britain* – the only surviving account of events in the post-Roman period.

This was not written as history, but is a resounding condemnation of the regional kings and clergy of his day in the western part of Britain that was familiar to him. His voice thunders like an Old Testament prophet as he castigates the wicked ways of the rulers, and condemns the clergy for their hypocrisy and worldliness, prepared to buy their office, but not fulfilling it, and acting more like wolves than shepherds. His robust denunciations are supported by copious Biblical quotations, particularly from the Old Testament. In his view the Anglo-Saxon invasions were a judgement on the native Britons for their wicked ways. Writing after Arthur's victory over the invaders, in an interval of comparative peace but very low moral standards, he foresees another catastrophic judgement on a corrupt Church and its people.

In the light of this it would seem St Illtud, St Dyfrig and St Cadoc were among outstanding exceptions, the avant-garde of the new movement in the Church, which favoured monasticism. *The Ruin and Conquest of Britain* had a powerful effect. Many identified with the anger and disgust Gildas had expressed against worldly Church leaders, and a movement of mass monasticism followed in the 540s. While others had recommended it before

Gildas, the response had been limited. Suddenly there was an enormous growth in the number of monasteries, particularly in South Wales, Cornwall, Brittany and Ireland. North Wales and northern Britain were also affected but to a lesser extent.

Monasticism shaped the Celtic churches and was the most common expression of Christianity in the period known as the Age of the Saints, but the Celtic practice was not like the eastern monasticism that preceded it, nor like the Benedictine model that followed it: Celtic monasticism was integrated with society and committed to serving it. It fitted into the existing social order where the kinship group was central.

To appreciate the nature of the Celtic monastery we have to abandon familiar ideas of both its physical aspect and of the participants. In that world there were no tidy categories of clergy, laity and monks. Nor was there one model: a community developed out of local conditions. Some communities may have been monastic in the sense we understand it, and the life of St Samson tells how he consecrated nunneries founded by his mother and aunt. In addition, and perhaps predominantly in Wales, large religious communities – or *clasau* – developed, where whole families lived together.

Communities were independent and self-sufficient, even tribal, under the direction of an abbot who was often a bishop too. His successor was usually a member of his own family. We can imagine the community meeting for worship, working in the fields to provide food for themselves and hospitality for guests, and educating the young, who in time went out to minister to the population of the surrounding area, rather like the canons of a collegiate church. In practice each monastery was autonomous; there was no common rule, nor was there any central organisation.

The big monastic foundations that developed were an important part of the Welsh tradition which continued for centuries, but initially there were many small foundations, not all of them monastic in origin, scattered over the country. Simple churches and cells were built of wattle and daub, or of timber, roofed with turf or thatch, and placed within an enclosure that was usually dedicated to its founder and so the *llan* came to refer to the church and thence to the settlement. The spread of Christianity depended on the wandering saints – a vital element in the Celtic tradition. For them the life of faith was a pilgrimage in a spiritual and a physical sense, being the Church, and extending the Church wherever they went.

There were also many hermits on islands or in secluded places. They were held in high regard: this was the peak of the monastic vocation, whether for limited periods or as a final retreat.

The sixth century is studded with the names of saints, but hard facts are difficult to come by. Stories of the lives of saints were often written centuries later, and are full of conventions and unlikely claims: a saint could not pass muster if he did not have several miracles, or a journey to Rome or Jerusalem to his credit. The earliest surviving life of the sixth-century St David was written in the eleventh century, though using older sources. Like many another, it had an axe to grind, which in this case was to boost the importance of the see of St David in the hope of ensuring its independence of Canterbury. It seems David came from noble stock. His mother Non is remembered at St Non's Bay in Pembrokeshire, where both a well and a ruined chapel bear her name. His most famous foundation was established only a few miles away, where the present cathedral of St David now stands. During his lifetime his monastery was renowned for its austerity. He is credited with many other foundations; in south-east Wales, the church of St David at Llanthony is reputed to stand on the site of David's original church there. Tradition claims he lived in the area for some time and other churches not far away are dedicated to him. He may have been responsible for the chancel known as St David's, which was built on to the ancient church at Glastonbury. Dedications to him exist in Cornwall and Brittany too, and he may have visited Ireland, where he is thought to have had an important influence on the Church: there were close links between Ireland and West Wales. As abbot-bishop he is recorded as presiding over two Church synods, one at Llandewi Brefi – now a small village, but then a religious centre – and another at Caerleon: an indication that there was some degree of organisation in the sixth-century Church, which *The Life of Samson* confirms. Acknowledged as a great churchman in his day, David was to become patron saint of Wales and his shrine early became a place of pilgrimage. In the later Middle Ages two visits to St David's were declared equivalent to one visit to Rome by papal decree.

In mid-Wales a monastery grew up at Llanbadarn, which may have had even greater prestige than St David's in the early days; it acquired a considerable reputation as a centre of learning for many centuries. Tradition has it that its founder, St Padarn, was from Brittany, like St Cadfan, who set up a community a little further north on the coast at Tywyn. The pilgrim path to Bardsey Island would have gone on to Llangelynnin, and from there to the *llan* of St Tanwg, as it approached the Lleyn peninsula.

In North Wales, Bangor became the main centre,

where Deiniol was an early bishop. It is thought he was educated at Llantwit Major and that a number of scholar abbots went from there to the north. Deiniol was buried on Bardsey Island, as was Dyfrig; it was already holy ground, and became the burial place for thousands of saints and a place of pilgrimage: the Welsh Rome. Clynnog Fawr, on the Lleyn peninsula, became the start of a "pilgrims' way" to the island, through settlements that provided food and shelter for the pilgrims. Near the end of the peninsula, at Aberdaron, is a memorial-stone from the late fifth or early sixth century, to one Senacus, a presbyter. It was at Clynnog Fawr that St Beuno was to establish the beginnings of a community that flourished. Early foundations exist under the present chapel of St Beuno, and on the outskirts of the village is Beuno's Well, with its steps and stone benches, where converts could be baptised and where pilgrims came for healing. In many places there is no sign of the church that existed in the early Christian centuries, but at Penmachno, south of Betws-y-coed, there are memorial stones that testify to the early Christian community that lived there.

On the island of Anglesey, at Penmon in the east, the stone remains of the cell of St Seiriol, a sixth-century saint, can still be seen, with a well beside it. At Holyhead, the Cornish St Cybi established his cell within the old Roman fort. Tradition has it that St Cybi and St Seiriol met regularly at the wells east of Llanerchymedd, an event described in Matthew Arnold's poem "East and West".

The church of St Asaph may have been founded at this time by the Scottish St Kentigern, though named St Asaph after his successor. So, as early as the sixth century, the Church was established in the places where the four major diocesan centres of Wales developed: Bangor and St Asaph in the north, and St David's and Llandaff in the south, the latter probably founded by St Dyfrig's successor, Teilo.

The picture of the sixth-century Church in Wales would not be complete without a mention of another great monastic foundation in the north-east, on the river Dee, at Bangor-is-Coed. According to Bede, this housed about two thousand monks around the year 600, when some twelve hundred of their number were slaughtered in a battle against the Anglo-Saxons under King Ethelfrid. They were unarmed and had gone to the battlefield to pray for protection from the enemy.

Not far away, at Holywell, St Winifred, who was a niece of St Beuno and one of the few female saints of renown in the early years, is remembered still each September. She had founded a nunnery there. After her death it became a place of pilgrimage where people came for healing.

The Church in Wales was widespread. It had developed a distinctive character, particularly in its *clasau*, its family communities, but it was not an inward-looking entity. It had turned its back on the Anglo-Saxon invaders, but relations with all its Celtic neighbours flourished. The sea was no barrier, rather a unifying force, and the Irish Sea was more like a lake with a community of nations around its shores, which brought Wales, Cornwall, Brittany, Ireland and southern Scotland into regular contact with each other, along with the Isle of Man, where many places and dedications bear the names of early Irish saints and where some two hundred sites of early chapels, or *keills*, are to be found.

The early *Life of St Samson* illustrates both the close links between the Celtic areas and the mobility of these sixth-century saints. Samson was educated and later ordained a priest by St Dyfrig at Illtud's monastery. He then spent some time at a monastery nearby, which may have been on Caldey Island, where he became abbot. This was followed by a period in a monastery in Ireland. When he returned he was made bishop, again by St Dyfrig, at Llantwit Major. However, that was not the end of his journeying: he made his way to Cornwall and thence to Brittany, where he founded a monastery at Dol and became bishop of Dol. From there he founded other churches in Brittany and spread the faith to the Channel Islands.

Gildas, likewise, did not confine his activities to Wales. Annals record a visit to Ireland, where he had some influence on monastic practice. An eleventh-century monk of Rhuis near Vannes in Brittany wrote the *Life of Gildas*, in which he describes him as the founder of the monastery there, who ended his life on an island nearby. The life of his friend, Cadoc of Llancarfan, seems to have followed a similar pattern.

In a culture where the sea figured large, small chapels were built around the coasts, as places to pray before and after journeys. Many hermits chose to live near the sea; St Govan's chapel at Bosherton in Pembrokeshire, built in a cleft in the rock, and measuring six metres by four and a half, challenges the imagination. Rebuilt possibly in the thirteenth century, its origins are thought to be earlier as St Govan was a sixth-century saint. St Tudno had his cave below the Great Orme at Llandudno. Islands became home to hermits or sometimes to communities, and estuaries were busy places.

None were busier than the estuaries on the Cornish coast where many saints arrived from Wales and Ireland, and gave their names to settlements, so that today's map of Cornwall reads like a litany of saints' names.

Celtic Christianity in the south-west was not confined

to Cornwall. In Somerset, apart from the church at Glastonbury, St Cyngar was active at Congresbury and Banwell around 530. Up to the eighth century Devon and Cornwall together formed the kingdom of Dumnonia, but the earlier conquest of Devon by the Saxons has made the Celtic legacy there less visible than in Cornwall. Yet, at least two early Celtic foundations survived the Saxon conquest in the north of Devon, at Hartland and Braunton, while the names of some saints are common to both Devon and Cornwall: St Kea and St Fili have left their names near Barnstaple and in the Fal estuary.

Nonetheless, it was Cornwall that was geographically well placed to feel the full impact of the saints of Ireland. Place names around the Hayle estuary commemorate the arrival of St Gwinear and some of his companions: Uny, Phillack, Erth and St Ives. Meryadoc, or Meriasek, may also have arrived with Gwinear. He became bishop of Camborne and his memory has been kept alive as the subject of the only medieval play to have survived in the Cornish language. There were many others from Ireland, such as St Buryan, who founded her church near Land's End.

Often a saint's place of origin is uncertain. Piran may have been Irish or Welsh; he was certainly very popular and became the patron saint of tinners and of Cornwall itself. The Cornish flag bears St Piran's cross, which is a white cross against a black background, and many place names recall him. The remains of a sixth-century chapel, thought to be part of his monastery, lie in the sand dunes near Perranporth, while at nearby Perranzabuloe his shrine was a place of pilgrimage up to the Middle Ages.

Of the many saints who came to Cornwall from Wales, Petroc's influence spread far and wide over the south-west peninsula, but particularly around his centre at Padstow and later his hermitage on Bodmin Moor. Bodmin was his last resting place and became the religious centre of Cornwall up to the Reformation. Often more than one member of a family came, as was the case with Samson. Docco came with his sister Kew from his monastery of Llandough, near present-day Cardiff, and together they set up a monastery north of Wadebridge, first known as Lan Docco and later as St Kew, where Samson called on his arrival in Cornwall. No family of saints was more numerous than that of Brychan, the semi-legendary king of Powys, who gave his name to Brecon. Dedications to the children of Brychan are many and widespread – perhaps they were "children" in the sense of being his converts or followers. From Hartland in north Devon, where the oldest, Nectan, settled, to the Camel estuary and southwards, St Minver, St Mabyn, St Keria and St Keyne, along with their numerous brothers and sisters, are part of the rich tapestry of early church life in Cornwall, as far as it can be discerned through the wealth of tradition that has accumulated in the intervening centuries.

Many Welsh saints moved on to Brittany; some, such as Samson and Paul Aurelian, founded bishoprics, as did the Cornish Tugdual at Treguier. Brittany was very much part of the itinerary of the travelling saints. In their turn, Bretons such as Budoc are remembered in Cornwall through church dedications at Falmouth and Plymouth, while the Breton Winwaloe established his hermitage almost on the beach at Gunwalloe.

Cornwall is rich in reminders of the saints in the names of settlements, churches and holy wells. Local festivals remain popular and serve to perpetuate the traditions of the past, as do the "pardons", the religious processions in honour of local saints, in Brittany.

The journeyings of the saints were an act of faith, at the mercy of the waves on their light craft – some made of hides stretched over wicker frames and tarred, others of timber. They lived frugally, dependent on simple hospitality, and knew the art of travelling light, with a staff and leather satchel for such books as they possessed, and a cloak to protect them from the weather. A handbell became part of the few trappings of the wandering saints – used to announce their arrival to a scattered population. The bell often became a treasure after the saint's death: Petroc's was kept at Bodmin and Paul Aurelian's at the cathedral church of St Pol de Leon in Brittany, just as the bell that may have belonged to St Patrick is preserved at Dublin's National Museum.

While simple travel, often alone and on foot, was the norm, it seems this was not always the case. The *Life of St Samson* paints a somewhat different picture of Samson's journey through Cornwall; by this time a bishop of some standing, Samson travels in a chariot brought from Ireland, harnessed to two horses, while his books and holy vessels are transported on a cart. A band of brother monks go before and after him as he makes his way to the south coast. En route, he passes a group of people worshipping an idol and descends from his chariot to teach them the error of their ways. At another unnamed place on his journey, he founds a church and leaves his father to care for it, with other members of their company. Golant may well have been one of his stopping places. Here there is a church dedicated to St Samson, with a holy well. The porch next to the well was perhaps a chapel for it and nearby Fowey could well have been Samson's port of departure from Cornwall to Brittany.

The *Life of St Samson,* because it is an almost-contemporary account, brings the sixth-century Church to life. It provides glimpses of the practices within church life: the oversight of the bishop in Samson's training, the role of the deacon assisting in services, singing the gospel, leading some of the prayers, administering the chalice, and the practice of confession and subsequent penance.

While the commitment of these early Celtic saints is impressive, a realistic view suggests that, at this stage, the instruction many converts received may have been very basic and their understanding coloured by previous beliefs. Magic and miracle lived side by side, as did superstition, legend and pagan ritual on the one hand, and Christian belief and practice on the other, sometimes overlapping. Notions of morality were only slowly modified. There are indications in the *Life of St Samson* that monasteries fell short of their early ideals: Samson pondered how he could leave Illtud's monastery without hurting his elderly master's feelings, since its reputation was no longer what it had been. Jealousy, greed and drunkenness all figure among the brothers in the *Life of St Samson*. Samson himself, on the other hand, is presented as not only totally committed but also as highly disciplined, frequently observing vigils and fasts, which sometimes lasted as long as a week, and never sleeping on a bed. The dedicated lives of the finest of these early saints reflected their conviction and vision, and the people responded with great devotion. The saints' annual festivals were times to remember their example and find encouragement in them. The cult of St Samson became widespread after his death.

It was not only in Wales and the south-west that the Church continued to grow in the west of Britain. In the north, in Galloway, the monastery of Candida Casa, founded by St Ninian, was attracting students and pilgrims from other Celtic areas, particularly from Ireland. St Serf was active in the Ochil hills, north-east of Stirling, and at his monastic school at Culross he prepared St Kentigern for his life's work. St Kentigern, or St Mungo as he was affectionately known, continued St Ninian's missionary work in the Strathclyde area and became a bishop. When his work there was interrupted for a while, tradition has it that he moved to Cumbria, where there are a few churches dedicated to him, then continued south into Wales, where he is credited with founding the church at St Asaph.

When the situation in Strathclyde allowed him to return north, he seems to have worked not only in the Glasgow area, but also to have spent some of his later years in Annandale and Dumfriesshire, where his name is particularly associated with Hoddom. His contribution as a missionary among the Britons in the north-west has earned him a respected place in the story of the sixth-century Church there.

Further north the Church was expanding dramatically in the sixth century, largely through a mission from Ireland, where Christianity was developing in a unique and powerful way.

III

TWO TRADITIONS – CELTIC AND ROMAN

The Age of the Saints in Ireland

In Ireland, the Christian Church, as it developed, acquired a quite distinct character. Circumstances there were different in that there had been no Roman occupation, so society everywhere had remained rural and tribal. There were many small kingdoms under local kings, with two more powerful over-kings at Tara and Cashel by the fifth century. Druidism was still deeply entrenched, but any initial resistance on the part of the druids to Christian ways of thinking would appear to have yielded over time without major difficulty, as one merged into the other. In converting to Christianity Ireland did not abandon her earlier culture. On the contrary, she developed and enriched it within the Church.

Just as in sixth-century Wales there were two forces at work shaping the Church – on the one hand the legacy of the Roman Church and its organisation and on the other, the new monastic movement – so a similar process took place in Ireland. St Patrick had evangelised within the Roman episcopal framework of a bishop with authority over priests and deacons, but the monastic movement took hold of Ireland in a particularly powerful way and, to a large extent, superimposed its own organisation, because it simply fitted in better with the existing social order, where the kinship group easily became the monastic family.

Whether monasticism came to Ireland via western Britain, or via the Mediterranean, it was different from the original movement in the Egyptian desert, both in its missionary outlook and in the value it set on learning. Already in the later fifth century, the church at Armagh had become monastic and at Nendrum on Strangford Lough a monastery had been established by St Mochaoi, a follower of St Patrick. We have some idea of what an early monastery may have looked like from excavations carried out at Nendrum in the 1920s. The stump of an ancient round tower led to the rediscovery of the monastery that was founded in the late fifth century on the island of Mahee in Strangford Lough. It consisted of three circular, concentric stone walls. In the inner circle were the remains of church buildings; between the inner wall and the second were remains of the monks' cells; while the space enclosed by the outer circle appears to have contained barns, workshops and animal shelters. Implements from a bronze foundry and the writing slates of a monastic school were also uncovered on the site, while an ancient bell, now in the Ulster museum, was found hidden in a wall. Further south, St Buithe had established Monasterboice, while in the west St Enda had founded a church on the Aran Island of Inishmore, the first of many there.

While there was no single pattern, a surrounding wall, or a bank and ditch enclosed each monastery with its small, simple buildings of wattle and daub, wickerwork or timber, and thatch or turf for a roof. Bede, writing in the eighth century, describes the Irish way of building as "hewn oak thatched with reeds". Some early buildings were of stone, particularly in the west. Gallerus' oratory in Kerry, whether of the seventh century or later, has stood the test of time. Built of corbelled stones and shaped like an upturned boat, it remains proof against the weather.

The sixth century saw an enormous expansion of monasticism. In central Ireland St Brigit founded her nunnery at Kildare, which was later to become a double monastery that maintained a high reputation for centuries. At Clonard, St Finnian pioneered the establishment of other houses in Ireland. There is a tradition that he trained twelve apostles who went out to found what were to become great monastic houses. Among them were St Columba and St Ciaran who founded Clonmacnoise. This grew into a flourishing centre of learning, where, at one point, it was claimed that three thousand monks and students lived.

Other great monasteries had their origins in this period: in the north St Comgall established Bangor on the coast, another great centre of learning that sent many missionaries abroad. It may have become even larger than Clonmacnoise. In the south Lismore developed similarly, with links by sea not only with Britain but also with southern Gaul and Spain. There were countless others. At some of these early sites there are no visible remains, as at Clonard, while at Glendalough in County Wicklow, the site offers a clear illustration of how an early monastery developed, with churches and other buildings added over the centuries, in this case along the length of the valley.

The small oratory there, known as St Kevin's Kitchen, with its steeply pitched roof, reminds one of later depictions of churches on stone crosses and also St Columba's oratory at Kells. This was where the sixth-century Columba was given a site to found a monastery and also where the monks from Iona in the ninth century found sanctuary when their island was attacked by Norsemen. Here the accumulated treasures of centuries can be seen, particularly the finely sculptured crosses – but these belong to a later stage in the story, as do the extensive ruins at Clonmacnoise and Monasterboice.

The large monasteries fostered many daughter houses and it was the federations of monastic communities that became the fundamental units of organisation under the jurisdiction of the abbot of the mother house. Each group was independent; there was no common liturgy and no central authority. In the course of the sixth century the abbot became a more powerful figure, not only in relation to the monks and the lay workers in the monastery but also over the land and people around it, providing for their spiritual needs. He became very much like a secular lord with a large estate. Often the abbot came from the local royal dynasty and his successors from his own family.

Occasionally the abbot was a bishop too, but more often one of the monks within the monastery was consecrated bishop though remaining subject to the abbot. While the bishop retained his sacramental role to ordain, confirm and consecrate, his administrative and disciplinary function was severely curtailed. This was a feature of the Celtic Church that was later to cause a great deal of friction in parts of the Church that followed Roman ways. It is also one expression of the very individual development of the Irish Church.

However, the Age of the Saints in Ireland, so called because of the vast numbers of holy men and women of this period (from the late fifth to the late seventh century), is a much more exciting story than one of mere organisation. The saints held before them an ideal of holiness which called for a total and passionate commitment. The rule of life was harsh, excessively so to present-day thinking, but there was in its practice an independence of spirit that expressed itself in exuberant, imaginative and even whimsical ways through poetry, manuscript illumination and voyages into the unknown. It was a way of life that profoundly affected not only Ireland but also Britain and, even more remarkably, Europe too, in one of its dark periods.

Where there are remains, the sites of these early monasteries are evocative, and we can imagine the life of prayer and praise, of learning and work of the early monks. At the heart of their life was the *Opus Dei*, the work of God, with several daily offices or services in which psalm singing was central. A sixth-century psalter known as the Cathach survives; it is thought to have belonged to St Columba and may have been written by him. The script is distinctive and there are simply decorated initials, outlined with red dots, a forerunner of the spectacular works of art that followed in later centuries. The daily worship of the monks culminated on the Lord's Day, which began at Vespers on Saturday, a time of preparation for the celebration of the Eucharist on Sunday.

From the beginning the monasteries set great store by learning and became centres where not only the Scriptures and the Early Fathers of the Church were studied, along with Latin, which was the language of the Church in the West, but also classical literature. As centres of learning, the Irish monasteries attracted large numbers of students from Britain and the Continent. Bede writes of the hospitality the visitors received, of how they were provided with food, books and instruction for which no payment was required. Through the Church, reading and writing entered a culture that had previously been purely oral, through books that had to be laboriously copied by hand. But even in the sixth century, Irish monasteries were beginning to produce writings of their own, in the form of Rules of Life to regulate monastic practice, such as the Rule of St Comgall of Bangor and the Rule of Columba, and there were the penitentials.

These penitentials were books that prescribed detailed penances for particular sins. Their very existence testifies to the importance of penance in the Irish Church, where a keen awareness of the holiness of God produced an equally keen consciousness of the failings of human beings. The penitentials represent an earnest desire to apply Christian teaching to daily living. In the practice of confession, which preceded the penance prescribed, the Irish Church made a very positive contribution to church life on a wider front. Whereas in the early Church confession for wrong-doing had been in public before the whole congregation, followed by exclusion from communion and subsequent public reinstatement, the Church in Ireland devised a different system: confession was made in private, often to a 'soul-friend', and penance at its best was designed to help the sinner move forward in his spiritual life in a constructive way, rather than simply to punish.

The rigours and asceticism of monastic life may paint a rather grey picture to our thinking, but for those with a sincere vocation, there were compensatory joys, and not only in the opportunities for worship. Craftsmen found satisfaction in exercising their skills, whether in manuscript copying and illustrating, or in metalwork; for others there was the joy of sharing new skills and knowledge. Many children of the upper classes were fostered by the monasteries, while the children of married lay brothers who farmed the land received some education too. As they grew, monasteries must have been very busy places. The spiritual needs of the people around the monasteries had to be met – basic instruction and opportunities for worship provided, along with baptism and burial.

Pagan practices and beliefs did not disappear overnight. Pagan festivals continued, gradually Christianised. As the Christian saints took the place of the old heroes, and new holy places were established in the form of churches, crosses and saints' shrines, so Christian teaching was slowly absorbed by the people.

Not all communities were large and busy; some were in isolated places. Skellig Michael off the coast of Kerry provided a site for a small community. The remains of six stone, beehive-shaped cells; two chapels; a graveyard; and a garden can still be seen. At Inishmurray, an island off Sligo, are the traces of cells and the enclosing wall of a monastery founded by the sixth-century St Molaise. But life in a community was only one side of the monasticism that had come from the East. The solitary life as practised by hermits, or anchorites, was embraced by many in Ireland. Freed from human ties the individual hoped to achieve a mastery of self in the practice of the presence of God. This was seen as the highest form of the contemplative life, usually preceded by life in a community and still under the direction of the abbot. The west of Ireland particularly, with its rugged coast and many islands, provided ideal sites for a life in isolation. In such places the sea provided the "desert" element, where there were few distractions from a life of closer communion with God. There were hermit settlements inland too, often indicated by the prefix "kil", meaning a cell, in a place name.

Linked with the anchorite movement was a peculiarly Irish form of pilgrimage – a voluntary exile from one's homeland, not necessarily alone nor explicitly as a missionary, but simply going "on pilgrimage for Christ", sometimes for penitential reasons. In this way many Irish saints found their way to Europe, as did Columbanus, who left the monastery at Bangor in the north around the year 590, in company with twelve followers, with St Gall among them. From the monasteries he founded in the Vosges mountains at Annegray and Luxueil, Columbanus went on to found another at Bobbio in Italy, which became a great centre of learning. Through his many disciples his influence spread throughout Europe and the strict Rule of St Columbanus was used in monasteries founded by these Irish monks for centuries, before yielding to the less harsh Rule of St Benedict. St Gall settled in Swabia, which is now St Gallen in Switzerland, where a Benedictine monastery with a famous library was later established.

It seems others were drawn to where these Irish pilgrims settled and led the monastic life, and a community would be established. Relations were not always harmonious with the diocesan-based Church in Gaul when the Celtic monks insisted on their own customs and calendar, which clashed with local usage, to the annoyance of the hierarchy, but they made a deep impression by their prayerful and ascetic lives.

St Brendan's travels led him in other directions when he set out with his companions in search of the promised land of the saints. It is thought he may have been responsible for taking Christianity to Iceland. A poem attributed to him recaptures something of the nature of these pilgrimages. In it he contemplates leaving the security of his native land to embark in his coracle on an unpredictable sea, trusting in Christ to help him.

Columba's Monastery on Iona

Of the Irish monks who came to Britain, it was undoubtedly Columba who made the greatest impact. Columba was born in 521 of noble stock: his father belonged to one of the ruling families of Ireland and Dalriada on the west coast of Scotland, which had been colonised by the Irish. Dedicated to the Church from an early age, he became known as Columcille, the Dove of the Church. He was one of the group of students at Clonard, under St Finnian, who became known as the Fathers of the Irish Church.

Among the churches and monasteries he founded in Ireland were Durrow, Derry and Kells, but in the year 563, he left his native Ireland with twelve companions and settled on the island of Iona. One tradition claims the move was a penance of perpetual exile for his involvement in a battle in which many died. Conflicts between large monasteries were not unheard of, but the idea of perpetual exile is perhaps a later gloss put on events. Iona was within a short sailing distance of his homeland and Columba returned many times to visit the foundations that remained under his authority. Iona was on the edge of territory ruled over by King Conall, a relative of his; it was also near the kingdom of the Picts who were not converted to Christianity at that time. Columba was the first abbot of the monastery at Iona. A century after his death, the ninth abbot, Adamnan, wrote an account of Columba's life in which he conveys something of the charismatic nature of the saint, inspiring both love and respect in his followers. This was perhaps not the whole story: Columba would appear to have been of a rather fiery and aggressive temperament in his earlier days, doubtless mellowed and humbled by a life of discipline and devotion to God.

Adamnan describes Columba's gifts of prophecy, his miraculous powers and his visions, and offers glimpses of life on the island of Iona, which then had little but the huts of the young community: glimpses of Columba sitting in his hut, sometimes transcribing the psalms; the occasional shout of a visitor from the other side of the Sound of Iona, prompting the ferry to cross over to Mull to fetch him; the grinding of corn for the barns; the white pack-horse carrying vessels of milk from the cowshed to the monastery.

However, life on the island was not just a pastoral idyll. Columba was concerned to spread the Christian faith. There were visits to King Brude of the Picts, near Inverness, and encounters with the King's druid, Broichan, and other druids whom he challenged to good effect, according to his biographer. There are references to the excommunication of destroyers of churches, and of missionary visits to the surrounding areas – to Ardnamurchan and Kintyre, and to many islands, Eigg, Skye, Islay and Tiree among them – establishing monasteries and cells, activities that earned Columba a reputation as one of the founding fathers of the church in Scotland. He returned often to Ireland and continued to wield power over a large area in both countries – a prime example of the powerful abbot in the Celtic Church.

Like most biographers of saints, Adamnan describes Columba's last hours movingly; how, having blessed the barn and the corn in it, he ascended the hill overlooking the monastery, blessed it and predicted that, small and humble as it was, Iona would be greatly respected. He encouraged his fellow monks to be at peace with one another. He rested a while on his bed, with a bare flag for his couch and a stone for his pillow, before he attended the midnight office that ushered in the Lord's Day. It was his last, but his influence and example were to linger for centuries. In the "Song of Trust", attributed to him, he dismisses pagan ways of thinking and commends faith in Christ, who is to him his druid, the Great Abbot.

In the early practice of Christianity in all the Celtic countries several strands were interwoven, from an appreciation of the contemplative life to the practice of faith in community, with whole families involved alongside clergy and monks. There was too the willingness to choose a life of austerity and the hardships involved in constant journeying. It was Christianity lived out in a pastoral context, a far cry from the sophisticated circles of the Mediterranean world, where a great deal of energy was spent on doctrinal debate in the early centuries of the Church. Only the background and culture were different; the central beliefs were the same and all were part of one universal Church. Christianity as it developed in Britain and Ireland was very much influenced by Gaul. Gaul itself had been greatly influenced by Eastern thinking and practice. In this way the Celtic Churches shared something of the tradition of the East and of the Church's early liturgy. But Celtic culture had its own distinctive contribution to make. In it there was no dichotomy between the material and the spiritual: the natural and the supernatural were interrelated, and worship often took place in the open air, with living water for baptism. The heart was engaged as much as the head as the people lived in communion with God, with others and with nature, which suggests an appealing wholeness. It was a period when all the Celtic peoples developed a strong sense of identity in which, over the years, race and place became intimately bound up with the Christian faith.

The Mission of St Augustine

In the year that St Columba died on Iona, St Augustine arrived in Kent. It was the year 597. He came with forty other monks from a monastery in Rome where he had been the prior. They brought with them interpreters from Gaul. It was the fulfilment of a plan Pope Gregory had cherished for some time: to take Christianity to the pagan tribes who had invaded Britain.

It had been a long journey. En route, the fears of the monks at the prospect before them crystallised: they sent Augustine back to Pope Gregory, begging that they might be released from the perilous task he had set them, but Gregory was not to be deflected. He encouraged them with a letter, telling them not to be influenced by the difficulties of the journey nor by the views of others. For good measure he made Augustine abbot, to increase his authority – a monk had to obey his abbot – and supplied him with letters commending them all to the rulers and bishops they would encounter as they made their way through Gaul, where relations were far from peaceful between Frankish kings. Thus armed, they survived the rigours of the journey, more than one thousand miles, and landed in Kent at Ebbsfleet on the Isle of Thanet. A stone cross commemorates the event.

They had come a long way from the Roman world of planned cities with their buildings of stone and marble, a world of books and written laws, where Christianity was established as the official religion. They came to a population in which many had only recently arrived, still fighting their way westwards and northwards, living in rival kingdoms under laws agreed by word of mouth. Their communities were smaller, their buildings made of timber, and in their sanctuaries they worshipped pagan gods – Thor, god of war and thunder, and Woden, father of the gods. Their allegiance was to their king, who was to them a descendant of Woden.

It is small wonder that the monks came in trepidation. They did not even have the experience of pastoral work that secular clergy would have had; their experience was of a life of prayer in community, but it was a life of total dedication and discipline. This was what Pope Gregory evidently thought was required.

From the Isle of Thanet their interpreters went to Ethelbert, king of Kent, to announce their arrival from Rome with the good news of Jesus Christ. He ordered them to stay where they were, while he considered what he would do. Ethelbert was not ignorant of the Christian faith: his wife, Bertha, daughter of the king of Paris, was a Christian, and on his marriage Ethelbert had agreed that she would be free to practise her faith under the guidance of her chaplain, Bishop Liudhard, who had accompanied her to Kent. Perhaps Ethelbert was sympathetic to the new faith, but although he was *bretwalda*, meaning the chief king among the Anglo-Saxons, it was a position he had established many years previously. He was now ageing; he had ruled for thirty-two years and he had to take into account the response of sub-kings and his pagan priests if he were to change allegiance.

When Ethelbert came to the Isle of Thanet, he summoned the monks to appear before him. The Venerable Bede, in his *History of the English Church*, describes how they came, carrying a silver cross and a representation of Christ, painted on a board, and singing a litany as they processed. The king received their message with courtesy: he and his people had their own beliefs, but he gave them freedom to preach theirs and offered to supply their needs, giving them a place to live in the capital of his kingdom, Canterbury, which was then still known by its Roman name of Durovernum. The mission was launched.

The old church of St Martin, which Bede suggests was built originally by the Romans, had been sufficiently repaired to allow Queen Bertha to use it for worship. A medallion found in the churchyard of St Martin's with the inscription "*Leudardus Eps*", a reference to the queen's chaplain, appears to confirm the link. This is where the monks based their work. For Augustine the time had come to be consecrated bishop, as Pope Gregory had planned if the mission proved possible. He went to Arles, an important episcopal see in Gaul, and returned as archbishop. His life as prior in the monastery in Rome had prepared him in some measure for his new position, but he had always worked under the direction of the abbot. He must have felt inadequate at the task before him and sought advice from Pope Gregory for the organisation of the Church committed to his care.

It was probably in the year 601 that King Ethelbert decided to accept the Christian faith and was baptised. This was a major step forward and must have given a fresh impetus to the young Church. The response from Rome was prompt and supportive in every possible way: more helpers and clergy, of whom Mellitus, Justus and Paulinus would play leading roles; vestments, relics, vessels and books for worship; a letter to King Ethelbert exhorting him to become a second Constantine for his people; and the pallium for Augustine, which was a gift from the pope for his archbishops to wear at Mass; together with instructions on how this new branch of the Church should be organised. Pope Gregory's plan was that there should be two archbishops, in London and York, each with twelve bishops under his jurisdiction, but political circumstances in the south did not allow for London to be the seat of the southern province: it was in the kingdom of an under-king who was not Christian, and it was Canterbury that Ethelbert had offered to Augustine as his base.

With the king's encouragement, Augustine had the Roman church, which stood on the site of the present cathedral, repaired, and dedicated it to Christ the Saviour. This became the new base for the mission, where worship was held, the clergy were trained in the bishop's household, and monks and clergy lived in community. There would have been pastoral work too: tending to the needs of the sick and the poor.

The king was further persuaded to provide a monastery for the monks among them, where they would be able to resume the life of prayer they had originally chosen. It was to be dedicated to St Peter and St Paul; there the kings of Kent and the archbishops of Canterbury would be buried. Its foundations can still be seen. These churches and all those built in the next half-century in the south-east were of stone, and followed a similar plan: a nave with a rounded chancel. They were almost certainly built by masons brought over from Gaul or Italy, since the Saxons had no experience of building in stone; even their kings' halls were built of timber.

A letter to the abbot Mellitus from Pope Gregory gave general advice on how to deal with the pagans, recommending that, while all idols should be destroyed, pagan shrines should be left, but purified with holy water, rededicated, and furnished with altars and relics. The old celebrations should be replaced with Christian festivals, so that the people were not deprived of their feasts, but led gently to the worship of the true God, step by step, just as they had been led through basic instruction to baptism, and incorporated into the body of the Church through sharing in the Eucharist and the general worship of the Church. Augustine had some freedom in arranging the liturgy. While his experience in Rome provided the basic pattern, Pope Gregory had suggested he should also use the best of the practices he had seen in Gaul. Central to worship would have been the Sunday morning Eucharist before the fast had been broken. The service had become widely known in the West as the Mass. The vigil in preparation for it started at Vespers on Saturday and was continued at the dawn office. The procession of clergy in their vestments, the candles and incense would have provided a spectacle for the new converts, for whom the chanting of the monks, the readings and preaching, and the communion itself, which they called the *husel* (meaning the sacrifice), would have been impressive, even though the language was Latin.

They would have been familiar with pagan rites and sacrifices to placate the old gods, but the solemn offering of blessed bread and wine in remembrance of the sacrifice of Christ, his resurrection and continuing presence, together with the teaching of the Christian faith were wholly new. They had their part to play too – they would have brought an offering in kind or coin, and they would have received the bread and wine, and a blessing on leaving. Marriage, the baptism of babies, sickness and death would have provided other points of contact with the Church, but particularly the feasts at festival times. For some it may have been a nominal acceptance of the faith, a form of loyalty to the king, for others, a great deal more for it to have survived in the less congenial times that followed the death of King Ethelbert.

As the work in Kent progressed, Augustine was looking further afield, mindful that Pope Gregory had given him authority over the British bishops in the west of the country, where the Christian Church was alive and well, even if not conforming to Roman ways.

A meeting was arranged in the year 603 near the Bristol Channel; Bede calls the place St Augustine's Oak. It would have been accessible to the bishops of the south-west and South Wales. The Anglo-Saxon Chronicle tells us that as recently as 577, only twenty-six years earlier, the king of the West Saxons had taken over the ruined cities of Gloucester, Cirencester and Bath, and extended Saxon territory over the Severn mouth and the lower Severn valley. For the Britons in the west then, the Saxons were still very much the conquering invader and they would surely have seen in Augustine someone allied to the enemy's chief king and wanting to extend his influence. They had no quarrel with Rome, nor had they any reason to suppose they needed instruction in the faith; they had been the first recipients of Christianity in Britain and had received the apostolic faith from their much revered fathers: David, Illtud and their company. Augustine may well have been unaware of the strength and tradition of the Celtic Churches. The Britons, for their part, had no experience of an archbishop. Augustine's overtures were received with suspicion, and his wish that they should join him in converting the heathen Anglo-Saxons and in adopting the ways of Rome made no headway. They asked for time to consult with their people and a second meeting was arranged, possibly further north since it was attended by many monks from the monastery of Bangor-is-Coed as well as by seven bishops. Before the meeting they sought the advice of a wise hermit, who told them to look for signs of humility in Augustine that would mark him out as a true man of God. If he remained seated when they arrived, they could draw their own conclusion. Augustine remained seated, for to rise would have ceded his authority to direct and teach. His wish that they should celebrate Easter at the same time as Rome and use the same form of the baptismal rite, as well as evangelise among the Anglo-Saxons, was rejected and his authority spurned. Augustine predicted that, as a result, they would suffer attack and death. For Bede the prophecy was later fulfilled at the battle of Chester when King Ethelfrid slaughtered some twelve hundred monks from Bangor-is-Coed, who had come to pray for protection. Reconciliation with the Celtic Church in the west was not to be achieved through Augustine.

Back in the south-east, the Church was beginning to expand beyond the bounds of Kent. In 604 Mellitus was consecrated bishop by Augustine and sent to preach to the East Saxons in the kingdom north of the Thames, which had London as its capital, ruled over by Ethelbert's nephew Sabert. On the success of his preaching Mellitus became Bishop of London, and Ethelbert had a church built dedicated to St Paul. Justus was made Bishop of Rochester; again the king provided a church dedicated to St Andrew and endowed both bishoprics with land and property.

Later in that same year Augustine died. His ministry to the English had lasted only seven years, but the small geographical extent of the Church he had established belies the significance of his achievement. The beginnings of an episcopate and a liturgy for the Church had been established, together with a pattern for the training of the clergy to be developed in the minster churches, which would be built on land given by the king, and later by bishops or lords, where clergy lived as a community. Books had been introduced: the Scriptures and sacramentaries for use in worship. The Gospel Book sent to Augustine by Pope Gregory is still used in the installation of the archbishops of Canterbury. The foundations had been laid for the monastic life. Stone architecture gave greater permanence to the setting of the Church. Society in a wider sense had also been affected: Augustine encouraged Ethelbert to draw up a code of written laws, which fitted the Church into society, giving clergy their "worth", like every other citizen, and protecting church property. The south-east was once again in touch with the civilisation of the Mediterranean countries, and in a relationship with the Church in Rome after a lapse of some one hundred and fifty years.

The epitaph on Augustine's tomb pays tribute to him and to the pope who had acted upon his missionary vision. Before he died, Augustine had consecrated Lawrence as his successor. Lawrence had been the only other priest among the first party of missionaries to arrive here. As archbishop he was able to build on the foundations laid by Augustine, but in 616, the still-young Church came under threat: King Ethelbert died after a reign of fifty years and was succeeded by a pagan son. King Sabert of the East Saxons, Ethelbert's nephew, also died soon after and his three pagan sons expelled Mellitus from their kingdom. It seemed best to all three bishops that they should return to their own country, since their task under pagan kings seemed impossible. Mellitus and Justus left for Gaul, expecting Lawrence to follow. But Ethelbert's son, King Eadbald, had a change of heart and resolved to accept the Christian faith. Mellitus and Justus were recalled; Justus returned to his former see at Rochester, but the rulers of the East Saxons had no change of heart so Mellitus could not return to his see. On the death of Lawrence in 619, Mellitus became the third archbishop of Canterbury.

Church building in Canterbury was increasing: in addition to St Martin's and the Church of the Saviour, the monastery of St Peter and St Paul, begun by Augustine had now been completed and consecrated by Archbishop Lawrence. King Eadbald had built a second church to the east of it, dedicated to the Virgin Mary in 620. Another church to St Pancras was built even further east; its lower walls still survive today.

Mission to the North

Then a completely new opportunity arose for the extension of the Church, this time in the north. King Edwin had become king of Northumbria and chief king among the Anglo-Saxons. He had sought the hand of Ethelburga, daughter of King Ethelbert, in marriage. A pagan himself, he had agreed to respect Ethelburga's Christian commitment and even implied that he would be open to persuasion. Justus, who had by this time succeeded Mellitus as archbishop, consecrated Paulinus as bishop and sent him north with Ethelburga and her attendants.

Paulinus hoped to convert Edwin's heathen people but his efforts were in vain; in those days the support and example of the king were vital to advancing the Church's mission. Eventually the persuasion of Paulinus, the example of Ethelburga and a letter from Pope Boniface encouraging Edwin to become a Christian bore fruit. He was already inclined to accept the Christian faith, but first he called a council of his chief men to discuss the matter openly. In Bede's account of the event, Paulinus waited to present his case to King Edwin and his nobles, as Augustine had done before King Ethelbert of Kent. Coifi, Edwin's chief pagan priest, spoke up without hesitation. He declared himself disillusioned with the old religion: his efforts in the service of the old gods had not procured him the personal advantage he had hoped for. Bede puts into the mouth of another counsellor a more philosophical view: he sees man's time on earth like the flight of a sparrow through the warmth and comfort of a banqueting hall, out of the harsh winter weather from which it came and to which it will return. In a similar way, what precedes our life on earth and what follows it is shrouded in mystery, which the new teaching might clarify. For that reason he feels it should be accepted. The other counsellors agreed and Paulinus was allowed to commend his faith. The king was persuaded and gave the same permission to preach that Ethelbert had granted to Augustine, while Coifi rode off eagerly with sword and spear to destroy the idols and shrines of the old order.

In 627 King Edwin was baptised, along with his nobles and many others at York, in a timber church the king had had built for the purpose. This was the city he gave to Paulinus as his see, as Pope Gregory had originally planned. After his baptism Edwin ordered that a greater church of stone should be built around the timber one. For six years Paulinus worked with Edwin's encouragement. At Yeavering, one of the king's residences, people came from all around to be instructed and baptised in the River Glen, and in the River Swale at Catterick. At the well at Holystone near Rothbury, it is claimed that Paulinus baptised three thousand people. We can imagine him, since one of those he baptised later passed on a description of him to an abbot contemporary of Bede: a tall, dark-haired man, ascetic-looking, a man with a presence. Paulinus's mission extended south of the Humber to Lincoln and, in the church he built there, Paulinus consecrated Honorius as the fourth successor to Augustine on the death of Justus.

Then disaster struck: Edwin was defeated and killed in a battle against Cadwallada, a British king in North Wales, and Penda of Mercia, a resolute pagan who ruled over central England for twenty-two years. The chaos that followed in Northumbria caused Paulinus to flee south by sea with Queen Ethelburga and her family, leaving behind him his deacon, James, to care for the Church. Edwin's immediate successors reverted to paganism, but they too were killed by Cadwallada. It was not until Cadwallada himself was killed by Edwin's nephew Oswald, that peace – and Christianity – was restored.

Oswald had spent time in exile on Iona; where better to look for help to restore the faith in his kingdom? The arrival of Aidan from Iona was a new beginning for the Church in the north. He chose the island of Lindisfarne to be his base. It was not far from the king's residence at Bamburgh and the two often worked together, with the king acting as interpreter for his new bishop. Other monks from Iona came to join Aidan, and a monastery was established on the island on the traditional Celtic pattern, with a small school where Anglo-Saxon boys could be trained for the Church. Other churches were built and monasteries founded on land endowed by the king. The wider Christianisation of the north by the Celtic Christians from Iona had begun in earnest. Aidan is seen as one of the model Celtic saints – a holy man of humility and compassion, whose wholehearted devotion to God inspired a similar devotion in King Oswald. The saintly king died in 642, as Edwin had died, in battle against Penda, the pagan king of Mercia.

Aidan continued his work until 651. On his death he was buried on Lindisfarne, which has remained a place of pilgrimage. His tireless evangelism, his simple life free of material possessions and his concern for the poor had made a deep impression on the people he worked among. The values and practices of the Celtic Church had, through him, made a profound impact in the north, which was to be maintained by others who followed in his footsteps.

Developments in the South, in the East and in Wessex

In Kent the Church was continuing to expand. Paulinus spent his last years as bishop of Rochester, while a monastery was founded for Ethelburga at Lyminge. Kings provided land and endowments for foundations at other places on the Kent coast – at Reculver, Folkestone and Dover, and, later in the century, at Sheppey and Thanet – most of them founded for royal princesses or by widowed queens, who assumed charge as abbesses. These religious houses were known as minsters and were at first the only churches: centres of what were in effect very large parishes, and the keystone of Church expansion. They contained either monks or nuns, or both, living under a monastic rule, or else clergy living communally under a bishop or a provost. Apart from their regular life of prayer, their task was to educate the young entrusted to them and prepare them for the service of the Church, and to provide a pastoral and evangelistic service to the surrounding area, in much the same way as the Celtic monasteries did.

The early churches in Kent were all built on the same Roman basilican plan. The site of the church at Reculver, built in 669 within an old Roman fort, clearly shows the plan of the original church: a simple nave without aisles and with a curved chancel, or apse, containing an altar. Around the apse would have been a stone bench for the bishop and clergy. Two projections, or porticuses, on the north and south sides of the building, overlapping both chancel and nave, opened into the church – one for offerings and the other for vestments and books; these were the beginnings of the transepts that were to develop to give the cruciform plan familiar to us.

Not very far away, at Bradwell-on-Sea, is another early church, this time still standing, seemingly in a world of its own on the Essex coast. Like Reculver, it was built on the site of an old Roman fort and on the same plan as the Kent churches. Only the nave survives but it is not difficult to imagine the apse at the east end, and the small porticuses to the north and south. The door to the one on the southern side can be seen from inside the church, along with the tops of three arches separating the nave from the apse, which was a feature common to most of these early churches.

The church was founded by a man from the north, Cedd, a monk from Lindisfarne, trained by Aidan and sent to help evangelise the kingdom of the East Saxons. After its reversion to paganism earlier in the century, there was now a new Christian king. Bishop Cedd spent eleven years working there, establishing churches; the church at Bradwell-on-Sea stands as a reminder to us of his faithful service.

In East Anglia, the Christian king Sigbert had done a great deal to convert his kingdom with the help of two men of very different origins: one being Bishop Felix from Burgundy and the other an Irish monk, Fursey. The king encouraged Felix to found a school to train clergy, with the help of teachers from Canterbury. As for Fursey, he had arrived in East Anglia from western Ireland with a small group of monks "on pilgrimage for Christ" and had set up a community at Burgh Castle, another old Roman fort, near Yarmouth. By his saintliness he drew many to the faith.

Many Irish monks were leaving their monasteries, which had developed a great reputation for learning, and were spreading their knowledge abroad. Around 635, one of their number, Maildubh, settled at Malmesbury and founded a school which was to develop into a flourishing monastery.

The kingdoms of the Anglo-Saxons were, in fact, being evangelised by Christians coming from many different directions in the first half of the seventh century: from Canterbury, Gaul and Rome on the one hand; and from Iona, Lindisfarne and Ireland on the other. The Celtic and Roman traditions were beginning to encounter each other on the ground as their missions spread. While their core beliefs were the same, their way of doing things and their church calendars were different, as was their general outlook.

Just as Bishop Felix had come from Gaul to work in East Anglia, two other bishops came from the Continent to the kingdom of Wessex. Bishop Birinus arrived around 634. His first task had been to convert the king; he was then given Dorchester-on-Thames as his see, where he built churches and worked to spread the faith in yet another Saxon kingdom. He died in 650 and was succeeded by Bishop Agilbert. He too was from Gaul and spent some ten to twelve years in Wessex, but it seems the king grew tired of Agilbert's foreign speech and appointed a second bishop, Wini, to a new see at Winchester without consulting Agilbert. The offended bishop resigned his see and went to Northumbria, where he was to be part of a Church synod that proved highly significant for the future of the Church in England.

Under successive kings the Saxons moved further west into Somerset. Now the Roman and Celtic traditions were meeting each other in the West Country too. Around the same time, the powerful pagan ruler of the central kingdom of Mercia, Penda, was killed, after years of wreaking havoc on all the kingdoms around him. He was succeeded by a Christian son, Paeda. In a calmer climate, communication between north and south became easier, and there were those who thought the time had come for the fusion of the two traditions, in the interests of Church unity. The impetus came from the king of Northumbria, Oswy, the new overlord, who in 664 convened a synod at Whitby to discuss the matter.

IV

UNITY UNDER AUTHORITY

The Synod of Whitby

During the course of the seventh century Christianity spread through all the Anglo-Saxon kingdoms. The year 664 was of special significance because it was the year of the Synod of Whitby. In itself this was an event of modest proportions, yet it contributed to the process of integrating different church traditions that had developed in these islands: on the one hand from Rome and Gaul, and on the other within the Celtic Churches, in which practice was far from uniform anyway. The differences had become increasingly apparent by the mid-seventh century as missionary efforts led to close encounters between them. In some places there appears to have been peaceful coexistence, as in East Anglia between Felix from Gaul and Fursey from Ireland. Bede tells us there had been some recurrent controversy within the community at Lindisfarne over the observance of Easter: some of their number were concerned that the Roman Church sometimes celebrated the festival at a different time from the Celtic Churches.

The problem of setting the date of Easter was not peculiar to Britain. It had dogged the Church from earliest times and took centuries to resolve. Many factors were involved, among them the date of the Jewish Passover and that of the spring equinox. It required the correlation of lunar and solar dates. Bede claims the Celtic Churches were still using a method of calculation that Rome had abandoned in the fifth century. This could result in a disparity of dates.

In the royal household of Northumbria there were unexpected repercussions: King Oswy, who had succeeded the saintly Oswald, had been brought up in the Celtic tradition; his queen, Eanfled, in the Roman tradition in her native Kent. It sometimes happened that they celebrated the chief Christian festivals at different times: while one observed Palm Sunday the other might be celebrating Easter; one fasted while the other feasted – a domestic reflection of the larger unsatisfactory situation.

King Oswy summoned the synod primarily to solve the problem of the dating of Easter, though Bede tells us that other church matters were also considered.

The significance of this early synod in the infant English Church has been a matter of much debate. Bede makes a great deal of it, but it has to be admitted that, at first sight, neither the venue nor the participants are impressive. Why Whitby? Why only three bishops? The clergy were mostly local, with one visitor who had only recently been made priest. Convened by the king of Northumbria, it might seem to be merely a local airing of the problem.

Closer examination suggests it was more significant than that: the king in question was an overlord whose influence spread well beyond the kingdom of Northumbria, which at its smallest stretched from north of the Humber up to the

Tweed. The monastery at Whitby was under the aegis of the see of Lindisfarne, which at this time was a more active centre of church life than Canterbury. Bishops were very thin on the ground: there were probably only five at that time in all the Anglo-Saxon kingdoms together. As for the new priest, Wilfrid, he was a formidable personality. He had spent his teenage years at Lindisfarne and had won the affection of the monks there. Then he had gone to Rome and Lyons for five years to study the Church there. The result was a complete change of allegiance from the church of his youth.

On his return to his homeland, fresh from instruction in Rome and experience of the Church in Gaul, Wilfrid was invited to Northumbria by Alchfrid, son of King Oswy and ruler of a sub-kingdom. Alchfrid may have seen political advantage in the establishment of the Roman tradition in Northumbria, with a bishop well disposed towards himself. In the early days, the local king and the Church benefited from the support each gave the other. He gave Wilfrid a monastery at Ripon, ejecting the Celtic monks he had previously given it to, and appointing Wilfrid abbot. At Alchfrid's request, the visiting Bishop Agilbert from Dorchester ordained Wilfrid as a priest. Together with the queen and her chaplain from Kent, they all championed Roman practice, as did James the deacon, who had come north forty years previously with Bishop Paulinus.

Defending the Celtic usage over Easter was the Lindisfarne community, supported by the much-respected Abbess Hilda and her community at Whitby, along with Bishop Cedd, who had been trained at Lindisfarne and often returned to Northumbria from his missionary work among the East Saxons.

It was the third bishop of Lindisfarne, Bishop Colman,

who would present the case for the Celtic practice. Irish by birth, he had been a monk at Iona, like his predecessors. Wilfrid would be the forceful spokesman for the Roman cause at the request of Bishop Agilbert, who was from Gaul and lacked fluency in English.

King Oswy opened the debate and declared its purpose: to decide, in the interests of church unity, which tradition should be followed in calculating the date of Easter, and everyone was directed to abide by the decision of the synod.

Invited by the king to present his case, Bishop Colman explained, in essence, that his community observed the customs learnt from the elders of his Church, believed to be derived from the Apostle John. With devastating eloquence Wilfrid proceeded to destroy Colman's case: it was the ill-informed practice of two remote islands foolishly opposing the whole world. While Colman had in all probability seen the whole question in terms of custom and loyalty to his forefathers in the Church, particularly St Columba, the thrust of Wilfrid's argument turned on the question of authority, which for him meant that of St Peter and his successors in Rome, and on the unity of the Christian Church. The confident, even ruthless presentation of the worldly-wise Wilfrid and his ungracious dismissal of the Church that had nurtured him seemed to confound his opponents. The inaccuracy of some of Wilfrid's claims went unchallenged. The climax of his argument provided the coup de grâce: could St Columba take precedence over St Peter, to whom Jesus had entrusted the keys of the kingdom of heaven?

It took King Oswy little time to declare in favour of St Peter, with a smile, according to Wilfrid's biographer and contemporary, Eddius Stephanus. No doubt the king thought he had not only made secure his place in heaven but had also made more secure his place on earth.

As a result of the decision, Bishop Colman renounced his bishopric and returned to Iona to consult with the community there. He took with him all among his fellows who shared his views. His departure from Lindisfarne came after thirty years of a remarkably successful mission by the Ionan monks to Northumbria.

Wilfrid's performance at the synod bore fruit for him personally within a short space of time, when Alchfrid chose him as bishop of his kingdom. Rather than be consecrated by Celtic bishops, Wilfrid elected to go to Gaul, where Agilbert, by this time Bishop of Paris, along with eleven fellow bishops, consecrated him with great splendour, bearing him aloft on a golden throne!

Bede, with his passion for order and unity in the Church, which for him meant conformity with Rome, gives us a detailed account of the Synod of Whitby. Even the pro-Rome Bede, however, recognised the qualities within the Celtic Churches, and was clearly impressed by the purity of life and love of God in the community at Iona. Any wrong practice, such as their dating of Easter, he attributed to a period of isolation from the rest of the Christian world. At the end of his account of the Synod of Whitby he pays generous tribute to the community at Lindisfarne – their frugal way of life, their generosity to the poor and the esteem in which they were held among the people, who flocked to the church to hear the word of God.

How significant was the decision of the Synod of Whitby? A small number of churchmen had agreed in principle to conform with Roman usage in certain respects. They were not the first to do so: the monastery of Bangor, alone in the north of Ireland, had adopted the

Roman Easter in the first decade of the seventh century. Parts of southern Ireland had made the same decision in the 630s. It was a whole century before conformity over the dating of Easter was achieved in most parts of Britain and Ireland, often after prolonged and heated debate, but the gradual process that led to the ascendancy of the Church of Rome over the essentially monastic Celtic Churches had undoubtedly received some impetus from the Synod of Whitby of 664.

When monasticism had first blossomed in Europe, there had been a degree of hostility towards it in Rome. One fifth-century pope had written deprecatingly of these "wanderers and strangers" with their different dress. They disturbed the establishment with their idealism and unworldliness. Monasteries soon became part of the establishment in Rome and Gaul, but they did not interact with the community in the way the Celtic monasteries did. Missions like Augustine's were controlled to some extent by the system and papal advice. By contrast, as Irish monks spread around the Continent "on pilgrimage for Christ", they brought with them their own practices and their own calendar. Their first obedience was to their abbot wherever they went, so they ignored local practice and the diocesan bishop, and caused much annoyance in official circles. The pope, though honoured essentially as the successor to St Peter, was not yet seen as the supreme authority of the Church in the West, but through correspondence with kings and church leaders, and through missionary endeavours, the papacy had been extending its influence. The Synod of Whitby helped the process. None did more to further it than Wilfrid, who, in the course of his tumultuous life, appealed more than once in person to the pope for a resolution of his many quarrels with kings and bishops, clearly setting the authority of the Apostolic See above theirs, and encouraging the growth of papal influence over the Church in England.

The Golden Age of the Church in Northumbria

Wilfrid's activities spanned all the second half of the seventh century. He was a dominant figure at a very formative time for the young Church as the conversion of the Anglo-Saxon kingdoms proceeded apace. When he eventually returned from Gaul three years after his heady consecration, he ruled for a time over a very extensive diocese. He had a talent for eliciting gifts from kings and queens, and from abbots and abbesses, to build and endow monasteries. In his enthusiasm for all things Roman, the monasteries he established followed the Rule of St Benedict. He ordained numbers of priests and deacons to assist him, and set about establishing an ecclesiastical empire in Northumbria, Mercia and Sussex, which was a confederation of monasteries under his authority: in this, at least, he was prepared to emulate the Celtic practice!

Small wonder that some kings viewed his progress with suspicion and some bishops with envy. In 678 he had a disagreement with King Egfrid of Northumbria and was exiled from his diocese. Three bishops were appointed in his place; moreover they had been trained in the Celtic tradition – double cause for grievance. This was the occasion for his first appeal to the pope for justice.

En route for Rome Wilfrid spent the winter in Frisia, present-day Holland, successfully evangelising among the people there and laying the foundation of a mission other Englishmen would build on. In Rome the pope supported Wilfrid's case and he returned with a written judgement in his favour, only to have it dismissed as a forgery. Imprisoned for a while by the king, then exiled, the undaunted Wilfrid made his way to the still pagan province of the South Saxons and converted them to the faith. He established a monastery at Selsey on land that the local king had given him. Another king gave him land on the Isle of Wight and Wilfrid set up a mission there. His years in exile were not wasted.

He was recalled to Northumbria by Egfrid's successor and restored to his bishopric. Five years later the story was repeated. This time king and bishops combined in accusations against him. They wanted him to surrender all his lands except Ripon, and also wanted to sever communion with him and his followers. Again Wilfrid headed for Rome, again to be acquitted of wrong-doing, but the pope referred the settlement to a synod of his fellow countrymen, where agreement was eventually reached: Ripon and Hexham, Wilfrid's chief monasteries, were restored to him and he lived out his remaining four years in peace.

Part of his legacy was a number of fine church buildings, much larger and more elaborate than earlier ones. Among them were St Peter's at Ripon, based on the basilican pattern used in the south-east, with a rounded apse at the east end, and St Andrew's Church at Hexham, which Eddius Stephanus, his biographer, describes as the greatest this side of the Alps, with a large nave and colonnades, aisles with chapels and galleries above, spiral staircases, and a crypt for relics. In each church the crypt is the only part of the original buildings to survive – all constructed by masons brought by Wilfrid from abroad.

At Hexham, the bishop's chair, which stands in the chancel, has been claimed as Wilfrid's; known also as the Frith (or Peace) Stool, it provided sanctuary for anyone who sat in it. It is placed where the apse of the first church reached, as a reminder of the original founder. Eddius describes how Wilfrid provided furnishings, including a Gospel Book at Ripon with letters of gold on purpled parchment, illuminated and placed in a jewelled case of gold. The church at Ripon was consecrated in 672 with great ceremony, in the presence of two kings and many dignitaries.

Church music too flourished under Wilfrid's influence; with the help of Eddius Stephanus, who was a singing-master in the Church, he set about training monks in the chant used in the Church in Rome and established two-part choirs singing antiphonally.

Wilfrid's monasteries on the Benedictine model differed in many respects from the Celtic type. St Benedict had originally devised his Rule for the community at Monte Cassino in Italy in the sixth century. Its use was to spread throughout the West in the centuries following. St Benedict himself described it as a rule for beginners that was "… neither burdensome nor harsh"; in its moderation it contrasted with the very ascetic and demanding Celtic monastic rules. In its original form, the Rule of St Benedict was meant to be for a self-sufficient community not greatly involved with the world outside, like the Celtic ones. Among the vows the monks made was that of stability, a commitment to one place, in sharp contrast to the wandering element of Celtic monasticism, and the existence of rather idiosyncratic communities or small groups with little regulation. The young Church in England was being offered an alternative kind of monasticism.

Wilfrid appears, in fact, to have made an impact on every aspect of church life, not only spreading the new-style monasteries but raising the profile of the papacy, extending the Church by his missionary work, developing church architecture, enriching the Church artistically and musically, and antagonising many in the process. While Eddius is filled with admiration for him and commends his charity and devotion to duty, one feels Bede's view of him lacks warmth – a character as contentious as Wilfrid could hardly be good for Church unity.

For our part, while we may not find his personality very engaging, we cannot but be impressed by his achievements and his resilience. Whatever his character, he did much to shape the seventh-century Church in England.

As he and others were busy introducing Roman and Continental ways into Northumbria, other churchmen there continued to embody in their lifestyle the values of the Celtic tradition. Most notable among them, and most dearly loved, was Cuthbert.

Born in 634, the same year as Wilfrid, his manner of life stands in complete contrast; indifferent to status, with a taste for solitude, but at the same time with a deep commitment to spreading the faith, he was a true shepherd of his flock. It was, in fact, as a shepherd in the Lammermuir hills that he felt called to the monastic life, which in Celtic terms meant a missionary life too. As prior of the Lindisfarne community, he saw it as his duty to persuade the brothers to adopt new ways according to the decision of the Synod of Whitby, which he himself had accepted. Bede describes how, as pastor and evangelist, Cuthbert travelled widely around remote villages, over rough hill country, living among the people, and accepting their poverty and squalor in order to win them to the faith, or to recall those who had fallen away at the onset of the plague, and reverted to spells and other pagan practices – some indication of the fragility of conversion in the early days.

After some ten years, Cuthbert fulfilled his heart's desire and withdrew to the island of Inner Farne to lead a hermit's life. There, among the animals and birds with whom he had a special affinity, he led a life of prayer and single-minded devotion to God, though still visited by many who sought his advice and by the monks from his community. It is possible, on a visit to the island, to imagine the simplicity of his life there, to imagine too the pain it must have caused him to leave his sanctuary when required by king and people to become Bishop of Lindisfarne. He was enthroned at York in the year 685 on Easter Sunday. For two years he dutifully fulfilled the obligations of his office. Then, sensing that his death was imminent, he returned to the solitude of his island to prepare himself.

As death approached, he encouraged his fellow monks especially to keep the unity of the Catholic faith, which meant keeping Easter according to the Roman calendar. Although he had wanted to be buried on his island, they persuaded him to be buried in the church at Lindisfarne and so his body was duly borne across the water to its resting place – for a while at least. When threatened later by Viking attacks, the monks left the island, taking with them the coffin containing the body of their beloved Cuthbert, along with other relics. After a long journey and a stay of more than a hundred years at Chester-le-Street, it eventually came to rest at Durham in the tenth century. In 1104 when his tomb was excavated, a sixth-century manuscript of St John's Gospel was found in the coffin. Other relics came to light in 1827, all now displayed in the cathedral treasury. Along with the original wooden coffin, with its carvings of the twelve apostles, the Virgin Mary and the seven archangels, was a pectoral cross of gold cloisonné work, together with a portable altar of embossed silver, which the saint may have used on his journeying. With them were parts of embroidered vestments, perhaps tenth-century gifts to St Cuthbert's shrine, and an indication of the skill in embroidery achieved by later Anglo-Saxons.

The shrine established in his honour became a centre of pilgrimage until it was destroyed under Henry VIII. Pilgrims continue to be drawn to where his remains still lie, under a simple marble slab marked "Cuthbertus", east of the high altar.

It seems Cuthbert had a charismatic personality. Bede describes him as a gifted speaker, with a light in his angelic face, a patient and kindly man with a compelling love of God and His creation, and a deep care for people. His style as a bishop must have been rather more comfortable to live with than Wilfrid's. Little wonder that the love and respect earned in his lifetime were perpetuated through the centuries.

There was in Cuthbert a fusion of Celtic and Roman virtues – on the one hand his simplicity, individuality and capacity for contemplation, and on the other a concern for order, discipline and the unity of the Church – so that his life can be seen as a force for reconciliation and a focus of unity in the post-synod period.

Since Aidan's arrival in 634, the community at Lindisfarne had flourished. It had been served by outstanding spiritual leaders, and had established a school to prepare boys for service in the Church, with Wilfrid, Chad and Cedd among them. It had also evangelised over a wide area. Only gradually did the Celtic influence there yield to that of Rome. From its scriptorium, towards the end of the seventh century, emerged an outstandingly beautiful work of art, the Lindisfarne Gospels, which is now in the British Museum. A note at the end of the manuscript describes how Eadfrith, a bishop of Lindisfarne, wrote the book; how one of his successors, Ethelwald, had it bound and covered; how Billfrith, a smith, decorated it with gold and silver and gems; and how, later, during their stay at Chester-le-Street, one of the monks, Aldred, had translated it into English and thus made the earliest surviving version of the Gospels in the language.

Written on two hundred and fifty-eight pages of vellum, most of the pages are plain with small decorated initials, but the glory of the manuscript lies in the six pages of ornamental text, which were illuminated chapter openings with a greatly enlarged initial letter in Celtic style, followed by a few words on a smaller scale, and in the five pages filled with an intricate cruciform design. In addition to these are the sixteen pages of arcaded canon tables and portraits of the Four Evangelists. The colours are soft; the flowing patterns are clearly Celtic, with the elongated animals an Anglian contribution found elsewhere, particularly in metalwork; while the figures are inspired by Mediterranean art – a fusion of many cultural influences. The whole is a monument to the devotion and artistry of its scribe and to the inspiration he found in his faith.

From the early monastery only a few inscribed stones survive in the Priory Museum at Lindisfarne. A statue of Aidan stands near the ruins of the later priory, to remind us of the man who inspired the community from its foundation. The monastery was always closely linked with Bamburgh, which was the royal seat. King Oswald and Aidan had worked together to establish the faith in Northumbria, a fact now evoked by Bamburgh Castle on the one hand and the parish church on the other. The latter is dedicated to St Aidan and its chancel is thought to be on the site of the Saxon church. The fine twentieth-century reredos in Caen stone, with its sixteen statues, pays tribute to those early Christians involved in the founding and consolidating of the Church in the north. They were remarkably successful.

The community at Lindisfarne continued until the monks were eventually driven out by Viking raids in 875, but after Cuthbert's death in 687 its most significant period was over. At the same time the twin monasteries of Monkwearmouth and Jarrow grew in importance. They had been founded by Benedict Biscop, a Northumbrian nobleman contemporary of Wilfrid who had, in fact, accompanied the young Wilfrid on his first visit to the Continent before the Synod of Whitby. He later took vows at the monastery of Lérins, which had played an important part in the early development of Western monasticism. Inspired by the communities he had seen abroad, in 674 he founded a monastery at Monkwearmouth, and in 681 one at Jarrow, seven miles away. He brought masons and glaziers from Gaul to supervise their construction.

An enthusiast for the arts, Benedict Biscop brought back from his five journeys to Rome many books and paintings, altar vessels, vestments and relics. On one of his return journeys he was accompanied by John, the arch-cantor of St Peter's, Rome, who trained the choirs at Monkwearmouth and Jarrow in the Roman chant. Singers came from monasteries around to learn from him. Like Wilfrid, Benedict Biscop was a promoter of the Roman liturgy. Monkwearmouth and Jarrow became two houses of one Benedictine monastery under Abbots Benedict and Ceolfrith, and were named after the apostles Peter and Paul. At Monkwearmouth only the lower storeys of the Anglo-Saxon tower remain of the early monastery, while at Jarrow the chancel of St Paul's Church, now the parish church, is the original Saxon church which was built with Roman stone. It has small, splayed windows, one containing Saxon glass, and the original Saxon aumbry in the south wall also remains – in all a simple and evocative sacred space.

A second, larger church was built in 685 on the site of the present nave. Still in existence are pieces of Saxon sculpture and the shaft of what is known as the Jarrow Cross, on which are inscribed the words "In this unique sign life is restored to the world". The nave was replaced in the eighteenth century and completely renewed in the nineteenth century, but many of the centuries between its foundation and the present time are represented in some way, whether by the tower, which was mostly built sometime between the eighth and eleventh centuries; the pre-Reformation bells; the choir-stall carvings from the fifteenth century; or by windows from many different periods, including one Norman window containing the work of a twentieth-century artist. The whole is presided over and unified by a modern carving of the risen and ascended Christ, which is suspended over the nave near the chancel end.

In the new kind of monastery that Monkwearmouth and Jarrow represent, which coexisted for a while with the Ionan Celtic type, there was a great emphasis on learning. This particular one held one of the finest libraries of its day. The Codex Amiatinus, the oldest complete Latin Bible known to exist, is thought to have been produced here. There were three copies; the abbot Ceolfrith set out to take one to Rome as a gift for the pope. He died on the way, but this Anglo-Saxon treasure eventually found its way to a library in Florence.

The monastery at Jarrow will forever be associated with the Venerable Bede, who spent his life there and put the library to such good use. A chair known as Bede's chair stands in the sanctuary of St Paul's at Jarrow, and a modern sculpture of him is a further reminder of the scholar-monk on whom we largely depend for our knowledge of the early history of the Church in England.

Before we leave Northumbria, there is one small building in the Wear valley from this early period that deserves special mention. It is the church at Escomb, near Bishop Auckland, which has been wonderfully preserved. Its origins – who built it and why it was placed in this particular spot – remain a mystery, but many features mark it out as an early Saxon church. It is a tall, narrow building with a variety of windows, irregularly placed, and a narrow, high chancel arch, which may be a rebuilt Roman archway. There are fragments of a fresco, scrollwork design and Roman inscriptions (there was a Roman fort at nearby Binchester, which may have supplied the stone). This unpretentious church, relatively unchanged since its origins and now in the middle of a housing estate, bears moving witness to a tradition of local worship that has spanned thirteen centuries, with only a brief interruption when it was restored in the nineteenth century.

The seventh century left the Church in Northumbria in good heart. Because the Synod of Whitby had taken place here, where the Celtic Church was loved and valued, something of its ethos could continue among those who accepted the Roman Easter and Roman ways. The Roman tradition was, in fact, enriched by the Celtic tradition, which, left to itself, might have become very idiosyncratic in comparative isolation. Instead, it was being more fully integrated into the universal Church. To move forward, perhaps each needed the other. Their combined strengths could conceivably make for a more effective body in a world where Christianity was still making its way. Whether the deep spirituality and self-discipline of the Celtic churches and their costly personal evangelism could flourish within a more centralised, authoritarian organisation was something only the passage of time would tell.

Developments in the other Kingdoms

From Northumbria the Church spread south into Mercia. Like Northumbria, this kingdom also covered a large area. With the constant conflicts between kingdoms in the seventh and eighth centuries, boundaries fluctuated, but Mercia extended roughly from Cheshire to Nottinghamshire at its northern end, south to Herefordshire and Gloucestershire in the west, and to Cambridgeshire in the east. Within it were smaller kingdoms. In the later seventh century it included also the kingdom of Lindsey, which was north of the Wash, and Essex, and dominated the south of the country. Penda, who ruled Mercia for twenty-two years, was a pagan, but before his death in 655 his son, Paeda, had married King Oswy's daughter and had become a Christian. He returned from Northumbria with four priests to convert the people of his sub-kingdom of Middle Anglia, which lay between Mercia and East Anglia. In 654 he founded an important monastery at Medeshamstede, which is now Peterborough. Paeda died in 656, but the monastery was completed by his brother and successor, Wulfhere. It was endowed with substantial wealth and consecrated by the archbishop of Canterbury with great ceremony. Daughter houses followed in places as far away as Bermondsey and Woking; closer to home were Repton, where parts of the chancel and the remarkable crypt survive, and Breedon-on-the-Hill, where some fine later Saxon carvings are to be found.

Wilfrid too founded monasteries in Mercia on land given to him by King Wulfhere. It may even be that Wilfrid was involved in the building of the church at Brixworth, which is on the same basilican plan as his churches at Hexham and Ripon. It has survived sufficiently well to convey something of its original magnificence for the period. The seventh-century building would have consisted of the lower part of the present nave, with side chapels beyond the double archways. Later in the Anglo-Saxon period these were made into aisles, the clerestory added to the nave and a tower built on. The final result must have been very impressive. A sunken ambulatory was also made around the outside of the apse, perhaps as an access to the crypt for pilgrims. The bone in the reliquary near the pulpit is said to have belonged to St Boniface, the eighth-century missionary to Germany; this may at one time have been housed in the crypt. Pilgrimages to places where famous relics were kept were very much part of the life of the Anglo-Saxon Christian. Sometimes the relics were displayed in the crypt and sometimes in shrines in the main body of the church; often they were sealed into the altar when a church was consecrated. The acquisition of a famous relic ensured the prosperity of a foundation as the pilgrims poured in. It was not unknown for the monks of one monastery to steal the relics of a saint from another monastery!

In 669 the Northumbrian Chad was sent from his monastery at Lastingham to be bishop of Mercia and made Lichfield his episcopal seat. He exercised his short ministry in true Celtic fashion, and was a force for reconciliation between Angles and Britons until he died in 672. In 700 the first cathedral at Lichfield was built and Chad's bones were enshrined in it: another great centre of pilgrimage had been born.

In the southern part of Mercia a new diocese was created and a monastery founded at Worcester, to which Bosel from Whitby Abbey was sent as bishop. He was one of five monks from Whitby who became bishops, all of whom had been taught by the Abbess Hilda. Like many another abbess of the time she was of royal blood; some were queens who had been widowed or who had taken vows in later life; some were sisters or daughters of kings. They made their mark on the fledgling English Church. Aelfled, a daughter of King Oswy, succeeded Hilda at Whitby. Ebba, aunt to King Egfrid, became abbess at Coldingham, north of Berwick. There were many of these royal abbesses in Kent, at Lyminge, Folkestone, Sheppey and Thanet. Like Kent and Northumbria, Mercia too had its share of royal princesses who became abbesses, notably the three daughters of one Mercian king. While two fulfilled their vocations in Kent, the third, Mildburg, took charge at Much Wenlock. Many of the abbesses had been prepared for their work in monasteries in north Gaul. Some of them returned there to serve as abbesses.

In East Anglia, another of the seventh-century Anglo-Saxon kingdoms, the daughters of King Anna fulfilled the same role. One of them, Ethelreda, was installed as first abbess at Ely. She was succeeded by her sister Sexburg, while her youngest sister, Withburga, founded a community at East Dereham. Before the high altar of Ely Cathedral, a stone slab recalls "Ethelreda, Saint and Queen, who founded this house AD 673". It marks the spot where her shrine once stood. It attracted countless pilgrims and made Ely a great religious centre. These very capable women made a great contribution to the conversion period through their leadership and spiritual example, and through their teaching and counselling.

The kingdom of East Anglia, where King Anna's daughters played a significant role during the latter half of the seventh century, had already been Christianised to some extent under a previous king, Sigbert. After their time the Anglo-Saxon Chronicle records a monastery being built by St Botolph at Icanhoh, thought to be Iken, near the estuary of the River Alde. It must have flourished because it was able to establish a daughter house at Much Wenlock. St Botolph had a great reputation for holiness, and many churches are dedicated to him; one of the most famous with which he was associated was at Boston, Lincolnshire. Four churches in London, at city gates, bear his name. A relic of St Botolph was given at a later date to Westminster Abbey; perhaps the procession that would have taken it to its destination passed through these places. The widespread diocese of East Anglia became more manageable in the 670s, when it was divided and a second episcopal seat established in the north at Elmham.

Close by, the kingdom of the East Saxons had recovered from its earlier reversion to paganism with the help of Bishop Cedd from Lindisfarne. His efforts were consolidated in the last part of the century by Earconwald, who was bishop of London for eighteen years. He restored a monastery at Chertsey and established another at Barking, where his sister became abbess. Together with the daughter houses of Peterborough at Bermondsey and Woking, they formed a group in the area of London. New monasteries were springing up in every kingdom.

South of the Thames, the seventh-century kingdom of Wessex extended roughly from the border of present-day Sussex westwards to Devon. The settlement of Saxons in Devon was a slow process, but towards the end of the seventh century, a religious community had been established in Exeter. West of Exeter still remained largely Celtic terrain, which was highly resistant to the advance of the newcomers.

Like the other kingdoms, Wessex was ruled by warring kings engaged, in turn, in defending their territory and seeking to extend it. The aggressiveness of these Saxon kings, to our minds, sits ill with their conversion. Yet, while many of them may have adopted Christianity initially out of political expediency, some went on to take their allegiance to the faith very seriously. Some went on pilgrimage to Rome in later life. Many kings renounced their kingship and retired to a monastery, perhaps war-weary or in a spirit of penitence, or perhaps as an acknowledgement that this was the highest calling of all. Their role in the conversion of England was vital, as without their cooperation missionary work would have been impossible.

In Wessex, with the encouragement of the king of the day, Bishop Birinus had laid the foundations of the Church there, working for sixteen years from his episcopal base at Dorchester-on-Thames. During the time of his successor, Bishop Agilbert, Wessex supplied the first native archbishop of Canterbury, Deusdedit.

In 688, a new king, Ine, became ruler of Wessex for thirty-seven years. He was a strong king, the strongest in the south, fighting to maintain his inheritance, but also a Christian concerned with strengthening the Church in his kingdom. One of his most notable achievements was a code of laws, like the one King Ethelbert had earlier introduced in Kent. Through such codes, civil life became imbued with more humane attitudes under the influence of Christianity. King Ine's code was also concerned with church matters, and sheds some light on Christian obligations at the time: a child had to be baptised within thirty days of birth, or a fine of thirty shillings paid; and the tithe of church scot had to be paid on time, or else multiplied twelve times and a fine paid! Ine is credited with building a church on the old site at Glastonbury and ended his reign by going on pilgrimage to Rome.

In 705, during his reign, a clear division of the diocese of Wessex had been made; Winchester was kept in the east and Sherborne established in the west, with Aldhelm of Malmesbury as bishop, the most significant figure in the Wessex Church of the later seventh century and a man of many gifts: scholar, writer, poet and music maker. In 654, at the age of fifteen, he had entered the monastery at Malmesbury, founded some twenty years previously by an Irish monk, Maelduib, whom he was later to succeed as abbot. During its early years it had gained a reputation as a centre of learning with a good library. Here Aldhelm was able to develop his scholarly gifts and establish himself as a writer. Most of his writings were in Latin and are now considered to be very tortuous in style. A treatise he wrote on keeping Easter at the right time confirms the topicality of the subject. King Alfred was lavish in his praise of Aldhelm's poems, which were written in English, but now are unfortunately lost. Through Alfred, a story survives of how Aldhelm would post himself on a bridge near his church and sing his poems, accompanying himself on the harp, to teach passers-by about the faith.

Like a number of his contemporaries, he was a builder of churches, not only at Malmesbury, where he built three, but also at Bradford-on-Avon and Frome. In 705 Aldhelm became bishop of the new see at Sherborne. His elevation gave him a reason for further building there. He continued at the same time to be abbot of Malmesbury, so that, in addition to supervising the community there and in the daughter houses, and observing the requirements of the monastic life, he had to fulfil the obligations of preaching and oversight incumbent on a bishop. He can have had little time left for writing! This busy period of his life came to an end in 709, when he died visiting the Somerset village of Doulting. His body was taken back to Malmesbury for burial, and crosses were built at each stopping-place, seven miles apart; these are known as the Bishopstones.

Part of the abbey that grew at Malmesbury survives and serves as a parish church today, while at Sherborne a more splendid building has taken the place of Aldhelm's church.

At the end of the seventh century the kingdom of Wessex was firmly set on the road to becoming the most important of the Anglo-Saxon kingdoms, but even before that, through the sons – and daughters – of the Church there, it was to make a significant contribution to the evangelising of northern Europe.

The Role of Theodore

Over all of the activity in church expansion in the latter half of the seventh century presided a Greek figure, Theodore, chosen by the pope in 668 to be archbishop of Canterbury. He was then sixty-six. He came from Tarsus, had studied in Athens and had spent some time in Rome. It would seem the pope had some doubts about his background and sent with him to England one Hadrian, a native of North Africa, a scholar and abbot in Italy. Hadrian was to keep a vigilant eye on Theodore's orthodoxy, lest he should introduce Greek customs not consonant with Western theology. With the arrival of Theodore and Hadrian a new dimension entered the Celtic-Roman equation in Britain. On arrival Theodore appointed Hadrian abbot of the monastery of St Peter and St Paul in Canterbury and, soon afterwards, they undertook a tour of every part of England, teaching and correcting wrong practice. Bede describes him as the first archbishop to win the obedience of all the Church in England. From his enthusiastic account he obviously regarded Theodore's time in office as a golden age in the history of the English church. His arrival was timely: the see of Canterbury had been vacant for four years and the bishop of Rochester had also died, so the Church in Kent was badly in need of leadership. One of Theodore's early acts was to install Putta, an expert in Roman chant, as bishop at Rochester. Another was to send the Northumbrian Chad as bishop to the Mercians. Theodore was perhaps more open to the qualities of those nurtured in the Celtic tradition than any product of a purely Roman tradition might have been and he made good use of them. When Wilfrid was exiled from Northumbria in 678, Theodore consecrated three bishops trained by the Celtic Church to take his place. Wilfrid may well have been a thorn in the flesh to Theodore: Bede writes of dissension between the two and between their clergy, and, much later, of reconciliation. As opportunity arose, Theodore split up the vast dioceses that existed into more manageable areas. Perhaps he also thought to curb the ambitions of any bishop in Wilfrid's mould. Whereas previously a bishop had been appointed to a people, now his diocese was intended to be a territorial one.

In 673 a Church synod was held at Hertford. Convened by Archbishop Theodore and attended by five bishops from the main kingdoms, along with other teachers in the church, it must qualify as the first general synod of the Church in England. There, the decision of the Synod of Whitby was restated and the dating of Easter firmly established. Practical guidelines were laid down, confining a bishop's activities to his own diocese and discouraging

THE STORY OF CHRISTIANITY IN THE BRITISH ISLES

his interference in monasteries. It dealt with the common practice of "wandering": in future, in order to move elsewhere monks would require permission from their abbot, and clergy permission from their bishop. Regular synods were to meet and the number of bishops was to be increased as the number of converts grew. In their pastoral ministry clergy were to encourage faithfulness in marriage. For the first time, the Church in England as a whole must have felt the direction of a firm and unifying hand, with a man of authority at the helm.

In 680 another synod took place at Hatfield. This time it was concerned not with organisation but with orthodoxy, and the English Church declared its official acceptance of the findings of previous General Councils of the Church, which had condemned certain heresies.

Theodore and Hadrian left another invaluable legacy: they had established a fine school at Canterbury, where both scholars taught what was a wide curriculum for the time. Benedict Biscop, who had accompanied them to England initially, was closely involved with the school at Canterbury. Aldhelm of Malmesbury also spent two periods of study there. Thus, Canterbury was linked with developments in the north and west.

Theodore was the author of many Biblical commentaries. What is known as Theodore's Penitential may have been collected together after his lifetime, but it incorporated his thinking and had a great influence on the penitential system in general. In Ireland, private confession and absolution, followed by counselling, had replaced the very public process of the early Church, which continued in Mediterranean countries. Theodore gave the Irish practice his official seal of approval. It was widely adopted.

In 690 at the age of eighty-eight, Archbishop Theodore

died; Hadrian died twenty years later. They had achieved a great deal. Theodore had addressed both church organisation and the content of the faith through his synods, and, with Hadrian, had made a lasting contribution to scholarship through his school at Canterbury. Together with the schools at Monkwearmouth and Jarrow in the north-east, Malmesbury in the west, and probably other smaller schools elsewhere, learning within the Church in England was increasing and offering an alternative to study in the Irish monasteries.

Great strides had been made in the course of the seventh century, largely due to the evangelising and pastoral activities of monks under cooperative kings. Secular clergy shared the task: in some cathedrals the bishop's familia consisted of clergy living communally and serving the pastoral needs of the surrounding area, as they would have done in any collegiate church.

As for the laity of the seventh century, the monasteries, sometimes known as minsters, provided the churches in which they worshipped for the most part. While the parish church as we know it had not yet come into existence, the minsters were in effect the mother churches of very large parishes, and in some places a preaching cross in an appropriate spot, sometimes at a crossroad, sufficed as a meeting place. However, it was not only through local worship that laity could display their devotion: the importance attached to relics and the creation of centres of pilgrimage at saints' shrines encouraged many to travel to them, perhaps not only out of piety but also as a welcome distraction from a life that was basically very insecure, and regularly threatened by outbreaks of plague, fighting and famine. Some of them even made the journey to Rome, in honour of St Peter. At home, they paid their annual tithe and took their babies promptly for baptism, to the church which offered them comfort and hope, and was modifying the harshness of daily life through its pastoral care and its influence on new codes of law.

We can only draw tentative conclusions about the mindset of the seventh-century Christian. From the place occupied by miracles, visions and prophecies in early writings, as in Bede's *History of the English Church and People* and in the increasing number of Lives of Saints written during this period, it would seem there was a general openness to the spiritual significance of events, and a clear expectation that individuals of deep spirituality and goodness would display gifts of healing and prophecy, and have visions. Such an openness and expectation were entirely in keeping with the experiences of the very early Church, though this was gradually lost to a large extent over succeeding centuries.

In the cultural life of seventh-century England, the Christian faith was becoming a great source of inspiration for artistic creativity at a time when many influences were converging from different quarters – from the Celtic areas, from Gaul, Rome and Mediterranean culture generally – all making an impact in many spheres. These influences were responsible for introducing a more complex style of building, and fine furnishings with which to adorn them: paintings, hangings, vessels, embroidered vestments for the clergy, and beautifully executed Gospel Books, with fine casings of gold and jewels.

The standard of music in worship had been raised too, through the efforts of gifted music makers. An increasing number of good schools and libraries were available for the preparation of churchmen. It was an exciting time for the young English Church, which was in a position to benefit from two very different strands of Christianity, with the opportunity to weld the best of both into a rich and unique expression of the faith. By the end of the seventh century, the results were most apparent where the Church was strongest – in Northumbria. Nonetheless, it was developing in all the English kingdoms, and, as a result of Theodore's devoted service and breadth of vision, the primacy and leadership of Canterbury had been re-affirmed in a very real sense.

V

EXPANSION UNDER THREAT

The Celtic Churches after the Synod of Whitby

While the conversion of England proceeded in the seventh century, Wales played no part in that process. Her land was still being encroached on by the advancing Anglo-Saxons, so conditions were hardly conducive to evangelism on the part of the Britons in the west. Bede is critical of their attitude, but they were what history had made them: the Anglo-Saxons had overrun much of their country and threatened the survival of their faith. They continued loyal to their own Church and were suspicious of Canterbury. It was more than a century after the Synod of Whitby before the Church in North Wales adopted the Roman Easter, according to an entry in the Welsh Annals for the year 768. It claims that Bishop Elfoddw, a bishop of Bangor, was responsible for the change. A Welsh Chronicle records that the bishops in the south of the country rejected his decision. Acceptance of the outcome of Whitby would be a long and uneven process.

Elfoddw had a pupil called Nennius, who gave his name

to a work called *History of the Britons*. In it he attempts to put events into chronological order at a time when the AD method of dating was only just becoming more widely used, and so his work represents a laudable achievement for the time. He adds little to our knowledge of Christian matters, but shows the significant role of the Church in bringing about the transition from an oral to a written culture. The monasteries, with their interest in learning and their writing skills, provided the circumstances to make it possible.

Throughout the course of the seventh century all of the west coast of Britain remained in close touch with Ireland. This was particularly true of West and South Wales. The anchorite movement was widespread in Ireland and it spilt over into Wales. The movement is seen, in part, as a reaction against conformity with Roman usage and a desire to preserve the traditions of the Celtic past. Their previous independence had made the Celts very conservative in outlook.

Yet Ireland had not been as slow as Wales to respond to the decision of the Synod of Whitby. Parts of southern Ireland had adopted the Roman Easter before the synod took place. There the greater traffic of students and pilgrims to and from the Continent and Rome would have made the Church more aware of differences in practice, and they had accepted the advice of the pope. After the synod pressure was brought to bear on the north of Ireland. The monk Egbert, a Northumbrian, spent most of his life trying to bring the area into conformity with Rome and eventually succeeded in 696. These acceptances represent the official voice of the Church; in practice it is likely they were implemented only very gradually in the Church at large.

This was because there were many aspects that

differentiated the Celtic Churches from Rome and the Continent. Apart from the dating of Easter, the Synod of Whitby had also dealt with the different form of tonsure each adopted. While the Roman style recalled the crown of thorns, allegedly worn by St Peter, monks in the Celtic Churches shaved only the front of the head. The style of the tonsure may not seem a matter of great import to us, but at that time a very large part of the Church consisted of monks. It was a visible difference and the debate engendered a surprising amount of heat.

There was also the more serious question of the role of the bishop, which had been modified in the monastic Celtic Churches. There he was subject to an abbot, and therefore his traditional authority and power to discipline were greatly reduced; a fact that appalled Bede. This was less true of Wales, where the notion of a bishop of a territory had survived from Roman times, and where the roles of bishop and abbot were more often combined.

In all the widespread Celtic areas there was no central leadership, no archbishop; consequently there was a lack of liturgical uniformity. Gildas, writing in the sixth century, mentions differences in the Mass, the word in general use in the West to refer to the Eucharist, which was derived from the Latin words of dismissal at the end of the service. Augustine, in his encounters with the British bishops in the early seventh century, raised the question of the differing practice of the baptismal rite too, which may have had to do with anointing, foot washing or threefold immersion.

In terms of faith the Celtic approach was deeply Biblical. Part of the veneration for the Old Testament was seen in the observance of the Jewish Sabbath, with all its restrictions, among the community on Iona, which is referred to in Adamnan's *Life of Columba*. Sunday was observed there without the restrictions of the Sabbath, once services had been attended. Confession and penance were of major importance among the Celts, as the number of penitentials bear witness. The Christian life was seen as a very disciplined life, illustrated particularly in the extent of the anchorite movement, with its extraordinary self-discipline. Fasting was one aspect of this discipline. It seems there were three Lents of forty days, before Christmas and Easter, and after Pentecost, which Bede describes as learnt in England from Irish teachers. Long prayer vigils were another form of discipline. These were all features particularly characteristic of the early Celtic Churches. Their beliefs were those of the universal Church, but the emphases in the practice of their faith were different. Some of these emphases, such as confession and penance, were absorbed by the Anglo-Saxon Church, reflecting their own social practice of paying compensation for wrongs done.

Faced with the threat of changes, there was a literary explosion in Ireland. It seems a need was felt to give authority to the native oral traditions that they held dear: the writing of Rules of monastic life, penitentials, Gospel Books, Lives of Saints, and poetry, together with pagan lore, would provide a record of past and present.

The author of the seventh-century *Life of Brigit*, Cogitosus, gives us a glimpse of the church that developed at Kildare out of the earlier foundation by St Brigit. Unlike the small churches of early monasteries, this was for congregational worship. It had many windows, paintings and linen hangings, and an ornate door. There were divisions in the church; men and women were separated, but all were united in spirit.

The setting in many Celtic churches may have been modest in terms of buildings, but there were splendid touches in the silk vestments; the gold or silver crowns of the bishops, Eastern in origin; in richly decorated Gospel Books; and the fine vessels of which the eighth-century Ardagh Chalice is a beautiful example: a silver bowl with gold, bronze and enamel ornament. The liturgy was enriched by music, both in singing and chanting, and in the use of instruments: harp, horn or bagpipes.

Early Gospel Books appear in Ireland. The Book of Durrow, the earliest of the fully illuminated manuscripts, is from the later seventh century; it is decorated in four colours, with carpet pages and canon tables, and with the symbols of the four Evangelists rather than the portraits of later manuscripts. There were pocket Gospels: the Book of Mulling and the Book of Diumma – both are now in the library of Trinity College Dublin.

The Antiphonary of Bangor in the north of Ireland from around 680 implies a liturgy with more Eastern and Gallic elements, than Roman. The influence of Gaul and the East had created a liturgy that was more elaborate and less sober than the Roman tradition, though they were similar in structure; variations were in use all over Europe.

The essentially monastic Church in Ireland had flourished, but contained within that success was a threat to its well-being. Native saints had always figured large in the Celtic tradition, and pilgrimages were made to their shrines. A monastery that housed the tomb of a great saint prospered; others would want to be buried there, at a price, and so wealth accumulated. Great monasteries that had pioneered the Christianisation of Ireland became power centres; with wealth and power their ethos changed. By the mid-eighth century there were even battles between ambitious monasteries, often over land disputes. In the north, Armagh was gradually extending its claims of primacy over all Ireland, in the name of St Patrick. Two accounts of his life, one by Muirchu and a more biased one by another priest called Tirechan, were written to support the claim, and incorporated, along with St Patrick's writings and a complete Latin New Testament, into the Book of Armagh, a much-respected collection, now at Trinity College Dublin.

In reaction to these bids for greater power, a desire grew in some quarters to recapture the early ideals of monastic life. In Munster especially, at the monasteries of Tallaght and Finglas near Dublin, the anchorite movement grew. In the later eighth century it seems some anchorites banded together, calling themselves Celi De, companions of God, later known as Culdees. They spread from there all over Ireland and to northern Britain. This was essentially a reform movement, deeply spiritual and disciplined; it was also associated with a great flowering of religious poetry.

The pattern of progress in the seventh century was quite different in Scotland, which had not yet taken the shape familiar to us. There were in fact four groups inhabiting the area. The Picts, as the native inhabitants were then called, were hemmed in to the west by the Irish, who had colonised the coastal area and its islands, to the south-west by the British kingdom of Strathclyde, and to the south by the Angles, who in time moved north as far as the Tay.

The southern Picts had first been evangelised in the early fifth century by Bishop Ninian from his base at Whithorn. In the sixth century Serf had worked in the Ochil hills and Kentigern in the Strathclyde area. Many Irish saints had been crossing the water since St Patrick's time, "on pilgrimage for Christ": Catan had gone to the Isle of Bute and his nephew Blane moved eastwards to found a monastery at Dunblane. There were many others,

Kenneth, Brendan, Finian among them, and Machar to whom the cathedral at Aberdeen is dedicated, but it is Columba who has claimed the place of honour among sixth-century missionaries, even to the extent of having more attributed to his efforts than is perhaps justified. Place names are not always reliable indications that a saint actually worked there, and dedications are not easy to date. It is also difficult to disentangle probability from legend. There were other very successful missions in the west, notably that of Moluag, a contemporary of Columba who came from the monastery of Bangor in the north of Ireland to found a monastery on the island of Lismore, which, in the thirteenth century, was to become the base of the Bishopric of the Isles. With the founding of a major centre at Applecross in the seventh century by Maelrubha, also from Bangor, there arose yet another important base in the west.

Moluag also founded centres in the north-east, at Rosemarkie in the Black Isle and at Mortlach in Banffshire. The names of Pictish missionaries emerge there too: Drostan, Colm and Medan recur in the north-east; their work probably centred on a community at Deer, which was to prosper for many centuries. Canisbay church, the most northerly church on mainland Scotland, is thought to occupy the site of a church founded by Drostan. Fergus, also a Pict, continued what they had started in the area.

The Scottish Lowlands, where the Angles had settled, then formed part of the kingdom of Northumbria. There were a number of monasteries in the area; some were early Celtic foundations and some were daughter houses of Lindisfarne. Cuthbert had first been a monk at Old Melrose. An Anglian bishop, Trumwine, was appointed to the Picts in 681, based at Abercorn, but his stay was short-lived because the whole situation changed in 685 when the Angles were defeated at the battle of Nechtansmere and their advance northwards was halted. There were other repercussions: in 710 the king of the Picts, Nechtan, aware of the findings of the Synod of Whitby, wanted his kingdom to conform with Roman custom. He wrote to Abbot Ceolfried at the monastery of Monkwearmouth and Jarrow to seek advice about Easter; he also wanted a church built in the Roman style, to be dedicated to St Peter.

A party was sent from Northumbria to help the king with his reform. It included a Pict named Curitan, who is credited with building the church in the Roman style, as King Nechtan had requested. Curitan continued the practice of dedicating churches to St Peter, renaming churches bearing the name of their founder. Dedications to other apostles followed, and to the Virgin Mary, though there may well have been some local resistance to losing the name of the founder. Curitan, or St Curdy as he was known, later moved north to Rosemarkie to renew St Moluag's earlier foundation. One of the impressive stone slabs commonly found in Pictland, thought to figure Curitan and two others, is in the National Museum of Antiquities in Edinburgh. It came from Dargie, near Invergowrie, where he had built a church.

In 717 King Nechtan took further his support for the Roman Church and expelled any clergy of the Columban Church who were not conforming with it. Iona had been deeply resistant to change; although Adamnan had failed to persuade his community over the Roman Easter date, the Northumbrian Egbert finally succeeded in 729. Under Nechtan the movement towards conformity with Rome had made some progress.

Aspects of the Developing Church in England

While the Celtic Churches were responding slowly to the Synod of Whitby decisions, the English Church was continuing to expand. Thanks to Archbishop Theodore's reorganisation, there were now seventeen sees; four of them in the north, at York, Lindisfarne, Hexham and at Whithorn where the bishopric was restored and the Saxon Pechthelm made bishop.

The Christian culture of Northumbria continued to flourish well into the eighth century. Of the manuscripts that emerged from the Lindisfarne scriptorium, the Durham Gospels are now in the Cathedral Library there and the Echternach Gospels found their way to the National Library in Paris. At Hexham one of the very few Anglo-Saxon chalices to survive can be seen. Made of copper gilt, it is barely more than seven centimetres high. We can imagine it used in conjunction with a portable altar, like the one found in St Cuthbert's coffin, to take communion to outlying areas.

One of the most remarkable expressions of early Christian art are the stone crosses that can be seen in the north. The Bewcastle Cross still stands on the moors north of Hadrian's Wall, in a remote village churchyard. The shaft, a single piece of stone, bears three figures on one face: in the centre is a Christ in Majesty, above is St John the Baptist and below what may be a representation of St John the Evangelist. A worn runic inscription suggests to scholars that it was made around 700. The other faces are inscribed with interlace and foliage. Only the head of the cross is missing.

A few miles away, in Dumfriesshire, is the Ruthwell Cross, also with carvings of figures and ornament, with scenes of St Paul and St Anthony in the desert, and runic inscriptions. Casts of both crosses can be seen in the Monks' Dormitory at Durham Cathedral. At St Andrew's Church, Hexham, is the shaft of Acca's Cross with its fine vine-roll decoration. Acca succeeded Wilfrid as bishop of Hexham.

These sculptured stone crosses mark the beginning of a very impressive art form that is a particular feature of these islands. They served many purposes: to mark a burial, to mark a place of prayer or preaching where there was no church, or else provided a landmark.

Devotion to the Holy Cross had developed in popular piety from the time of Constantine, who was inspired by his vision of the cross, and after the alleged finding of the true cross by his mother, the Empress Helena. Relics of it were sent across Europe. Elaborate crosses appeared on altars, and a cross was used as a rallying sign in battle. It inspired hymns and poems, and special feasts in honour of the cross had become part of the liturgical year.

The beginnings of a tradition of Christian poetry appear. Bede attributes the earliest example to Caedmon, a cowherd at the abbey of Whitby. Saddened at not being able to share in the communal verse-making accompanied by the harp, Caedmon was surprised to receive the gift of poetry and composed many poems about the Christian story. Only a version of his poem on the creation survives. Aldhelm of Malmesbury also practised this verse-making to music in the tradition of the Anglo-Saxon minstrel. Bede himself offers us a poem on the approach of death. But it is *Beowulf* that takes pride of place. Possibly written down first in the eighth century, perhaps later, it is a sixth-century story that crosses the divide between two worlds: the Norse Heroic Age of brave warriors and their deeds, and a world of mostly nominal Christians. The hero is a

Swede who lives by the sword in a setting where evil takes the form of monsters and hobgoblins, but the author presumes a knowledge of Christianity in his audience to whom the poem would have been sung. Ideas of Fate run alongside the providence of God, who is seen as the creator and sustainer of His world, to whom thanks are due. His story is in part a reflection on the transience of human life and power, and man's ultimate destiny. Through its poetry the language of the Anglo-Saxons was being expanded and enriched. It was also expressing a changing set of values under the influence of Christianity.

The life of Guthlac of Crowland illustrates this change. He was a descendant of the royal house of Mercia and sufficiently inspired by stories of brave warriors to start his adult life as a soldier. He showed a gift of leadership and acquired large quantities of booty from those he defeated. However after nine years his success palled; he gave up all the wealth he had accumulated and became a monk at Repton. There he spent two years, finally resolving to take up the ultimate challenge of the monastic life and become an anchorite. He chose the island of Crowland in the Fens, then a desolate spot in the middle of a swamp, to build his hermitage.

For fifteen years he led a very harsh existence, overcoming his initial fears and hallucinations through prayer and fasting, and attaining to a degree of saintliness that brought many to the door of his hut, some for healing and some in search of counsel. Wilfrid himself was a regular visitor, as was Aethelbald, the future king of Mercia, then in exile. Guthlac died in 714, at the age of forty. A shrine was erected in his memory and later an abbey was built at Crowland. One aisle of the medieval abbey serves as the present parish church. A nine-foot long roll of parchment dating from the twelfth century, known as the Guthlac Roll, now in the British Museum, depicts eighteen scenes from the saint's life. These have been copied in a nineteenth-century stained-glass window in the church of Market Deeping, once part of Crowland Abbey and one of nine churches to be dedicated to the Saxon raider turned saint, who earned his place in the history of the Church of the conversion period. His choice seems an alien one to our world, yet such endurance and perseverance in the search for God presents a challenge to the way of life and thought of any age.

For the most part the Church was developing in less dramatic ways; in some cases in less idealistic ways. Bede expresses his concern that some monasteries were being founded for wrong motives, simply in order to keep land in the family, where the so-called monks had no true vocation. He describes too how one monastery at least had lapsed into wayward habits: the life of prayer had given way to one of indulgence and gossip, and the nuns spent their time weaving fine clothes for themselves.

Another, more positive, development was the building of churches by Saxon thegns on their estates. They would then appoint a priest to serve the church. This must have been a welcome expansion for those who had to walk great distances to reach a church. This was another of Bede's concerns, expressed in a letter to a friend of his, Egbert, who became bishop of York around 732. He urged the need to ordain more priests to teach and baptise, and to consecrate more bishops for some of the minster churches. When Egbert's brother became king of Northumbria, Egbert was able to carry out many reforms. One of his achievements was to establish a cathedral school at York, where he himself taught. Some of his writings also have survived. His Pontifical, the liturgical book of a bishop, is a source for early liturgy and for the English coronation rite.

Another cause very dear to Bede's heart was that the newly converted should understand their new faith better. The Anglo-Saxon Church must have found it necessary from an early stage to use the native language for its teaching, in an otherwise Latin liturgy. Bede went a step further by translating the Lord's Prayer and the Creed into Old English. The crowning act of his busy life was to complete his translation into English of St John's Gospel on the very evening of his death on the Feast of the Ascension in 735.

One of his scholars, Cuthbert, describes the event: how Bede had become weaker since before Easter of that year, but had continued cheerfully in the monks' daily routine of prayer and praise, and in teaching. Sensing the end of his life was near, he shared such possessions as he had with his fellows (some pepper, some linen and some incense), consoling them at his imminent departure and assuring them that he simply longed to see Christ his King. He completed the remaining sentence of his translation of St John's Gospel, chanted the Gloria and departed this life.

From the age of seven onwards, he first spent his life at Monkwearmouth and then at Jarrow, where at nineteen he became a deacon and at thirty a priest. In the autobiographical note at the end of his *History of the English Church and People*, he tells us that his chief delight had always been in studying, teaching and writing. He wrote many commentaries on the Scriptures, compiled extracts from the Early Fathers of the Church, and wrote histories of saints and abbots, many letters, hymns, poetry, and two books on the subject of time.

He came to the writing of his history of the English

Church after many years of critical study of the Scriptures, and brought to it a meticulous concern for accuracy. Abbot Albinus, successor to Hadrian at Canterbury, provided him with information about Kent and nearby areas. A London priest, Nothelm, a later archbishop of Canterbury, went to Rome, where he studied the archives and copied letters to provide Bede with material. Bishops and monks made contributions. The assembling and checking of material at a time when communication was slow and the physical conditions of writing in a monastery of that time, particularly in winter, make his achievement all the more remarkable.

His account shows him very much as a man of his time and place. As a Benedictine monk living in an area with a Celtic tradition, he reflects something of both traditions, but he was especially keen to show how unity under Rome would benefit the Church and how the Church in its turn could be a means of uniting all the kingdoms. Many have seen in Bede the first signs of the idea of Englishness.

At the same time he is very much a Northumbrian, writing for the king of Northumbria, with more first-hand material about Northumbria than any other area – this may account, in part, for his very detailed account of the Synod of Whitby, which was on home ground, compared with his comparatively cursory treatment of the first general synod of the Church in England at Hertford in 673. It must also be said that the debate at Whitby involved two of his abiding passions; one for church unity, the other concerning calculations of time. He had already written two books on time and became the acknowledged expert on the dating of Easter. He was also among the first to use the BC/AD method of noting dates in his writings and helped establish its usage, through the many manuscripts and translations made of his history book. His reputation in Europe was secured, even in his lifetime. Posterity owes much to him. He was buried at the monastery where he had lived and worked, but in the eleventh century his bones were taken, by somewhat devious means, to Durham, where he is now remembered in the Galilee Chapel of the cathedral where Cuthbert also rests.

During Bede's lifetime, the position of Northumbria as first of the English kingdoms had been taken over by Mercia. The reign of King Aethelbald, a powerful and aggressive king, dominated the first half of the eighth century there, giving to the Church on the one hand and appropriating church lands on the other. He was present at the Church synod of 746, where the duties of bishops to visit and priests to teach their flock were made explicit, and pagan practices of divining and reading auguries were condemned. It took place at the unidentified venue of Clovesho, which may have been situated in Mercia. Politically powerful though Mercia became, there was no cultural golden age to compare with that in Northumbria, either there or in any other English kingdom in the seventh or eighth centuries. Mercian churches founded earlier, such as Brixworth and Repton, continued to be added to and altered. In the church at Breedon-on-the-Hill, where the nave walls may be part of the original monastery, there are examples of fine eighth-century carving: friezes that may have gone round the whole church and panels with carved figures. There is also the Breedon Angel, built into the south wall of the tower, which is a full-length figure with folded dress similar to drawings in the Book of Cerne (a book of prayers that was probably written at Lichfield in the early ninth century). Both works give some indication of Mercian artistry before the arrival of the destructive Danes.

The remarkable Hedda Stone at Peterborough, which was probably the cover of a shrine, may be contemporary with the Breedon carvings, since there are some similarities in its decorative panels and the twelve figures in arcades on the sides. There are a number of stone crosses in Mercia that date from the early ninth century. Two are in the market place at Sandbach, and one with deeply carved scrolls is at Bakewell, where there may have been a workshop: the impressive cross at Eyam also displays the same distinctive scrollwork. It may be that preaching crosses were common in this area due to a lack of churches.

From the kingdom in the south-east some manuscripts survive from the eighth century. The Canterbury Bible in the British Library has purple pages with gold lettering, a full-page portrait of St Mark and Canon Tables. Just as the Irish Celtic influence predominates in the manuscripts produced in Northumbria, here the Mediterranean and Continental influences are more apparent. Like the northern manuscripts, some of the southern ones have travelled: the Codex Aureus to Stockholm and the Barheim Gospels to the Vatican.

The Anglo-Saxon Mission to Europe

Arguably the most outstanding achievement of the eighth-century Anglo-Saxon Church came through her missions to Europe. Mindful of the Gospel command to teach the faith to all nations and of the benefit that they had received through Pope Gregory's mission under Augustine, men of great calibre and endurance set out to evangelise the pagan tribes on the Continent. The example of Irish monks must have been some encouragement to them, as the enterprise was not without risk: two Anglo-Saxon priests were murdered at the outset of their mission to Old Saxony.

The Northumbrian Willibrord was among the first of the Anglo-Saxon missionaries to achieve considerable success during his almost fifty-year mission to Frisia, the Holland of today. This was where Wilfrid had spent some months in 678 on his way to Rome, evangelising and baptising converts. Willibrord had in fact been educated in Wilfrid's monastery at Ripon. In 690 he set out on his life's mission with twelve companions, a practice common among the Irish. Having first obtained papal approval, he and his party made their base in Utrecht and worked to good effect. Willibrord was made archbishop of Frisia, with Utrecht as his episcopal seat. He tried to extend his work into eastern Frisia but the pagan king was not cooperative, and Willibrord moved briefly, and at some risk, to Denmark and Heligoland. Of the monasteries he founded, the best known was at Echternach in present-day Luxembourg, where he was obliged to stay during times of political turmoil. The Echternach Gospels, almost certainly written by a Northumbrian scribe, are now in the National Library in Paris. In 719 Willibrord was able to return to Utrecht, and, in the twenty years that followed, rebuilt the church that the pagan king had tried to destroy; he remained there until his death at Echternach in 739 at eighty-one years of age.

The most famous of the Anglo-Saxon missionaries, Boniface, first went to the Continent to help Willibrord, but the political situation was volatile and he returned to England. He was a Wessex man, born around 675 at Crediton and named Wynfrith. After an early education at the monastery in Exeter, he entered that of Nursling, Hampshire, and became a much-respected scholar and teacher. He felt called, however, not to serve the Church in his native Wessex but to evangelise among the Germanic tribes on the Continent. On his second visit there in 718, like Willibrord, he made the journey to Rome to ask – and receive – the pope's approval for the work he planned in Germany, then part of the Frankish Empire. Obedience and loyalty to the pope were integral to the whole of his missionary work. It was around this time that he seems to have taken the name Boniface. After three years spent sharing in Willibrord's work in Frisia, and no doubt learning from the older man's experience, he moved on to Hesse and Thuringia. At Geismar in Hesse, he made a dramatic and courageous stand against pagan belief by felling an oak tree sacred to the god Thor. With the timber he built a chapel to St Peter. He went on to found Benedictine monasteries and schools on land given by new converts, and worked with great success, first becoming a bishop, and then becoming archbishop in 731. He must have been sixty when he extended his work into Bavaria. Throughout his mission he received constant support and advice from the papacy. By acknowledging papal authority from the beginning of his mission and by seeking advice on many matters, Boniface extended the influence of the pope, consolidating the latter's position.

He enjoyed the protection of the leaders of the Franks, who invited him to help carry out reforms in the Frankish Church. Some clergy at the Frankish court viewed this Englishman on a mission blessed by Rome without enthusiasm, but he was able to achieve some changes through a number of synods. He was given land at Fulda in Hesse, where one of his followers founded an abbey. There he was able to take some rest. It became the most famous of the foundations associated with him. At almost eighty, he sought the appointment of a successor, and, on his recommendation, another Englishman, Lull, who had come from Malmesbury, was duly appointed archbishop of Mainz. But Boniface had not finished his work; he decided to make a last visit to Frisia and led a successful mission over two summers. Sadly his life and that of fifty followers came to a brutal end when they were murdered by some resistant pagans. Boniface was taken for burial at Fulda, which became a great centre of pilgrimage and Christian culture in the centuries that followed.

During his long years abroad, Boniface kept in touch with the Church in England, which was, in fact, an active partner in his mission, giving him every kind of support and encouragement. Letters came from all levels in the Church, from bishops, from abbots and from nuns, and practical gifts too.

Many of the letters from Boniface contain requests for books – to the archbishop of York for the commentaries and homilies of Bede, to one Abbot Duddo for a treatise on St Paul and his own notes, and to Eadburga, Abbess of Thanet, for a copy of the Epistles of St Peter in letters of gold, to show to his people.

Other gifts came from his supporters, including vestments, altar cloths, money and cloaks, which he describes as a great comfort to the missionaries, for the circumstances in which they worked were very demanding. A priest, recently arrived in Hesse, writes to the monks of Glastonbury that the life was dangerous and harsh, and under threat from the heathens around them. He asks for their prayers – a request echoed in many letters to England. Many responded, some of them nuns who had met Boniface and who write with great affection, as to a brother or a father. Even the king of the East Angles writes to him promising support through the prayers of the monasteries. The support he received from the Church in England was greatly valued by Boniface as he faced the difficulties and dangers that surrounded him. Most valuable of all were the offers to help him in his work. He had a high opinion of the contribution of women and appealed for some to go to Germany to help him. He specifically asked that one Leoba, a relation of his and nun at the minster of Wimborne, might come. Her arrival, in company with several other nuns, must have encouraged him greatly. As abbess of the community at Bischofsheim, she established a centre of learning, where other abbesses were trained, and she influenced many beyond its walls.

Another Wessex man, Willibald, came to share in Boniface's work in Bavaria. After a grand tour of Rome and the Middle East, followed by some years at the monastery of Monte Cassino, where St Benedict had been a monk, the pope sent him to work under Boniface's direction at Eichstatt in Bavaria, to make it a missionary centre. Eichstatt was on the Danube and provided a base from which to evangelise among the Slavs. The success of the monastery he established there, on the same lines as Monte Cassino, led to his becoming bishop of Eichstatt in 741, where he served for forty years; like Willibrord and Boniface reaching a ripe old age. Not far from Eichstatt, his brother became abbot of the double monastery of Heidenheim, where his sister, Waltpurgis, who had been a nun at Wimborne like Leoba, later became abbess. Willibald's story comes from an Englishwoman, Hygeburg, another of Boniface's recruits who became a nun at Heidenheim. We can only wonder just how many English men and women became part of the mission to the Continent. It speaks well for the Church in England, which had nurtured Christians of such commitment.

Nor was the English Church ever very far from the

thoughts of Boniface. As an archbishop and a churchman of great stature on the Continent, he felt able to write a letter of censure to King Aethelbald. He had been disturbed by unfavourable accounts of the king and wrote to persuade him to mend his ways – to treat nuns with respect and to honour the privileges of the Church. After the Frankish Church Synod of 747, which marked the climax of his missionary career, he was keen to share its conclusions with Archbishop Cuthbert of Canterbury, as well as his concerns over some scandals associated with the English Church: laymen seizing monasteries and directing them, drunkenness in parishes, extravagance in the dress of clergy, and the behaviour of matrons and nuns journeying to Rome, which was a practice he thought should be forbidden as it tarnished the image of the English Church. His letters fill out our picture of that Church and of the man himself. He emerges as a man of warmth, faithful to old friends, and with a gift for inspiring the same faithfulness in his followers and giving them a sense of being members of one family, embarked on a communal enterprise, whether they were working with him on the Continent or supporting his mission from England. At his martyrdom Archbishop Cuthbert paid tribute to him and the dangerous mission he had undertaken. Other Englishmen followed in the footsteps of Boniface, Willibrord and their fellow-workers. Among them was the Northumbrian Willehad who became the first bishop of Bremen.

Leoba survived Boniface by some twenty-six years and continued her work until 780, supported by the new king, Charlemagne, and never returned to England. She was, like Boniface, buried at Fulda.

Charlemagne, who began his impressive reign in 771 and was crowned Roman Emperor by the pope in Rome in the year 800, took an active part in the continuing reform of the Church and in the education of the clergy. He invited scholars to his court to help him in this task, among them Alcuin, a Northumbrian who had been trained at the school in York founded by Bishop Egbert and that was then one of England's leading schools. There he had become master and librarian. Charlemagne made him head of the Palace School at Aachen, where this English scholar made a significant contribution to education and the development of the liturgy, exercising considerable influence over the reforming movement of Charlemagne's empire.

There were further contacts between this empire and England through Aethelbald's successor, the powerful King Offa of Mercia, and Charlemagne. Perhaps through Charlemagne's influence, the pope sent legates to England in 786, for the first time since Augustine's mission, to look at the state of the Church there. Offa's power extended over much of the south of England, including Kent, and he also had ambitions for his kingdom's status within the Church. The Anglo-Saxon Chronicle records a lively synod in 787 when it seems King Offa exercised his power and the archbishop of Canterbury ceded part of his metropolitan area so that a new metropolitan see might be set up in Mercia at Lichfield. For a short time England had three archbishops, but the move had not met with general approval in the Church and the see was short-lived.

The seventh century had seen the conversion of the Anglo-Saxons to Christianity. The eighth-century Church in England, still dominated by the monasteries, had not only expanded and blossomed in many directions under sound leadership among the bishops, it had also produced outstanding Christians – scholars such as Bede whose works were widely disseminated at home and on the Continent,

Alcuin at the heart of an increasingly powerful empire, and outward-looking missionaries who inspired many others to join them in the conversion of pagan tribes. Together they had created a growing awareness on the Continent of England as an emerging nation. Through its role in the Christianisation of Germany and the reform of the Frankish Church, the English Church had, in fact, made a significant contribution to the formation of a Western Christian empire, the precursor of medieval Europe. In the same way, countless Irish monks "on pilgrimage for Christ" had been making their mark on the Continent for more than two centuries and were continuing to do so, founding monasteries and schools famed for their learning. Through their combined efforts, Fulda, Utrecht, Eichstatt and lesser known places joined Luxeuil, Annegray, St Gall and Bobbio on the Christian map of Europe.

Viking Attacks Begin

At home, however, by the end of the eighth century, all the achievements of the Church were seriously threatened: the Vikings were on the move, and they were pagans. The year 787 marked the beginning of their raids. In 793 Lindisfarne was sacked; other attacks followed on Jarrow, Iona, Whithorn and Melrose. Monasteries were particular objects of attack – unprotected, vulnerable sites, often on the coast and on islands, where valuables had been amassed. Their contents were plundered, buildings destroyed and their occupants treated with scant regard, often being murdered.

After the early raids in Northumbria, many Vikings, for the most part Norwegians, settled in the Shetlands and Orkneys, which remained part of the Norse kingdom until the fifteenth century. In the west they settled in the

Hebrides and from Carlisle south to Lancashire, and on the Isle of Man, which formed a good centre for raiding and where the Vikings left many marks of their culture. Coastal areas of Wales suffered too. Others went on to Ireland, where they would create a kingdom around Dublin, which became a base for attacks inland.

In 835 a new wave of Danish raids began in the south of England. From Kent, where Canterbury and Rochester were attacked, the raiders continued into Lincolnshire and began to winter inland. As the century progressed they went on to raid York, Mercia, East Anglia (where King Edmund was martyred) and Northumbria. In Wessex they met with persistent opposition. After repeated attacks, in 878 King Alfred was victorious and came to an agreement with the Danish leader, Guthrun. England was to be divided: north of a line roughly from Chester to London would be under Danish rule – called the Danelaw – and Guthrun was baptised with Alfred as his sponsor: a token beginning of the conversion of the Danes. In 883 Danes and Norsemen settled in York.

The destruction of countless monasteries left the Church impoverished, both in manpower and material goods. Church land was appropriated and given by kings to thegns. Diocesan organisation suffered: in the north, Hexham and Whithorn ceased to be bishoprics; York was occupied and the diocese impoverished; and Lindisfarne was abandoned in 875. Further south, in middle and eastern England, several sees were affected; that of Dunwich was never restored. The monastery schools that had educated the clergy and the libraries with their precious hand-copied manuscripts were lost. Yet in all the confusion and fear of the late eighth and early ninth centuries, the very precious manuscript of the Book of

Kells was preserved. Its provenance is not certain, but it may well have been written largely at Iona and taken to Kells for safety when the monks left the island for the small monastery in central Ireland. It now resides in the library of Trinity College Dublin.

The manuscript is an outstanding masterpiece, in which the four Gospels are illuminated with a wealth of complex and varied decoration, both in terms of whole pages and within the lines of the text. There are full-page portraits of Christ, and the Madonna and Child, as well as portraits of the Evangelists and many versions of their symbols: the man for St Matthew, the lion for St Mark, the calf for St Luke and the eagle for St John.

In addition there are fully illustrated pages of the temptation and of the arrest of Christ. The introduction to each Gospel is highly decorated and specially significant moments are highlighted. Hidden away in the intricacies of the patterns lurk cats and mice, fish and birds, plants and faces.

The text used is a mixture of the Vulgate and the earlier Old Latin translation of the Bible, still used by the Irish Church in the eighth and ninth centuries; scholars claim to recognise a number of hands both in the script and in the illustrations. There are similarities with the Book of Durrow, the Echternach Gospels and the Lichfield Gospels, which may present problems to those wanting to identify its source, but perhaps illustrate most of all the cross-fertilisation that must have taken place among monasteries with their different styles and influences. In the end, one can but wonder at this awesome achievement and at its survival.

The Vikings had wreaked widespread havoc throughout Britain and Ireland, and had brought to an end the first flowering of the Anglo-Saxon Church, yet that Church was able to survive even in the Danelaw, while in the southern part of the country King Alfred provided a beacon of light at a very dark time.

VI

RECOVERY AND RENEWAL

The Church Fights Back in Every Area

When Viking attacks were at a peak, Alfred became king of Wessex at the age of twenty-two. This was in 871. During his twenty-eight year rule, he came to be acknowledged as king of all England not under Danish rule; that is, of all the south including London and south-west Mercia. In the remainder of the country, the Danelaw, with York as its capital, the pagan Danes and Norsemen settled and ruled. Nevertheless, somehow the Church there survived.

In his kingdom, Alfred was intent on preserving a Christian society and on redressing the effects of Viking devastation. Even before the arrival of the Vikings, standards of scholarship had lapsed, so a revival of learning was to be at the heart of the process. With this in view, Alfred invited scholars to his court just as Charlemagne had done, set up schools to ensure the education of clergy and nobles, and stimulated the development of English as a literary language in its own right, alongside Latin. In this he played an active role himself, learning Latin, and with his scholars translating works he valued into English, such as Bede's history and Gregory the Great's *Pastoral Rule* on the work of bishops, copies of which were sent to every diocese. He encouraged the compiling of the Anglo-Saxon Chronicle, in English, subsequently kept up to date, right up to the twelfth century, in different monastic centres: a very valuable resource. A new code of laws, with an introduction that makes clear their Christian context, was drawn up and translated into English.

He gave generously to the Church and attempted to renew the monasticism which, in its heyday, had made such a valuable contribution to Church and society. He founded a nunnery at Shaftesbury and a monastery at Athelney, the place where he and his followers had taken refuge from the Danes before their successful battle at Edington. But in this his efforts were premature: England was not ready for a renewed monasticism and monks had to be found in Gaul for his monastery.

Alfred's achievements were considerable, given that his early reign was dominated by Viking attacks, which resumed again in the years before his death. He was a dedicated Christian king and felt accountable to God for the power he held. Perhaps his greatest legacy was a new and nobler idea of kingship, which saw faith, learning and justice as the keys to the betterment of his people, along with a stronger sense of English identity, achieved particularly through his nurture of the English language.

The south of England did not have to face the problems of concentrated Danish settlement. Initially the Anglo-Saxons had made only slow progress into Devon, in the face of Celtic resistance. By the tenth century, with the encouragement of kings, there were many minsters serving as bases for evangelism. In addition to Exeter, in time Crediton and Tavistock were added, and a little later Buckfast, among the larger foundations. There were also a number of local churches: the parish system was in fact establishing itself here as elsewhere, with the older Celtic foundations absorbed into it.

The same was true of Cornwall. In addition to local parish churches, a number of collegiate churches had grown up, which were communities of priests and canons with a set rule of life, who acted as parish clergy. In some cases it was a Celtic-type monastery that converted into a collegiate church, as at St Buryan's. King Athelstan founded a bishopric at St Germans and appointed a Celt, Conan, as bishop. Conan even submitted to the authority of the archbishop of Canterbury – a submission his Celtic compatriots in Wales resisted for a long time. From the other main centre at Bodmin, which went back to the sixth-century St Petroc, and had continued to be a centre of pilgrimage and learning, emerged a tenth-century illuminated copy of the Gospels.

Devon and Cornwall had been integrated into the pattern of the Church in the rest of England, but in Cornwall particularly, the past had not been abandoned. Dedications to Celtic saints remained, as did the people's attachment to wells and islands, and to the preaching crosses that had served as meeting places for worship before churches were built. At Cardinham, three miles north-east of Bodmin, a very fine tenth-century cross stands in the churchyard.

Wales in the Ninth and Tenth Centuries

The other Celtic areas weathered the Viking attacks to a greater or lesser extent. In Wales, during Alfred's reign, there were some signs that the southern part of the country was becoming more open to relations with England. Not only did they have a common enemy in the Vikings but they also sought help against the power of Mercia. The same openness was not apparent in North Wales, where a strong, new dynasty had been established. Rhodri the Great, who ruled in the middle of the ninth century, was still fiercely anti-Saxon and determined to keep at bay the Mercians on the one hand and the Vikings on the other, with some degree of success. Though Wales was subjected to many attacks, and her monasteries repeatedly sacked and restored, the raiders did not settle there to the extent that they did in some other parts of the west, such as Lancashire, Cheshire and Cumbria.

Rhodri the Great had united most of Wales and a sense of nationhood was developing, as it was in the English kingdoms under King Alfred. His court in Gwynedd had become a centre of culture, and was in contact with Continental courts since it was on the route that Irish travellers took to and from the Continent. The traditions and genealogies of the Britons and their poetry, preserved orally over many centuries by professional bards at royal courts, could now be written down. In the centuries preceding the Norman Conquest it was through poetry, much of it written by monks, that the Church in Wales gave finest expression to its faith. In South Wales, the thirteenth-century Black Book of Carmarthen contains early ninth- and tenth-century poems conveying the native spirituality in the native language.

The Age of the Saints in Wales was now well past and Celtic monasticism was generally beginning to decline. Some of the old *clas*-type monasteries continued – these were the religious communities where whole families were involved. Clergy continued to marry, although the papacy had for some centuries recommended that priests should be celibate, and the hereditary principle still operated in these communities. At Llanbadarn and Llancarfan clerical dynasties kept up the tradition of learning. From St David's monastery King Alfred invited the monk Asser to his court, to help in his crusade towards literacy. In other places, the *clas* churches gradually became the parish churches of the wider organisation of the Church, in which bishops took their undisputed place as leaders. Their numbers are uncertain. In addition to the diocesan bishops at Bangor and St Asaph's in the north, and at St David's and Llandaff in the south, other major monastic houses, such as Llanbadarn, may have had an abbot-bishop at their head.

Relations between Wales and England improved through the grandsons of Rhodri the Great and King Alfred, when Hywel the Good and Athelstan joined forces. Danish raids resumed in the late tenth century: St David's was raided four times in the 980s, Llantwit Major and Llancarfan suffered too, and the island of Anglesey proved very vulnerable.

In all the Celtic areas, the most widespread tangible legacy of the ninth- and tenth-century Church are the sculptured standing crosses. Some examples have survived in Wales. At Margam Museum in the south, the cross of Einion and the cross of Cynfelin are the best examples of the local style, both disc-headed and heavily patterned. The latter once stood in the village street outside the church. Its shaft is now greatly reduced, but the figures of Mary and John standing at the foot of the cross are still clear. There are later, more slender, examples in Pembrokeshire in the closely patterned Carew Cross and St Brynach's Cross at Nevern, while the church at Llanbadarn contains one of the finest of the Welsh stone crosses.

Ireland in the Ninth and Tenth Centuries

However, it was in Ireland especially that this art form reached its finest expression against a background of regular devastation inflicted by the Vikings. The first raid was in 795. By 830 Vikings were trading not only from Dublin, but from Waterford, Wexford and Limerick too. Large parts of central and southern Ireland in particular were under repeated attack in the ninth century; in the north, the monastery at Bangor had already been destroyed. Only slowly were the invaders being Christianised.

Whereas during earlier centuries travellers went to study in Ireland, away from the wars and disturbances in Britain and on the Continent, in the ninth century the Viking invasions encouraged Irish scholars to go to the Continent, in some cases taking valuable manuscripts with them for safety. There they made a significant contribution to education, sometimes at royal courts as Alcuin had done at the court of Charlemagne. John Scotus Erigena, a philosopher, poet and notable scholar, became head of the palace school at Laon, while Sedulius Scotus, a poet and theological writer, established an Irish cultural centre at Liège. Irish Christians went to many European countries, from north-east France where they had been very active, to Hungary and Czechoslovakia, and even further to parts of Poland and Russia, establishing settlements and schools, and founding hospices on pilgrim routes. Their tendency to ignore the diocesan system continued to cause friction, as did their wandering ways, so directly opposed to the stability prized by the now well-established Benedictine Order, and attempts were made to modify their ways.

Back in their homeland, in spite of the turmoil of the period, this was when many of the finest of the high crosses were produced, all of them painstakingly crafted sermons in stone. At Monasterboice is Muiredach's Cross with its panels of figures: on the west face the crucifixion, and on the east face Christ judging the world; also the West Cross, which is more than six metres high with twenty-two sculptured panels of Biblical scenes and a representation of the crucifixion on the head of the cross. Equally impressive, at Clonmacnoise are the South Cross, with its abstract designs and a crucifixion, and the Cross of the Scriptures, with its carved panels of figures. Through these, along with some five hundred grave slabs from the eighth to the tenth centuries and the remains of several early churches, Clonmacnoise offers a fairly comprehensive memorial of the Irish Church of the first millennium. Both sites have a round tower, which is common to many early Irish Christian sites: a product of the precarious living conditions in the ninth and tenth centuries –a combined belfry and lookout point, which also provided some shelter from attack.

At Kells too, where the monks of Iona found shelter when they fled from Viking attacks on their own island, a number of ancient stones and structures, together with a round tower, stand in the churchyard. The Cross of Patrick and Columba is possibly the oldest of the crosses, and has a rich mixture of carvings. It may have been the Ionan monks who built St Columba's church with its steeply pitched stone roof. Inside the present church is a copy of the Book of Kells, one of the finest treasures of early Christian art. These survivors of violent times, when so much was destroyed, tell us something of the devotion of Christian artists and craftsmen at a time when insecurity was a way of life. They stand as a memorial to the faithfulness of the Church of their time.

After a lull of some thirty years, towards the end of

the ninth century, the Vikings returned in force, bringing another century of fighting and destruction to Ireland, until their power was finally broken by Brian Boru, who became high king of Ireland in 1002. The battle of Clontarf of 1014, in which he died, was a decisive defeat for the Vikings. They had brought significant and lasting change to a country with an essentially pastoral base, not least through the establishment of towns and ports, where the Norse continued to live in their own communities. Closer links were developing in the early eleventh century between the Church in these communities and Canterbury; priests were going there to be consecrated as bishops, first from Dublin, then from Waterford and Limerick. In response the archbishop of Canterbury was showing a growing interest in the Irish Church.

Scotland in the West and East

In Scotland, as in Ireland, the art of the sculptured high cross flourished. On Iona, St Martin's Cross, which stands in front of the present abbey, is an outstanding example of the crosses to survive from this period. Its carvings are still wonderfully preserved: on its east face, figures of the Virgin and Child, Daniel in the lion's den, and Abraham about to sacrifice Isaac; on the west face a decorative panel. A replica of St John's Cross, which had weathered badly, stands nearer the entrance to the abbey, patterned on both sides. The monastery at Iona sustained many Viking attacks but was repeatedly rebuilt. The graveyard, Reilig Oran, goes back to the early Christian period; many carved fragments and early cross-marked gravestones are displayed in the museum of the medieval abbey. It is claimed that there were many hundreds of standing crosses on the island before the dissolution of the monasteries.

Other islands bear reminders that the art was widespread, such as the Kildalton Cross on Islay. The craft continued over many centuries. Schools of sculpture grew up on the mainland around Loch Awe and Loch Sween, and on the Kintyre peninsula.

When some of the monks left Iona for Kells, fleeing from the Vikings in the ninth century, others moved east to Dunkeld, which became a centre for the Columban Church. In the middle of the century, the Irish in the west, and the Picts in the east and north became united to form the kingdom of Alba, north of the Firth and Clyde, and a national bishop emerged with his seat at Dunkeld. In the early tenth century the centre moved from Dunkeld to St Andrew's, where there had been a monastery at Kinrymont since the sixth century. The move to St Andrew's may be seen as a change of direction in thinking in the new kingdom. King Nechtan of the Picts had started the process of aligning the Pictish Church with the Roman order. Gradually the role of the bishop was becoming more important and the number of secular clergy was increasing. Later in the tenth century the kingdom of Alba expanded when Malcolm II won back the lowland area between the Forth and the Tweed, and his grandson Duncan acquired the Celtic kingdom of Strathclyde: mainland Scotland as we know it had come into being.

While the contribution of the Ionan Church in the west, from its beginnings in the sixth century, has tended to dominate the scene thus far in the area that became Scotland, both in terms of evangelism and artistic achievement, the Picts in their area had also used their skills to express their Christian allegiance. Their skill in metalwork is evident in the treasure trove of silver objects found at St Ninian's, Shetland, in 1958. It had been buried beneath the floor of a tiny church in about 800, perhaps in response to Viking attack. Some Pictish crosses survive, such as the eighth-century examples at Aberlemno in Perthshire: a magnificently patterned cross in the churchyard and another at the roadside, almost three metres high with mourning angels each side of the inscribed cross. Other massive cross slabs come from Meigle in Angus. St Vigean's in Arbroath has a museum of Pictish stones, as does Groam House Museum at Rosemarkie. Strange symbols and animals proliferate, which have led some to see Pictish influence in the Book of Kells, or even the hand of a Pictish scribe, particularly in the animals, and the human figures and faces. From the ninth century comes an illuminated manuscript, the Book of Deer, from the community in the north-east. In addition to the Gospel texts, it provides further interest in that it contains glosses and notes in the Scottish Gaelic language. What has survived from this period may be only a fraction of what was produced in the very distinctive Pictish style.

Christianisation of the Vikings

Further south as we move into the tenth century, there are signs of the slow Christianisation of the Viking settlers, as crosses and gravestones begin to display Christian symbols alongside Scandinavian motifs and elements of Norse mythology. One of the finest crosses is in the churchyard of Gosforth in Cumbria: a slender, tapering cross almost three metres high with a carving of Christ with arms outstretched, the only Christian sign among representations of Norse mythology. The same juxtaposition of symbols appears on the Sigurd Cross in the churchyard at Halton, Lancashire: on the one side scenes from the life of Sigurd the Norse hero, on the other a cross with two figures beside it. Did the sculptor see them as of equal value, or was there a struggle of loyalties? The Nunburneholme Cross on Humberside depicts a similar conflict: on one side are a warrior, sitting and holding a sword, and the Virgin with the Christ-child holding a book. These crosses suggest two very different worlds of belief struggling, it seems, to achieve a resolution.

A similar example can be found on the Isle of Man, where the Vikings established roots at an early stage. There was already a school of sculpture on the island before their arrival that had produced the eighth-century Calf of Man Crucifixion. Among the concentration of Viking-age sculpture is Thorwald's Cross, at Kirk Andreas, with a Christian scene on one side depicting the triumph of Christ over Satan, and on the other a scene from the last battle in Norse mythology.

The Norwegian Vikings on the Isle of Man may have been slower to adopt Christianity than the Danes in England. As the dominant group in a confined area they would have felt no need to comply with local customs. Early burials with grave goods, and a ship burial that disturbed earlier Christian burials suggest they continued pagan practices for a time, but, as other generations succeeded, differences in burial practice disappear. Christianity did not become the official religion of Norway until the early eleventh century. The Isle of Man remained part of the Norse kingdom until 1266.

King Alfred's successors gradually reconquered the Danelaw, though there was often trouble with the Danes at York. English rule was restored, but there was an established Danish settlement in the east and the north with a Danish ruling class, from which emerged in 942 a Danish archbishop of Canterbury, Oda, a reforming bishop.

Reorganisation in the English Church

English Church leaders were concerned with rebuilding the diocesan structures disrupted by the Vikings: some bishoprics were restored and some new ones established. Efforts were made to ensure that pastoral care was provided for the people through the communities of canons or priests, rather than to re-establish monasticism. Some new communities were founded. In addition to the Old Minster, Winchester acquired the New Minster.

In the seventh century no great distinction had been made between canons and monks. Differences became clearer with the drastic reduction in monastic life brought about by the Viking invasions. Now, the canonical communities were making a vital contribution to the life of the Church. Their clergy spent a great deal of time outside the community, organising the work of the Church in the locality, but also providing a monastic type of worship. From time to time discipline became lax, many married, some held property and lived in their own houses, and attempts were made to impose stricter rules in the late eighth century. In the early eleventh century they experienced a period of renewal in the north, at York and Beverley, at Ripon and Southwell, as well as in the south at St Paul's and the cathedrals of Exeter and Wells.

At the same time the parish system was evolving. The Viking settlements had contributed to the fragmentation of big estates previously held by king, Church or nobles. Many smaller estates centred on a manor came into being. To build a church to serve the manor and the village that usually developed around it, lent some status to its lord, who then appointed a priest – and thus lay patronage flourished. In some cases the new Scandinavian lords built or restored churches: at Kirkdale in North Yorkshire, the inscription on the sundial tells us that Orm, son of Gamal, had the church "rebuilt in honour of Christ and St Gregory in the days of Edward the King..."; while at York, in 1055, one Earl Siward was buried in the church he had built and that he had consecrated to the Norwegian Saint Olaf.

There was a spate of church building in the tenth and eleventh centuries. The Domesday Book records two thousand six hundred local churches. By then, London had some thirty churches. Numbers had grown in many cities. The rise of parish churches lessened the significance of many of the old Minster churches, which gradually lost their monopoly on burial rites, and the parish churches began to receive the benefit of burial and baptism dues. Similarly, the communities of canons increased their spheres of influence as the role of the early monasteries was diminished.

Renewal of Monasticism and Anglo-Saxon Culture

Monasticism was not a spent force. The tenth century saw a great movement for renewal, which began at Cluny in France around 910 – an attempt to recover earlier ideals. The influence of Cluny spread, giving rise to a large family of monasteries and reaching England, particularly through those at Fleury-sur-Loire (now St Benoit-sur-Loire).

It is Dunstan who is usually credited with leading the reform movement in England. Born of a noble family in Glastonbury and educated by the community there, he appears to have been involved at the royal court from his youth, sometimes in and sometimes out of favour, or even exiled. He was a man of many gifts: he played the harp, illuminated manuscripts and was a skilled metalworker. Under the influence of an uncle, the bishop of Winchester, he became first a priest, then a monk. At the wish of King Edmund, he became abbot of Glastonbury, which he restored and established as a Benedictine abbey. Under King Eadwig he was exiled and went to St Peter's, Ghent, which was a reformed abbey in the Cluny tradition, but was recalled from exile on the accession of King Edgar. His career in fact spanned four reigns, but it was his partnership with Edgar, in a time of comparative peace from 955 to 975, that bore most fruit for the Church. Dunstan first became bishop of Worcester, then bishop of London and finally, in 960, archbishop of Canterbury. He re-founded monasteries at Malmesbury, Bath and Westminster, and founded new ones in ways that freed them from lay ownership and interference. It was, in fact, due to royal influence and the generosity of Edgar in granting land that this new spate of monastery building got under way. Some of these Benedictine abbeys became the churches of bishops and the mother churches of large areas. It was from the monasteries that most bishops came almost up to the Norman Conquest.

During Edgar's reign, society was organised into shires and the shires divided into hundreds. Local courts enforced the law. All the people were ordered to pay tithes: in addition to the offering known as church scot, there was now soul scot, payable at death, and plough alms. These were to provide a living for the clergy and there were penalties for non-payment.

As archbishop of Canterbury, Dunstan was able to wield an influence over a wide area of church life, but in the reform of the monasteries there were other major figures involved. One was Oswald, who had been a novice at Fleury, where he had experienced the influence of Cluny. He became bishop of Worcester, and later he held the sees of both Worcester and York together – a practice known as pluralism, later much decried. He founded monasteries at Westbury-on-Trym and at Ramsey in the fens, with daughter houses at Winchcombe and Pershore. *The Life of St Oswald* tells of the rededication in grand style of the abbey at Ramsey, when bishops, princes and abbots attended a celebratory service of Vespers with antiphonal singing and organ music.

Outstanding in monastic reform was Aethelwold, whose zeal earned him the description "father of monks". He had taught the young Edgar at the monastery of Abingdon, which Aethelwold had restored. When Edgar became king, Aethelwold continued as his counsellor. He became bishop of Winchester and expelled the secular clergy from the Old and the New Minsters. Many of them were married canons whom he replaced with Benedictine monks. In restoring the monasteries of Ely, Peterborough and Thorney, he re-established monasticism in the Danelaw. Over a period of fifteen years some forty houses were restored or founded throughout the dioceses, contributing greatly to the regeneration of the Church.

From a Church synod held at Winchester about 970 a significant document in the history of English monasticism emerged. It was intended to ensure the same observance of the Benedictine Rule in all the reformed monasteries and was known as the *Regularis Concordia* – the Monastic Agreement. From its details we can conjure up a picture of daily life, dominated by the liturgical round, and of the celebrations on feast days: the procession with palms on Palm Sunday, the foot washing of the poor and among the brothers on Maundy Thursday. On Good Friday, a cross, wrapped in a cloth, was laid in a representation of a sepulchre and placed on the altar, with curtains around it.

Brothers kept watch over it in turn, singing psalms, until Easter Sunday, when the discovery of the empty tomb was enacted – the beginnings of medieval religious drama. It ended with the singing of the "*Te Deum Laudamus*" and the pealing of all the bells.

After Edgar's reign and the death, in the last decades of the tenth century, of the three prime activists for reform, the movement slowed down. The number of monasteries did not reach the level of the pre-Viking period, but other aspects of Church life had benefited.

In the monastic schools, children received an education for which books in Latin and English were needed. In his monastery at Cerne Abbas, the schoolmaster Aelfric, once a pupil of Aethelwold, busied himself both producing books for children, and translating books of the Bible into English, writing commentaries on them and composing Lives of Saints. For the clergy, he wrote around a hundred sermons in English for use during the Christian year. His Easter Day sermon on the Holy Communion was to prove of interest to the Protestant Reformers centuries later.

Another writer was Wulfstan, a scholar, statesman and archbishop of York, who wanted to offer guidance to the laity in their daily lives as well as to clergy. It was a time of renewed Danish attacks and ever-increasing demands for tribute money – called Danegeld – imposing further strains on society. In his *Institutes of Polity*, he addressed everyone in positions of responsibility in society, outlining their duties in practical terms. As archbishop of York, in the area of Scandinavian settlement, he must have been very aware of continuing heathen worship and practice, a concern expressed in his sermons and in the Codes of Law he helped to draw up. In his Sermon to the English People, known as the Sermon of Wulf (his pen name), written in 1014, he chided them for their faithlessness to God and His Church. At the time, many thought the end of the world was imminent, as the first millennium after the crucifixion of Christ approached. Just as the sixth-century monk Gildas had seen the coming of the Anglo-Saxons as a punishment on the Britons, so Wulfstan saw the onslaught of the Vikings as a punishment on a country where the Church – both people and buildings – was treated with scant respect, and where men were made slaves and often sold out of the country.

His concern reminds us that slaves were still a significant part of the population. St Patrick, in the sixth century, had been a victim of the slave trade when he was taken to Ireland; similarly, some of his Irish converts were captured and sold as slaves. There were a number of reasons why people became slaves. Many were captives in war. Some were paying the penalty for an offence against the law not serious enough to deserve hanging. In a society where there were no prisons and the poorer classes had no money for fines, this was an alternative punishment. The guilty man's family became slaves with him. Others gave up their freedom in times of famine in return for food and shelter. Hence, there were large numbers of slaves, who formed the basis of the rural economy, possibly a quarter of the population.

But attitudes were changing. From the ninth century onwards, it is clear from the evidence of wills that many who owned slaves – kings and bishops among them – felt, as they approached life's end, that it was right to grant them freedom.

It was not only in works of prose by churchmen such as Wulfstan and Aelfric that English as a written language was blossoming, but also in poetry. Four manuscripts have come down to us from the tenth century that include a great variety of verse, some of it first composed in earlier centuries. In addition to the poetry, one of the manuscripts, compiled at Worcester and now in the Bodleian Library, contains a Benedictine Office in which parts of the Latin liturgy have been put into Old English prose and verse, including the Lord's Prayer, the Creed, the Gloria and some of the psalms, all of which the laity would have been expected to know. The Benedictine reformers had continued the work that Bede, King Alfred and others had been keen to forward: to make an otherwise Latin liturgy more accessible to the people.

Another manuscript, the Exeter Book, given to his cathedral by the eleventh-century Leofric, the first bishop of Exeter, contains poetry on a wide range of themes. In much of it, life and history are given a Christian interpretation. The transience of human life is seen against a background of eternity. Faithfulness and endurance are encouraged as Christian virtues. There is a growing sense of the worth of the individual, so central to the Christian faith.

In the manuscript described as the Vercelli Book is the poem called "The Dream of the Rood", a remarkable and moving piece of writing in which the poet imagines he sees the tree that became the cross on which Christ was crucified. The poet hears the tree speak of its experience: its sorrow at having to fulfil that grim role, the sadness of the created world and, finally, the triumph of the resurrection, which will lead ultimately to the Second Coming. Some of the words resemble those on the Ruthwell Cross in Dumfriesshire, which dates from around 800.

In this period of renewal of Anglo-Saxon culture, very much centred in the south, Winchester was a pivotal point. As the royal seat of the kings of Wessex and the see of its bishop since the seventh century, it was a political and ecclesiastical centre. It had also become a very popular place of pilgrimage. Miracles of healing were believed to take place at the shrine of St Swithin, a ninth-century bishop of Winchester. Aelfric, the monk at nearby Cerne Abbas, wrote a life of the saint, claiming that many cures took place at the shrine and that the crowds of pilgrims made it difficult to get into the cathedral. Winchester was important as a cultural centre too. The art of manuscript illumination was revived in a style known as the Winchester School. It had new features, notably the acanthus-leaf motif, and a generous use of gold and bright colours, all seen to effect in Aethelwold's Benedictional, a book of blessings, now in the British Museum. The acanthus leaf also appears on St Cuthbert's stole and maniple, both products of the tenth century when England had a reputation for fine embroidery.

What has come down to us in works of art of the time is probably a very small part of all that was produced. An incident referred to in the margins of an eighth-century Gospel Book made at Canterbury sheds an interesting light on how some objects survived. It seems this book, the Codex Aureus, was stolen by Vikings, but bought back by an earl and his wife for gold, and returned to Christ Church, Canterbury.

The Anglo-Saxon Church as Seen Through Its Buildings

Surviving church buildings, in all their variety, offer us another window onto the later phases of the Anglo-Saxon Church. In the Sussex Downs, the small village churches of Saxon origin may be typical of those built by lords of small estates, such as St Andrew's, Jevington, with its Saxon tower and sculpture.

They stand in contrast to the imposing mass of St Mary's, Stow, in Lincolnshire, where the central crossing retains its eleventh-century arches, the tallest and widest to survive. St Ethelreda is said to have rested at Stow on her way to Ely. Also in Lincolnshire stands the Saxon tower of Barton-on-Humber. As at Earl's Barton in Northamptonshire, the floor of the tower formed the nave of the church. Outside, both churches display many Saxon features: the pilaster strips and arcading, the stages divided by string courses, and small double windows.

Much of this kind of decoration can be seen in one of the most complete and substantially unaltered Saxon churches to survive – St Lawrence's Chapel at Bradford-on-Avon, only recognised as a church in the nineteenth century: the nave had been used as a school and the chancel as a cottage. While its history is uncertain, we know that in the seventh century Aldhelm founded a monastery at Bradford-on-Avon and this may have been a chapel built in the precincts at a later date. Experts judge it to be tenth century. The outside decoration is surprisingly complete. Inside, both the narrowness and the height of the building are striking, as is the darkness, lit only by a few high, splayed windows. Above the narrow chancel arch, two finely carved angels have been wonderfully preserved. To step into this chapel is to savour something of the atmosphere of the Saxon past.

While what survives of church buildings from Saxon times is almost exclusively in stone, the nave of the church at Greensted in Essex suggests that there may have been other timber churches.

Each surviving Saxon church, however partial it may be, adds something to our appreciation of how they looked and how they may have functioned. The large minster church of St Mary at Breamore in Hampshire, built in the tenth century, retains an inscription in Old English over an archway. It is outlined in red pigment and is interpreted as "Here the covenant is manifested unto you". Churches of the time were probably more colourful than we might imagine, with wall hangings like those brought back from the Continent by Benedict Biscop in the seventh century, and painted walls and sculptures.

Pieces of sculpture from the time have an unelaborate and moving quality, such as the Virgin and Child at St John's Church, Inglesham, in Wiltshire, with the hand of God over the Child's head; this is also a feature of the Ramsey Rood, a life-sized representation of Christ, with eyes open and head upright. At Langford near Lechlade, where only the tower of the church remains, there are two contrasting roods. The large one is of Christ triumphant, the smaller one of Christ in agony, with the heads of St John and Mary turned away. One of the finest late Saxon sculptures is at St John the Baptist's Church at Barnack in Cambridgeshire, which is of a seated Christ with the folds of his garment defined in detail. The Saxon love of decoration is sometimes displayed to good effect on fonts: the font at Melbury Bubb in Dorset has a frieze of lively animals, while that at Deerhurst in Gloucestershire is beautifully patterned with spirals and vine-scroll ornament.

In this Priory Church of St Mary at Deerhurst many Saxon features have been preserved. The earliest part of the church, a simple rectangle, may in fact have been the pre-Saxon Celtic church. In the ninth century it became the chief monastery of the area, and was much extended, both outwards, with side chapels alongside the nave, and upwards; the west wall of the nave has a blocked doorway above ground-floor level as there was probably a gallery in front of it. The choir also has doorways at first-floor level. Were these upper doorways and gallery used to good effect musically during the course of worship? The church has other unusual features in the five triangular windows and the elaborate double window in the west wall. At the chancel end an apse was added, as in the early Kent churches. The only surviving part of it has happily preserved the carving of an angel. Other Saxon churches, such as those at Wing in Buckinghamshire and Worth in Sussex, share some of these features, including an apse. As time went on, the English preference for a square chancel in the Celtic style prevailed over the curved apse the Romans had introduced.

Deerhurst's most famous son was Alphege, a monk there in the tenth century, who became archbishop of Canterbury and was murdered by the Danes in 1012. By that time the prestige of Deerhurst had waned, ousted from its former pre-eminence by monasteries at Gloucester and Winchcombe. Under Edward the Confessor it became simply a cell of the monastery of St Denis in Paris, but it still serves as a parish church and so provides a continuous story of some fifteen hundred years since its foundation.

St Mary's is not Deerhurst's only treasure. A simple Saxon chapel, Odda's Chapel, was discovered near the priory in the nineteenth century, next to a farmhouse. It had been used as a barn and later as a house. The original doorway, the splayed windows and the chancel arch remain as they were built. The dedication stone, at one time over the doorway, is now in the Ashmolean Museum. A copy tells us that the chapel was founded by Earl Odda, a friend of Edward the Confessor, in memory of his brother Aelfric, who died at Deerhurst. It was dedicated in 1056.

It is not difficult to imagine the impact of a church building, its size and ornament, and the drama that unfolded inside it, together with the singing and vestments, on people living in small dwellings of timber and thatch, whose lives were often short and humdrum. In an uncertain world, the Church provided a constant backcloth. With the increasing use of English for parts of the service, worship was becoming more meaningful. From Vespers on Saturday to Sunday evening was now a holiday. Time was measured by the Church's festivals and fasts, and by its saints' days. The saints were ever present, their shrines and relics visited by kings and subjects alike, in a spirit of devotion, sometimes as an act of penance, and in the belief that prayer in these places was particularly efficacious; it could even bring healing. There was a special devotion to Mary, as the mother of Jesus; a number of festivals in her honour had developed by this time.

The Church was present at all the significant moments of life – birth, marriage and death – but it was also concerned with other aspects of daily life. It cared for the poor, it encouraged alms-giving, and it was involved with law and order. In a society without prisons or police, the judging of lawbreakers depended on oaths. Oath-taking was very serious at all times; oath-taking over relics, before God and the saints, was especially solemn. In cases of difficult judgements, the accused had to face an ordeal inside a church, supervised by a priest, in which he had to perform a painful feat, such as lifting an iron bar from a fire or a stone from boiling water, to prove his innocence.

The church porch may already have had many functions, both Church-related and purely secular; it was where betrothals and part of the baptism rite would take place, where business might be transacted, and where matters of concern to the community might be dealt with by civic dignitaries.

Not only did the Church permeate many areas of life, it must have employed a large section of the population: clergy and monks, and lay workers in the monasteries, but also builders and craftsmen, as new churches were built.

The renewed English Church was not insular. It had many links with European courts. Its traditional loyalty to Rome continued, as well as the payment of "Peter's Pence", a tax paid to Rome since the time of King Offa. The pope, for his part, exercised a degree of oversight through legates and councils, including granting privileges to monasteries and approving the occasional change of episcopal see, as when the bishop of Crediton moved to Exeter.

Just as in the eighth century Boniface, Willibrord and others had taken Christianity to Germany and Holland, in the later tenth century English missionaries helped to Christianise the Scandinavian countries, first Denmark and Norway, and later Sweden. They built on the lead of converted Scandinavian kings, and went to instruct and nurture the new Christians.

The Last Decades Before the Norman Conquest

In 980 a new phase of Danish raiding began. When King Aethelred was rash enough to order all Danes in England to be killed, there followed a ten-year war. In 1012 the archbishop of Canterbury, Alphege, the former monk from Deerhurst, was murdered when he offered some resistance. A period of Danish rule followed. King Canute, who regarded himself as a Christian, built churches and honoured the memory of Alphege and Edmund, both martyred by the Danes. As king of Denmark and also Norway, he spent a lot of time abroad and noblemen became an increasingly powerful class in his reign, a state which continued under Edward the Confessor.

Edward became king in 1042 with the support of Earl Godwin and his followers. He had been brought up in Normandy and during the course of his reign there was already a considerable degree of Norman infiltration into England. Normans were given positions at court and estates in the country.

There were changes in the episcopate too. Edward had brought with him from Normandy the abbot of Jumieges who became archbishop of Canterbury. He appointed six foreign bishops, two of them Normans – a cause for resentment in monastic circles – though he did also appoint a few native monk-bishops. Wulfstan, bishop of Worcester, a man of great personal piety and a reformer, would be one of the few native bishops to survive the Norman Conquest that was to come.

In 1052 Robert of Jumieges was ousted from Canterbury through devious means by Stigand, who had been a king's priest under Canute. Stigand assumed the role of archbishop of Canterbury but still retained his see at Winchester. As holder of the two richest bishoprics, he was very wealthy and also very worldly. He provided little leadership at Canterbury. The pope disapproved and advised other bishops not to acknowledge him.

Edward himself was a pious man. One of his achievements was to begin the rebuilding of Westminster Abbey in the Norman style. However, he was distracted by many problems, so neither king nor archbishop provided the direction the Church needed, and the monastic revival had already lost its impetus. In 1066 Edward died. He had no son, so Harold, son of Earl Godwin and the most powerful man in the land, was crowned king. Across the Channel, William, duke of Normandy, who claimed that Edward had named him as his successor, prepared to challenge Harold, but not before he had asked – and received – the pope's support.

More than a thousand years after the birth of Christ, the Church was firmly established in spite of the reversals caused by successive pagan invaders. Over time the latter had adopted Christianity. However nominal the allegiance of many may have been, however inadequate the response of a Church that had had to struggle to build and rebuild itself, the truly great Christians – the saints – were recognised and honoured. They kept before the people the heart of Christian belief and practice, and their influence continued long after their earthly life. Many of the saints of the first millennium had been monks; the role of the early monasteries had been crucial and those of the reform movement of the tenth century had helped stimulate the recovery of the Church after the Viking depredations. In contrast, the later Benedictine monasteries were less committed to involvement with the populace at large than the earlier ones had been and their role among the people was already diminishing. The task of providing worship and pastoral care was being shared by the collegiate churches with secular canons and by the parish churches.

On the wider canvas the fragmentation of the universal Church had begun. For ten centuries the Church in all the countries where it had been established was one united body. In 1054 came the Great Schism when the Byzantine Church of the East and the Church in the West separated, having failed to resolve their differences over liturgy and doctrine. For a while there were hopes of a reconciliation, but these were dashed in 1204 when the Crusaders sacked Constantinople.

The West had already received not only the faith itself but a great deal else from the East. Eastern liturgies had been the source of Western ones. From the East, too, had come an early form of plainsong, which influenced the chants that developed in the West. Especially important in Britain and Ireland, the Church had taken to its heart the monasticism that came from Egypt. The seventh-century Archbishop Theodore of Canterbury, born in Tarsus and at one time a student at Antioch, had brought to Britain something of the Byzantine culture that had nurtured him, an influence expressed through his teaching and writing. Some books had travelled: the *Life of St Antony* of Egypt was popular. Illuminated manuscripts in the Byzantine style had found their way here and inspired the development of figurative art, which enriched the intricate patterning of native Celtic art. Eastern influence had been very much part of the story of the developing Church in these islands.

In each country there was now a stronger sense of nationhood, and in each case the Church would develop in a very distinctive way, given the particular mixture of history, temperament, geography and political circumstances.

Change was imminent as the Norman Conquest of 1066 approached, in spite of the fact that the invaders this time were Christian. The longer-standing Christian cultures of the Celtic countries were now matched by the equally distinctive Anglo-Saxon Christian culture, and it was the latter that would initially bear the brunt of the coming invasion.

VII

NEW MASTERS

The Norman Conquest of 1066 marks a watershed in the two thousand years of Christian history in these islands, coming as it does at almost the halfway point. The material legacy of the Conquest to the Church is particularly apparent in England, where there is a wealth of fine architecture in the distinctive Norman Romanesque style – rounded arches with ornamental carving, solid pillars, thick walls and small windows – seen in endless variation, from the massive and imposing grandeur of cathedrals such as Durham to countless parish churches. The Norman style influenced building in the Celtic countries too, most notably in Scotland.

Nonetheless, the actual experience of conquest in the Church of the time was in many ways a humiliating one. The Church had successfully ridden the Viking storm, but had been deprived latterly of strong leadership. Stigand, the archbishop of Canterbury, had assumed office irregularly and was unacceptable to the papacy; the episcopate lacked authority and cohesion: some of the bishops were English-born, others had been appointed by Edward the Confessor from the Continent. While William the Conqueror single-mindedly addressed the process of conquest, things remained unchanged in the Church.

It was not until 1069 that he was forced to turn his attention to it. The archbishop of York had died and the Church had effectively no archbishop, given Stigand's doubtful status. A number of councils followed; Stigand was deposed, along with three other bishops. Thomas, a canon of Bayeux in Normandy, was made archbishop of York, and in the same year William appointed a new archbishop of Canterbury. His name was Lanfranc and he had worked under William's patronage in Normandy.

Lanfranc was first and foremost a monk, but no ordinary monk. Born in northern Italy, with a lawyer's background, he was a scholar and an outstanding teacher. After his conversion he had chosen to go to Bec, a very poor monastery in Normandy with a strict rule of life. At Bec he had founded a school that drew students from all over Europe. He had experience in leadership and administration, too, having first become prior at Bec, then abbot at William's new monastery at Caen. He had a great deal to offer as leader of the English Church, but at the age of sixty-six it is unlikely that he welcomed this new challenge. Sometime after his appointment he wrote to the pope of the day, begging to be rescued from a people he describes as barbarians, fearing that he could help neither them nor himself spiritually if he stayed. The pope ignored his plea and Lanfranc went on to prove himself more than adequate for the task, and his new flock were perhaps not as impossible as he had thought.

In eleventh-century England, Church and state were to a large extent one, and it was the king who was seen as the head of the Church, with the right to invest bishops with their office and to summon councils. Lanfranc exercised his office within these parameters. Both he and the king wanted a strong Church, if from different motives, and in their attitude to the papacy there was no conflict between them: neither wanted too much interference. In Normandy, William had been actively involved in reforming the Church. By contrast the English Church may have appeared, or was presumed to be, a provincial backwater that was in need of being brought back into the mainstream of church life as practised on the Continent.

From the beginning Lanfranc was intent on establishing himself as primate of all Britain, the ecclesiastical equivalent of the position William had assumed, and he set about reforming the Church through a series of councils. The structures of the Church were streamlined, with dioceses divided into archdeaconries and they in their turn into rural deaneries. Each bishop would hold no more than one see. Some bishoprics were transferred from rural places which were seen as unsuitable. New centres of dioceses were created at Norwich, Lincoln, Ely and Chichester.

A stricter discipline was urged on the clergy through attempts to enforce celibacy, to stop the buying of ordinations and benefices, and the holding of more than one living. These were reforms in line with papal policy, but when the authoritarian Pope Gregory VII required greater submission from the English king, William would have none of it. He promptly imposed severe restrictions on all kinds of communications with Rome.

With the king's encouragement ecclesiastical courts were established. Lanfranc compiled a textbook of canon law for the English Church. In future Church affairs and the clergy would be dealt with by bishops according to canon law rather than civil law – a process that became known as the "benefit of the clergy". This was a major change that achieved greater independence and status for the Church.

Lanfranc was not impressed initially with English monastic standards. According to Eadmer, a monk of Christ Church, Canterbury, at the time, he found the monks there very worldly. To Lanfranc the remedy was clear: when William died in 1087 only three English abbots remained. Norman appointments came from Bec, Caen and other monastic houses, as did a number of monks. The English element was being diluted and English ways modified, but Lanfranc went too far when he removed English saints such as Dunstan and Alphege from the Canterbury calendar. It caused such ill-feeling that he thought it politic to reinstate them.

He drew up a set of rules for his monks at Canterbury, his Constitutions, which replaced the tenth-century *Rule of the Anglo-Saxon Church*, and were adopted by other communities. A fresh discipline entered these monasteries. He was fiercely protective of their rights and was frequently involved in long legal battles to recover estates lost when land changed hands after the Norman Conquest. Meanwhile the English tradition of monastic historical writers continued in many places.

In 1070 there had been some forty Benedictine houses in the south, but none in the north. In the next two decades that situation changed. The first of a number of northern monasteries to be founded was at Selby. Here, William's son Henry – the future Henry II – had been born in 1068. Some of the old foundations, such as Jarrow and Whitby, were revived. New ones were founded; one at Shrewsbury; another at Chester, where the refectory of the monastery, complete with wall pulpit, survives in what is now the cathedral and provides sustenance for today's pilgrims. Another was founded in the south at Battle, just one year after the Norman Conquest, in thanksgiving for victory.

The imposing abbey churches we know at Gloucester, St Albans and Tewkesbury were begun at this time, as was the priory at Christchurch. Almost half of the cathedrals of the time were or became monastic in the Benedictine tradition. Magnificent cathedrals were built, with Durham, Ely and Norwich among them, all part of the Norman signature on the English landscape; to us an impressive legacy, but to contemporaries a rather more intimidating presence, and perhaps a source of nostalgia for the more modest, familiar buildings that had been destroyed to make way for the new.

Lanfranc had already had to supervise the rebuilding of his own cathedral at Canterbury after a fire had partially destroyed it. He extended his influence into the city with new hospitals, almshouses and a school, so providing for social and educational needs as well as for spiritual welfare. A new model of bishop was evolving. In addition to their spiritual role, they were now builders and administrators, responsible for very large estates and for the execution of justice under canon law, with military duties as well. Like Lanfranc, other bishops were building and reorganising, and re-establishing their rights to properties; Gundulf in Rochester, Wulfstan in Worcester and Walkelyn in Winchester.

The same was happening in the cathedrals served by secular clergy: Thomas was restoring York to its former glory after its near-destruction in the post-Conquest uprising in the north, and new building was taking place at St Paul's, Hereford, Chichester, Lincoln, Lichfield, Exeter and Old Sarum, all under the direction of their respective bishops.

The conscientious bishop had a heavy workload, given the size of dioceses and the vast numbers of clergy to oversee: not only priests and deacons but also many clerics in minor orders. Some clergy had no vocation and held benefices through family connections or through favours; many had little education; and others set no example in their private lives. It was hoped the reforms that aimed at celibacy and the elimination of the selling of offices would give clergy greater authority and a new professionalism. Church life under the Normans was set to move forward.

To contemporary able English churchmen, however, things would have appeared somewhat differently. The top layer of the hierarchy – bishops, archdeacons and abbots – had become almost exclusively Norman. The social and economic gulf between bishops and clergy, already considerable, was widened still further by the difference of race and language. Englishmen had very little hope of promotion or opportunity to influence the development of their national Church. Old English ritual, liturgy and calendars came under scrutiny. The change of language dealt a blow to the developing vernacular – in this respect England had been way ahead of other European countries. Now English took third place, with Latin the language of the Church, of government and scholarship, and French the language of daily conversation among the upper classes.

In many villages, however, it is possible that change came very slowly, with perhaps the same priest following the old ways and customs. Even at a higher level English influence continued at least in one area: at Worcester, Wulfstan, the only English bishop to survive for long after the Norman Conquest, was a respected and effective bishop for more than thirty years until his death in 1095. The distinctiveness of the English Church was not erased.

It was only a matter of time before it emerged again in its individuality.

The Celtic Countries Following the Norman Conquest

The immediate impact of the Norman Conquest on the Celtic countries varied in each according to its accessibility. In eleventh-century Scotland the Church was coming out of a period of comparative isolation. Malcolm III of Scotland had married an English princess, Margaret, whose brother Edgar was a descendant of the royal Saxon line. Given that fact, the Scottish king found himself obliged to pay formal homage to William at Abernethy.

Queen Margaret was a staunch Christian who had been brought up in the Roman tradition. The form of the Eucharist in the Scottish Church gave her some concern; she wanted to end the use of what she described as a "barbarous rite" – presumably how she saw the legacy of the Celtic Church and possibly the use of the Gaelic language. At Dunfermline she decided to found a small monastic community and turned to Lanfranc for advice. He sent three monks to establish what was probably the first Benedictine house in Scotland. Dunfermline would replace Iona as the burial place of Scottish kings. Queen Margaret was generous with her gifts to other establishments, with Iona and St Andrew's among them. She died in 1093, but her influence was to live on in the next century, when three of her sons, in turn, became king.

In the same period, Wales was still beset by conflict through continuing Norse raids and internal fighting among native leaders. Now, in addition, it was easy for Norman warlords to cross the border with their armies. In 1081 William the Conqueror visited St David's and came to an agreement with the local princes that they should be allowed to settle affairs in south-west Wales, in return for a nominal loyalty to himself.

The Church the Normans found in Wales was not like their own, but the *clasau*, the old family communities in the monastic tradition with hereditary clergy, were coming to an end. The one at Llanbadarn still survived with the clerical dynasty of Sulien maintaining its long tradition of learning. Its senior member was the bishop of St David's, whose son Rhigyfarch became famous as the author of the earliest surviving *Life of St David*. This was a work of great significance for the Church of the time in that it embodied a desperate bid on the part of the Welsh Church to maintain its independence from Canterbury. With little supportive evidence, it left no stone unturned to promote St David's as a former archbishopric and St David as an archbishop; the quintessential Celtic saint qualified in every respect for the role being thrust upon him. It did a great deal to popularise St David and was only the beginning of the fight to preserve the heritage of the Welsh Church.

Like Wales, eleventh-century Ireland was still suffering the effects of prolonged conflicts, both with the Norse settlers and between native tribes, but the Irish Sea initially offered some protection from Norman incursions. Churches had been destroyed and the numbers of priests depleted. The monasteries and their abbots were still a powerful influence, but the bishops' role was emerging from its secondary status. The Norse who had been Christianised did not want to be subject to the Irish abbots, and the see of Dublin, founded earlier in the eleventh century, was the first to send priests to Canterbury to be made bishops. The influence of the reform movement on the Continent was spreading, and there was a desire in

Ireland for closer contact with the wider Church in the West, encouraged by Canterbury and Rome, which would be realised in the twelfth century. Among the people, cults of relics and pilgrimages to shrines were very much part of their devotional life; pilgrimage to Rome increased and by the end of the century there was an Irish monastery in Rome.

The Church and the Crown

In 1087 William the Conqueror died and his son William Rufus inherited the throne. For him the Church was primarily a source of revenue: when bishoprics became vacant he took the income and was in no hurry to fill the vacancies. After Lanfranc's death in 1089 there was no archbishop of Canterbury for four years, until the appointment of Anselm. Like Lanfranc, he came originally from Italy, via Bec, where he had become abbot, and, again like Lanfranc, he came reluctantly. As a scholar and theologian he was outstanding, sometimes described as the greatest theologian between the fourth-century St Augustine of Hippo and the thirteenth-century St Thomas Aquinas. His writings have continued to be greatly respected. In his *Proslogion* he argued the existence of God on grounds of pure reason. His maxim was "*Credo ut intelligam*" – "I believe so that I might understand".

From the beginning Anselm was in conflict with the king over the land rights of Canterbury and the bishops did not trust him. He viewed the authority of the pope rather differently from Lanfranc, and supported papal efforts to make the Church more independent of the king. In England the relationship between kings and Church leaders had been close from the time of the conversion – they had given each other support – but bishops had become powerful landowners and kings felt the need to control their appointment. But was it really the right of the king to choose and invest bishops, or that of the Church? And was a bishop's first loyalty not to the Church? As a result of his firm stance Anselm spent two periods in exile, first under William Rufus, then under Henry I, until a compromise was reached – bishops would pay homage to the king, but he would not invest them with their office. Some power had passed to the Church.

Anselm died in 1109. Eadmer the monk, who had worked closely with him and had shared his exile, wrote a biography of him, in which he is full of praise for his subject as a pastor and a man of prayer, able to communicate his faith to all kinds of people. He encouraged private devotions and his collection of *Prayers and Meditations* was greatly valued. Anselm had been much more accepting of local traditions than Lanfranc, so more affirming of the English heritage. In his final years he was concerned with furthering the reforms introduced after the Norman Conquest – reforms that were not simply the product of Norman policy. Both Lanfranc and Anselm were European in outlook and experience, and they were part of a movement for reform throughout the Church in the West, encouraged by a stronger papacy. They had also begun a renaissance of learning in England.

The struggle for power between king and Church that had so influenced Anselm's time in office resurfaced again dramatically in the twelfth century between Henry II and Thomas Becket. Becket was of Norman extraction, the well-educated son of a London merchant. At a fairly early stage of his career he became part of the household of Archbishop Theobald of Canterbury. It was a training ground for his future in the Church. In 1154 he became archdeacon of Canterbury. Then followed his appointment as chancellor by the king, which lasted eight years; during this time he enjoyed wide-ranging powers and a lavish lifestyle, and became very close to the king.

When Theobald died, Thomas was appointed archbishop of Canterbury in his stead, being ordained priest the day before his consecration. The king wanted to recover royal authority over the Church. He was particularly opposed to the ecclesiastical courts, which were often lenient, but he had miscalculated in thinking that his new archbishop would comply with his aims. Becket refused to sign the Clarendon Constitutions proposed by Henry, which contravened some of the rights of the Church. The king responded by trying to ruin Becket financially and brought him to trial. He was condemned and escaped to France in 1164. The pope gave him his support, while Henry took action against Becket's family and clerics, and disposed of his Canterbury estates.

There were many attempts to reconcile the two, none of them successful. In the meantime Henry tried to break all links between England and the papacy. In 1170 Pope Alexander III ordered Henry to allow Becket to return and to restore all his property, and Becket to submit to the king, without sacrificing the freedom of the Church. After a meeting of the two in July some reconciliation was arrived at. Although the king had not revoked the Clarendon Constitutions or returned estates to Canterbury, Becket returned to England and was welcomed en route to Canterbury as a hero. In his uncompromising Christmas Day sermon he excommunicated unlawful holders of church property. He had previously excommunicated some of the bishops for disloyalty. Exasperated by the situation, Henry wished himself rid of his archbishop in the hearing of some of his barons. Four of them complied: they rode to Canterbury and killed Becket at the high altar of the cathedral.

There was widespread horror at the deed, not only in England but on the Continent too. Sympathy for Becket, already seen as fighting for the Church, increased. Miracles were reported at the site of his murder. In 1173 he was canonised and a shrine was set up, which became one of the most visited in Western Europe. King Henry, for his part, came to Canterbury to do penance and was scourged by the monks. The following year a cardinal came to England, and many of the church matters under dispute were resolved and the status of canon law reinforced. Becket had won his battle for the authority of the Church.

Not that the matter rested there: thirty-seven years after Becket's murder, fresh controversy arose when Pope Innocent III consecrated Stephen Langton as archbishop of Canterbury. King John had wanted another candidate and refused to accept Langton. As a result, in 1208, England was placed under an interdict that officially meant the Church was restricted in its functioning – a puzzling time for the faithful when access to the services and comfort of the Church was curtailed. The king himself was excommunicated. It was only when he submitted to the pope after six long years, and agreed to the appointment of bishops and abbots by the Church that the interdict was lifted.

Since the middle of the eleventh century, the papacy had become much more active, becoming a central force in Europe in the twelfth and thirteenth centuries. It had its finger on the pulse of Church affairs everywhere in the West through its legates and through vast correspondence. Several ecumenical councils were held, most of them attended by representatives from Britain. The most important was the fourth Lateran Council of 1215, which affirmed the doctrine of transubstantiation – that the bread and wine of Holy Communion become the body and blood of Christ – a significant moment in the story of the Church, which would have repercussions in the Reformation. The Lateran Council also laid down that everyone must take Holy Communion once a year at Easter and that it should be preceded by confession.

The papal curia became the centre of an international system of ecclesiastical law, the supreme court of appeal, with many legal experts; most of the popes of the period were lawyers. The faithful flocked to Rome, with requests for benefices, for personal cases to be heard and for disputes to be settled, all at a price. It became primarily a place where business was transacted, to the detriment of its spiritual role.

New Orders of Monks and Canons

In the monastic world, where the Benedictines had held a virtual monopoly for some centuries, new orders of monks were appearing and aiming to recover early ideals. Foremost among them were the Cistercians, founded at Citeaux near Dijon in France. An Englishman, Stephen Harding, from Sherborne Abbey, was one of the founder members of the order. Their basic rule of life was Benedictine, but their aim was to observe the strictest poverty: their food and clothing, and their churches were to be as simple as possible. Their white robes distinguished them from the black-robed Benedictines, as did their choice of sites for monasteries – remote places, often overgrown, to be reclaimed by their own labour or by the many lay brothers who came to share their life, though at a less demanding level. Cistercian houses spread widely, each autonomous to a degree, but inspected regularly, and each year the abbots of all the houses met at the mother house at Cîteaux to regulate the discipline of the order. One of the earliest foundations was at Clairvaux in France; its abbot, Bernard, exercised a great influence throughout Western Europe in the twelfth century through his eloquent preaching, and his books and correspondence. He had a special influence on the Irish Church through his friendship with the reformer Bishop Malachy.

The Cistercians in England flourished quite spectacularly, largely through sheep rearing on a grand scale. The ruins of Fountains Abbey, Rievaulx and Tintern, all founded in the mid-twelfth century, impress us by their grandeur rather than their simplicity, as well as by the beauty of their setting. There were many others. Part of the Cistercian abbey of Dore in Herefordshire has been restored for use as a parish church. At this stage the even more austere Carthusian Order did not gain much foothold – only two houses were founded in Somerset.

Comparable to the growth of the Cistercians was that of the canons, particularly the Augustinian or "regular" canons, communities of priests who took vows of poverty, celibacy and obedience, but were more involved with the outside world than the monastic orders. They took as their pattern the life of the early Church, as described in the New Testament. They cared for the spiritual needs of the laity and served the needy in society, living by a Rule devised by St Augustine in the fifth century. For the most part they lived in more modest buildings than the Cistercians.

Unique to England were the Gilbertines – a smaller order founded by a priest, Gilbert, of Sempringham in Lincolnshire. He encouraged a group of his women parishioners to live according to the Cistercian Order. Numbers grew, but Citeaux refused to admit them to their order. Instead the communities were directed by the regular canons, and the houses became double houses for men and women, like some of the old Anglo-Saxon foundations; there were nine in all at Gilbert's death. A marked increase in the number of nunneries was a feature of this more diverse monastic development.

Part of its diversity was the formation of orders that combined the monastic life with the life of the soldier, brought into being by the Crusades. When the Holy Land was invaded by Muslims and Jerusalem captured, the response was emotive. In 1095 the pope appealed to Christians in the West to reclaim the Holy Land and offered indulgences to those who responded – the remission of all penance for confessed sins and a guarantee of heaven as martyrs. Kings and great numbers of their people took up the challenge. Richard I spent most of his reign crusading. The Knights Templar were founded to provide protection for pilgrims travelling through the Holy Land. They had their headquarters in Jerusalem and houses in most European countries; their chief house in England was the Temple in London, one of the oldest churches to survive there. Like their other churches it was circular, following the plan of the church of the Holy Sepulchre in Jerusalem. The other crusading order was that of the Knights Hospitaller, which began by providing hospitality for pilgrims and care for those wounded in the First Crusade in a hospital in Jerusalem. They became a military order in the twelfth century and many commanderies were set up in England.

The First Crusade culminated in the recapture of Jerusalem in 1099. Less successful Crusades followed and Jerusalem was lost. The sack of Constantinople by Crusaders in 1204 only served to reinforce the earlier schism between the Eastern Church and Western Church. Christendom had been prepared to make war against those they saw as enemies of the faith, a concept totally alien to the New Testament and the thinking of the early Church. The cruelty, plundering and loss of life incurred led to some change in public attitudes. In 1312 the Order of the Knights Templar was suppressed. By the end of the fourteenth century crusading in the Holy Land had come to an end.

Back at home the idealism of the Cistercians was not sustained. The growth of the population, and of towns and trade led to their increasing involvement in farming for profit; they were being diverted from things spiritual. Monastic orders generally remained significant – the Benedictines had continued to expand alongside the new orders – but they were losing the role of spiritual leaders that they had held for so long. Very few new houses were established among the big orders. Hailes Abbey in Gloucestershire was one of the last Cistercian houses to be founded, dedicated in 1251. The Augustinian canons, meanwhile, were maintaining their position and acquiring new priories. Most were relatively small, so within the means of the moderately wealthy to establish, and their practical involvement with society ensured their popularity.

Developments in the Celtic Countries

In Scotland the twelfth century saw increasing links with England during the successive reigns of Queen Margaret's three sons: their sister married the English king Henry I, and the first son, Edgar, was helped to the Scottish throne by the English. When he wanted a further supply of monks for Dunfermline he turned, as his mother had done, to Canterbury, where Anselm was now archbishop.

Alexander, who succeeded him, was particularly supportive of the Augustinian canons and established their first priory at Scone. But it was their brother, David I, who made the most impact on the Church in Scotland. He had spent some time in England and was a powerful baron there, his wife an English countess. When he came to the throne he brought with him to Scotland Anglo-Norman nobles, and appointed them to positions of rank in state and Church. He was actively involved in reorganising the Church. The parochial system was taking shape, as were dioceses. By the end of his reign in 1153 there were nine bishoprics. He wanted the Scottish Church to be independent of Canterbury and York, and St Andrew's to be an archbishopric, but the pope was opposed to this.

In 1137 the cathedral church of St Mungo in Glasgow was dedicated; in its crypt was the shrine of St Mungo. Edinburgh's St Giles Cathedral was also a twelfth-century foundation, as was Dunblane Cathedral, and on Orkney, still in Norwegian hands, the building of St Magnus Cathedral in Kirkwall had begun.

At Dunfermline the king re-established his mother's Benedictine priory as a major abbey, in a style similar to Durham cathedral. Many houses were set up for the Augustinian canons, the most substantial at Jedburgh and Holyrood. Another was St Rule's at St Andrew's, where the new Augustinian community was probably intended to supplant an earlier one of Culdees. Originally from Ireland and a survival of the Celtic Church, the Culdees were still active in many places in Scotland, often as colleges or groups of clergy, serving a local church or attached to bishops' churches at places such as St Andrew's, Brechin and Abernethy, all of them sites of early monasteries.

The king was keen to introduce new, strict monastic orders. Cistercian houses were founded; the first was at Melrose. His generosity to the Church through his foundations and endowments was impressive. The new orders brought economic as well as spiritual benefits: they worked the land and some of them, the Cistercians in particular, became involved in European markets. The canons served the community, providing help for the poor and hospitality to all levels of society. New centres of learning had been created through the new orders and some Scotsmen were going to Oxford to study.

By the mid-twelfth century the Scottish throne had become stronger, but kings made little impact on the Highlands, and the Western Isles would remain in Norwegian hands for another century. The Church was in better shape structurally but parish churches were being adversely affected by the growing practice of appropriations. Many founders of parish churches gave them to monasteries, which took the tithes and offerings but were obliged to provide a clergyman. This they often did at minimal cost – those they appointed might be ill-qualified, so the parish church not only lost revenue, it was frequently badly served. In some cases, an abbey might receive tithes from as many as thirty appropriated churches; cathedrals too benefited from the practice.

The building of abbeys continued, with some changes from the earlier Romanesque style; pointed arches and piers of many shafts made for a lighter effect, a transition to the Gothic style that would follow. The cathedral church and priory at St Andrew's, the largest church built in Scotland, was started around 1160. Before the end of the century, in 1192, part of King David's ambition for the Scottish Church was realised when it became a special daughter of Rome, subject only to the pope. Its governing body was a provincial synod, convened by a papal legate and presided over by bishops in turn. The Church had become independent of England but, without an archbishop, was not yet fully a province.

In Wales, the Normans became actively engaged in the changes taking place in the Church, as they moved aggressively across the country. In the south, Norman bishops were appointed and the extent of dioceses established. The old *clas* churches were becoming parish or collegiate churches, or priories, which often passed into the hands of Norman Benedictine houses. Llanbadarn and its endowments were given to the Benedictine Abbey of St Peter's, Gloucester, as was Llancarfan. Other churches and monasteries, including Llantwit Major, were given to Tewkesbury Abbey. Such moves explain the zealous attempts of the Welsh Church to counter this appropriation by the Normans.

In the twelfth century the building of the present church at St David's began. It became a cathedral under the Norman Bishop Bernard, and the old *clas* clergy became a chapter. St David was formally canonised. This was when the chapter made its claims to be a metropolitan see.

The fight to be independent of Canterbury was not the only one to be played out in South Wales at the time. At Llandaff another strong Norman bishop, Urban, had built an impressive new cathedral, and was intent on proving Llandaff to be the most prestigious of the Welsh churches with an older tradition than St David's and once the see of an archbishop. The remains of the sixth-century St Dubricius were brought from Bardsey Island to make the point. At his consecration Bishop Urban had sworn obedience to the archbishop of Canterbury, and in the course of the twelfth century all four Welsh bishops eventually followed suit.

The Cistercian Order had spread to Wales. There were early foundations at Tintern and Margam, where much of the twelfth-century building has survived, including the façade of what is now the parish church. As the century progressed many houses were established. One community was at Strata Florida only a few miles away from the old foundation of Llanbadarn, which it superseded. Further east was the abbey of Villa Crucis near Llangollen, where there are substantial remains of what became a very rich abbey. In their asceticism the Cistercians were closer in spirit to the old Celtic saints and became better integrated into the community than the Benedictine priories. These were often established near Norman castles and most of the monks were not native Welsh. Many of these priories were given to English monasteries, those at Brecon and Carmarthen to Battle Abbey, while the defensive priory the Normans built at Ewenni in west Glamorgan and the church of St Woolo in Newport were both given to Gloucester Abbey. In Powys, at Pennant Melangell is a curious survivor in the form of a late twelfth-century shrine, dedicated to an earlier local saint, Melangell. It was dismantled and hidden at the time of the Reformation, and is now reassembled in the shrine chapel. The shrine itself is rather exotic looking in structure and decoration, and adds something to our appreciation of the medieval veneration of the saints.

Numerous Augustinian houses were founded in the south, at Llanthony in the south-east, and at Haverfordwest and Carmarthen, where Norman power in south-west Wales was concentrated. Old foundations in the north at

Bardsey, Beddgelert and Penmon converted to Augustinian to ensure survival. Therefore, new centres of learning arose, where the writing of history continued, and links were maintained with Welsh princes and court poets. A number of Welshmen went to Paris to study and many to Oxford, but education was for the very few.

The resistance of the Welsh to the Normans continued with many uprisings under the leadership of local lords. Henry II invaded Wales on three occasions. Churches and villages were burnt and hostages murdered. In 1175 there was a vicious massacre at Abergavenny. All this and much else we learn from the pen of the ebullient Gerald of Wales, Giraldus Cambrensis.

He was born in Manorbier in Pembrokeshire in about 1145, and was three parts Norman and one part Welsh. A learned churchman and writer, who had studied for long periods in Paris and at one stage was court chaplain to Henry II, he had one consuming ambition: to become archbishop of a St David's independent of Canterbury and ultimately to be made archbishop of Wales. It was not to be. His personal ambition in an independent Welsh Church and his powerful position in South Wales, related to many ruling families, made him a quite unacceptable choice to any English monarch.

His book *Journey through Wales* describes how Gerald, as archdeacon of Brecon, was required to accompany the then archbishop of Canterbury, Baldwin, on a preaching tour of Wales to encourage support for the Third Crusade. Leading churchmen, such as Bernard of Clairvaux, were doing the same thing in other European countries.

The two set out with their party from Hereford at the beginning of Lent in 1188. They made their way across South Wales and around the west coast to North Wales, arriving at Chester for Good Friday and the Easter celebrations, and finally, coming south along the Marches back to Hereford. They went to towns and castles, to churches and cathedrals, to abbeys and monasteries commending the Third Crusade, sometimes preaching in the open air, joined by local churchmen and nobles. Archbishop Baldwin visited all four Welsh cathedrals and said Mass at each one; he was the first archbishop of Canterbury to do so, implicitly making his authority over them clear. In all three thousand men, most of them Welsh, offered themselves for the crusade and were signed with the cross. The volunteers ranged from high-ranking churchmen, such as Gerald himself, to assorted lawbreakers.

In the spring of 1189 Gerald duly set off on the crusade with Archbishop Baldwin and was at Chinon with the English court when Henry II, who had also undertaken the crusade, died there. The new king, Richard, ordered Gerald's return to England and he was absolved from his vow. Archbishop Baldwin continued on his journey and died at the siege of Acre in 1190. It was more than seven centuries later that Gerald's dream of an independent Church in Wales with its own archbishop came true in 1920.

While the activities and rivalries in South Wales give it a high profile in this period, Bangor and St Asaph were making their own efforts to preserve the Welshness of the native Church. At Bangor the first Norman bishop was driven out, one native bishop was consecrated in Ireland, and there were long vacancies and occasional Welsh appointments. At St Asaph there was no bishop until 1143 and a succession of short episcopates. Nowhere were the Normans welcomed.

In Ireland the twelfth century spelt the end of the

Celtic Church through the combined efforts of the Anglo-Norman barons, the English throne and the pope. The Danes, established mainly around Dublin, sent their prospective bishops to Canterbury for consecration and, in response, Canterbury took an interest in the Irish Church. Anselm wrote to the king of Munster encouraging reforms in specific areas: in the organisation of the episcopate, in the practice of selling offices and in the lax marriage laws. The king responded by organising the diocese of Limerick and gave the Rock of Cashel, an ancient royal fortress, to the Church. Here Cormac's Chapel was built and consecrated in 1134; it was a miniature cathedral in a very fine Irish Romanesque style, more ornate than previous architecture: a nave and chancel with steeply pitched stone roofs buttressed by square towers, and beautifully ornamented doorways.

In the early years of the century, Gilbert, bishop of Limerick, had proposed Ireland should have a similar episcopal system to England, but independent of it, with two archbishops and twenty-four bishops in charge of sees with fixed boundaries – a new feature in the Irish scene – all under one primate, all commissioned by the pope. For decades council followed council until finally in 1152 at the Synod of Kells, presided over by the papal legate, the Irish Church emerged with four archbishops at Armagh, Cashel, Tuam and Dublin, and with thirty-two bishops in all. Thus Dublin became integrated into the system, though many of its early archbishops were of English birth. One of the tasks of the bishops was to cultivate the growth of parishes, a slow process, particularly in sparsely populated areas where it was difficult to finance clergy.

Outstanding among Irish churchmen in the first half of the century was Malachy, a scholarly and reforming bishop.

En route to Rome for one of his many visits, he met with Bernard of Clairvaux and was greatly impressed by the way of life of the Cistercian monks there. A strong friendship grew up between the two, which led to the establishment of the Cistercian Order in Ireland. Bernard sent monks from Clairvaux to help establish Mellifont Abbey. Soon there were some fourteen Cistercian houses. Malachy also encouraged the Augustinian canons who were active in the movement for reform. By 1170 there were sixty Augustinian houses, mostly in the north. Malachy died at Clairvaux, which had been his wish, again on his way to Rome.

One of the problems the Irish Church faced was the need to raise moral standards, lowered by years of conflict. In 1171 Henry II went to Ireland. Before the king's arrival there had been successive landings by Anglo-Norman barons, which brought more devastation as they appropriated land and divided it among themselves; disputes continued for centuries. The king stayed for six months, during which time some of the Irish lords submitted to him. At the Council of Lismore the Irish bishops accepted English laws, in the hope of reform and peace.

The Anglo-Norman lords who came were only slowly absorbed into Irish society; their main stronghold was the area around Dublin, which later became known as the Pale. They contributed to the development of the parish system, dividing their estates into manors with a church and parish priest. The system of appropriations became a problem here too and clergy, particularly rural clergy, were very poor. The incomers supported the Cistercians and Augustinians, and added to them the military orders, the Hospitallers and Templars, as well as the more pastoral Brothers of the Cross, who provided hospitals.

At the Council of Cashel in 1172, under a papal legate, the Irish Church was brought into the Roman Church, and details settled regarding tithes and church property, and the position of clergy under canon, rather than civil, law.

In Dublin, Christ Church cathedral, originally founded by the first bishop of Dublin and its Norse king around 1038, was rebuilt by Anglo-Normans when O'Toole, a former abbot at Glendalough, was archbishop. His successor, John Comyn, appointed by Henry and the first Anglo-Norman archbishop of Dublin, thought to supplant Christ Church by building a castle and cathedral church of St Patrick outside the city walls. In the event Christ Church has maintained its role over the centuries as the cathedral church of the diocese of Dublin and Glendalough, while St Patrick's bears the title of the National Cathedral of the Church of Ireland.

Monasticism with a Difference

In the thirteenth century the Church in the West was presented with an entirely new phenomenon when the friars broke in on the scene. This was monasticism in a new guise. They brought the Church to the people and fresh life to the Church. The Franciscans and Dominicans were the main orders; there were also Carmelites, Augustinian friars and smaller orders. Their lives were based on monastic discipline and community living, but they chose the growing towns and cities as their mission field, and went out to preach to the people. They became very popular through the devotion of their preaching, and by their way of life and personal poverty. They were known as the Mendicant Orders, depending on alms and the food they could grow.

In England, they went first to Canterbury and London,

to Oxford and Cambridge, then spread widely to Scotland, Ireland and Wales. The Dominicans made their first base in Edinburgh in 1224 and in Cardiff before 1242. The Franciscans followed. In time, some towns had houses belonging to all four main groups of friars.

The early Franciscan emphasis was on poverty and preaching in the tradition of their founder, St Francis of Assisi. The Dominicans started as a preaching order intent on opposing heresy; from the beginning they stressed the need for study and training, and produced great theologians, including St Thomas Aquinas. In time the Franciscans came to share their view, and from their ranks came scholars such as William of Ockham and Roger Bacon. They frequented the new universities that had been growing up in the twelfth and thirteenth centuries. Many English scholars went to Paris, which was a centre for theological study, as well as to Oxford and Cambridge. The Franciscan John Duns Scotus studied at all three. This was the age when scholasticism was at its peak – a great tradition of learning in medieval times, an attempt to arrive at a deeper intellectual understanding of church doctrine through analysing and defining, using philosophical and theological argument. Anselm was one of its early proponents in England, and the thirteenth-century Thomas Aquinas one of the most influential. His *Summa Theologica* became the basis of modern Roman Catholic theology.

There was, however, a problem with the friars: they were not subject to the bishops. They went where they chose, to preach, say Mass and hear confessions. Ill-feeling arose between them and the parish priests and bishops. Monks also saw them as rivals. There was even rivalry between the friars themselves. They made a great impact but much more might have been achieved through a spirit of cooperation. Both orders acquired fifty or more houses in England. Numbers were smaller in the Celtic areas. They brought a new dynamism to the Church and did a great deal to revive the art of preaching, but, by the end of the thirteenth century their most successful period in most places was over.

Spiritual leadership, which for so long had lain with the monasteries, had passed in every area largely to the bishops. Among them were outstanding men who addressed some of the current problems. Bishop Grosseteste of Lincoln, when he visited his very large diocese, deposed abbots for their inadequate provision for parish churches. On a visit to Rome he openly criticised papal appointments of Italians to rich English benefices. John Peckham, when he became archbishop of Canterbury, visited every diocese in his vast province, and set about reforming abuses such as pluralism, the practice by many clergy of holding more than one living. He tried to raise the standards of clergy, encouraging them to preach at least four times a year, as preaching had declined to such a degree. Better education and training of the clergy were clearly part of the solution, which the growing numbers of schools in towns might help to address. In the meantime his treatise on the catechism provided them with a valuable teaching aid. The deeply spiritual Bishop Richard of Chichester and the reforming Bishop Thomas de Cantilupe of Hereford, both former chancellors of Oxford University, were canonised.

Church Building and Church Life

The Normans continued to make their mark on the landscape in a variety of buildings in their very distinctive style. Among them the collegiate church of Southwell

Minster, now a cathedral, has preserved its original external outline and its chapter house with a fine star-shaped vault. An imposing new abbey at Romsey replaced the Saxon nunnery founded by King Alfred's son, and a massive almshouse church was built at St Cross, Winchester. Sometimes, parts of churches have retained their original style: the chapter house at Bristol cathedral has survived from the twelfth-century Augustinian abbey.

Countless parish churches form part of this extraordinary legacy bequeathed to us. Some are imposing, such as the Church of St Michael and St Mary at Melbourne in Derbyshire, built as a place of retreat for the bishop of Carlisle when the Scots threatened, or St Mary's Church at Iffley in Oxfordshire. Others are on a smaller scale, like that at Barfreston in Kent with extensive carving. In Herefordshire a well-preserved gem of a church has survived in the village of Kilpeck. There was a flourishing school of carvers in the area, their art displayed not only at Kilpeck but in the stone fonts of the churches at Eardisley and Castle Frome.

Over the latter part of the twelfth century and the early thirteenth century the style of building was changing to Early Gothic, with its pointed arches, more ambitious vaulting, slender pillars and larger windows. When the bishop of Old Sarum moved his see to New Sarum, Salisbury, in 1218, and laid the foundations of the new cathedral, the main body was built entirely in the Early Gothic style. The unity of style enables us to appreciate its graceful elegance.

Most of our great cathedrals and churches display a variety of architectural styles as succeeding builders responded to new ideas and skills, or to disasters such as the all-too-common fires, the collapse of towers or even damage from an earthquake in the case of Lincoln, where the magnificent Norman-built west front miraculously survived.

In the thirteenth century the abbey at Peterborough, with its Norman nave and rare painted ceiling, acquired its west front with its three great arches. At Wells the remarkable west front of the cathedral, which still has almost three hundred sculptures, was built. Serious rebuilding began at York. In many places stained-glass windows of great beauty were created, complementing the stonework with their rich colours – York and Canterbury still have extensive collections from the period.

What must have been the impact of such size and splendour on the vast crowds of pilgrims who came to visit the shrines housed within the walls of these great churches? Some shrines were long established, such as St Chad's at Lichfield and St Swithin's at Winchester; others honoured recently canonised bishops. Buildings were changed and extended to accommodate the crowds of pilgrims. At Canterbury Becket's remains were moved to the newly created Trinity Chapel at the east end, while at Lincoln, out of the damage caused by the earthquake, came the Angel Choir where the shrine of the much-loved Bishop Hugh was set. At Westminster Abbey Henry III had a magnificent new shrine built to honour Edward the Confessor. The popularity of these shrines continued right up to the Reformation.

In many churches wall paintings were becoming a common feature. Like the stained-glass windows they were not purely decorative, but for the instruction of the congregation. In the chancel of St Mary's Church at Kempley in Gloucestershire is a fine set of twelfth-century frescoes of angels and apostles, surmounted by a figure of

Christ. At Clayton in Sussex there is a Christ in Majesty over the chancel arch, ready to receive the crowds moving towards him along the walls of the nave. Many churches still have at least traces of the figure of St Christopher, the protector of travellers, usually placed so as to be seen through an open church door – a pledge of safety for that day.

We can try to imagine the services that took place in these spaces, devoid of pews, chairs and pulpits – no hymns, few sermons, very little involvement of the congregation, but the spectacle of the Mass, in which people increasingly received only the wafer and not the wine. The Eucharist was central to the worship and teaching of the Church, recalling the passion, crucifixion and resurrection of Christ. The Lateran Council of 1215 had affirmed the doctrine of transubstantiation. The Dominican scholar Thomas Aquinas elaborated the doctrine: at the prayer of consecration the whole substance of the bread and wine becomes the whole substance of the body and blood of Christ; only the "accidents" (i.e. the appearance) remain the same. Later in the century, the introduction of the feast of Corpus Christi, with a procession, served to promote the doctrine. Heaven and hell figured large in medieval thinking, as did purgatory, where the soul, it was thought, suffered after death and was purified of its sins. The building of chantry chapels in large churches began, where Mass could be said for the souls of the departed to ease their passage through purgatory. The Virgin Mary and the saints were major realities in the lives of the faithful.

By the end of the thirteenth century the parish system was up and running almost everywhere. If there was a competent clergyman actually living in the parish, the system could work well. Other parishes suffered neglect in varying degrees, in the standard of services and pastoral care, and in the physical state of the church. Out of his share of the tithes, the rector paid such staff as he had, whether vicar, deacon, clerk or sexton; provided books and vestments; and took care of the chancel, while the congregation took care of the nave. In addition, parishioners were encouraged to bring Mass pennies, and pennies for confession and for other occasional offices. At festivals they might bring other offerings, traditionally eggs at Easter and fowl at Christmas. If they were fortunate in their clergy, they learnt the basics: the Creed, the Ten Commandments and the Lord's Prayer. Only some clergy had a Bible – they were too costly for many. The people received some guidance through the confessional, and they received communion at Easter, and perhaps on one or two other occasions in the year.

There were many other aspects of church life: drama within the context of the liturgy, but also masques and mystery plays, performed inside the church and in the churchyard. The church itself was used for many secular activities, such as for banquets and dancing, while the churchyard served as a venue for fairs and markets. "Scot ales", feasts to raise money for a church, were organised on the Sunday before Michaelmas, and on the fourth Sunday of Advent and Lent. The Church in its many aspects was at the heart of parish life.

The Celtic Countries As They Approached 1300

In thirteenth-century Scotland the building of religious houses had not abated. Work continued at St Andrew's and Holyrood. On the island of Iona the building began of a Benedictine abbey, on the site of St Columba's early monastery. A little remains of it in the present abbey. An

Augustinian nunnery was established there too, both in the early decades of the century. In 1250 Queen Margaret was canonised and a new shrine chapel built at Dunfermline. Yet another strict Benedictine Order, the Valliscaulians, unrepresented in England, arrived on the scene, founding three major priories. The last of the Cistercian houses, Sweetheart Abbey in the south-west, was founded in 1273.

The early thirteenth century had seen the arrival of the friars, and Scotland had acquired a very full complement of religious orders, but by 1300, as a movement of power and influence, monasticism had passed its peak.

In Ireland one of the most important developments for the Church had been the rehabilitation of the role of bishops. After centuries of being subordinate to the abbots of the monastic churches, bishops could now be elected by churches and chapters, and their authority was firmly established within more clearly defined sees. By the mid-thirteenth century half of the episcopate of the Irish Church was Norman. The composition of the population was complex: native Irish, Norse, Anglo-Norman and, through intermarriage, Anglo-Irish, with a large number of English immigrants. English law did not extend to everyone, in spite of efforts by the archbishop of Cashel in 1280 to make it do so – a situation that did not make for cohesion.

The style of building was changing in Ireland, as elsewhere, to the Early Gothic, with traces still of Irish Romanesque motifs. The site at Cashel offers a picture in stone of the period: the twelfth-century Cormac's Chapel, the thirteenth-century cathedral with its lancet windows, the ruins of a Dominican priory of 1243 and those of the Cistercian Hore Abbey of 1272.

In Wales, dissatisfaction with English rule simmered and the country was impoverished by conflict. Apart from the cathedral churches at Llandaff and St David's, where building continued, elsewhere it was limited and modest. At Brecon rebuilding began of the Benedictine priory established by the Normans. The chancel, with its narrow lancet windows, was rebuilt in the thirteenth century and is the oldest part of the present church, which became a cathedral in 1923.

Advances in administration had been made: the boundaries of dioceses were clearer, archdeacons and rural deans were in place and contributing to the oversight of clergy, and organisation into parishes was well established in the south, though slower in the north.

Most significant of all for the Welsh Church, the native language was strong. The Creeds and key passages of the Bible were being translated into Welsh. An increasing amount of Welsh literature was appearing – Lives of Saints, devotional works, and most especially, poetry, much of it by clerics. There were some effective bishops. John of Monmouth, bishop of Llandaff, invited scholars to the cathedral and established a centre of training for clergy at the end of the thirteenth century. Bishop Bek of St David's founded two collegiate churches in his diocese to improve the level of ministry. The bishops of Bangor and St Asaph encouraged the friars in their ministry.

Two cultures with different languages lived in unwilling coexistence. The situation became more clearly defined when Edward I, after establishing law and order in England, turned his attention to Wales. He campaigned there from 1274 to 1284 and made the English presence and its implications very visible in the many castles he built. In 1284 Archbishop Peckham of Canterbury visited all four Welsh dioceses to encourage and reform. He was followed soon after by Edward, whose journey through Wales took him to all four cathedrals. Welsh independence had come to an end and the Welsh Church had become even more subject to England. It was the only one of the three Celtic countries in that position. The Church in Scotland and Ireland was under the pope's aegis.

In Scotland, the death of Alexander III in 1286 created a power vacuum and an opportunity for Edward to prove himself the "Hammer of the Scots", asserting his authority over Scotland as he had already done over Wales. As Edward threatened, a Franco-Scottish alliance was formed which would prove a significant element in Scottish life for the centuries following.

By 1300, two and a half centuries after the Norman Conquest, the papacy was strong, with far-reaching influence, not only in matters of doctrine and church practice but over appointments and general regulation. Monasteries were a ubiquitous presence, still of significance, though some were increasingly involved with the secular world. Bishops were taking charge of spiritual direction, many of them aware of the need to tackle abuses and improve standards, but they had an unwieldy workforce of varying competence, and communication was slow. Implementing reform took time. For the people, the Church was the dominating influence at all levels of society and allegiance to it was, for the most part, unquestioning. Voices of dissatisfaction, dissent or scepticism were as yet muted; in the centuries following, they would make themselves heard as their numbers increased and as the miracle of the printed word disseminated new ideas, often at great cost to the individuals concerned.

VIII

NEW IDEAS

In the fourteenth and fifteenth centuries the Middle Ages moved into a different and final phase, in many ways a period of unrest. For two and a half centuries a strong papacy had given a certain stability to the Church in the West. When it moved from Rome to Avignon in 1309 and stayed there for some seventy years, that stability was disturbed. There followed the Great Schism from 1378 to 1417, a period when there were two, sometimes even three, popes – a situation that inevitably reduced the prestige of the papacy. Its financial activities and the extent of its involvement in the Church everywhere in the West produced a reaction; England found it necessary to make it illegal for the pope to appoint foreigners to the English Church and tried to reduce appeals by her clergy to the papal court. Secular rulers were questioning the power of the papacy to interfere in national affairs. Crucially it was providing no spiritual leadership.

What it was offering was an increasing number of indulgences, a practice that would have widespread repercussions. The Church maintained that, even after confession of sin and repentance, a penance was still required on earth or after death in purgatory before the soul was admitted to heaven. Through certain pious acts the faithful could draw on a "treasury of merits" of Christ and the saints, which the Church administered in the form of indulgences. These reduced the penalty owed and people at every social level took advantage of the opportunity. Indulgences could be bought for the practice of certain devotions, for pilgrimages to Rome and other holy places, and for helping to build or restore churches. An individual could buy a full indulgence from a confessor on his deathbed. A great deal of money was raised for the Church in this way, but, as they became widely available, so their value was called into question. The role of the pardoners, who made a business of selling indulgences, brought the system into total disrepute.

In Germany in 1517, Martin Luther nailed his ninety-five arguments against indulgences to the church door in Wittenburg, the beginning of the Reformation there. Things would move more slowly and take a different path on this side of the English Channel.

In the fourteenth century the monasteries, once so vital to church growth, were in decline. While there were undoubtedly communities where men and women followed their vocation with sincerity and devotion, in many others this had ceased to be the case. Many had become very wealthy, sometimes discipline was lax, and some had to close down for lack of recruits. The popular view of the monk's life was changing; at one time it had been seen as the only way to lead a life totally committed to God; anything less was second best. The daily prayer life of the monks had been seen too as a kind of bastion against evil for everyone. The fearful experience of the Black Death of 1348, when somewhere between one-third and one-half of the population died, may have confirmed the feeling of disillusionment.

In England only the Carthusian Order expanded. Two houses of this strictly contemplative order had been established in the twelfth century. After the Black Death, eight more Charterhouses were founded. The Carthusian monks lived as virtual hermits in individual houses clustered around a cloister, an arrangement preserved at Mount Grace Priory in North Yorkshire, founded in 1398. They observed a strict rule of silence and met together only for worship and for meals on feast days.

A new order, founded by St Bridget of Sweden, made its appearance in England in a double community at Brentford on the Thames in Syon House, founded in 1415 by Henry V. This and the modest growth of the Carthusians were exceptional features in the monastic scene, and both were influential through the devotional literature that they produced for lay people and religious alike.

A new attitude was developing among some lay people, which recognised the spiritual value of the secular, as opposed to the monastic, way of life and saw the potential of individual discipline in quite ordinary circumstances. There was a new recognition of the value of manual work.

Critical voices could be heard – Chaucer, in his *Prologue to The Canterbury Tales*, written towards the end of the fourteenth century, is scathing in his character sketches of the pilgrims. He takes as an example the monk who neglects the Rule of Benedict for the pleasures of the hunt. The friars he describes as guilty of every sin from adultery to usury. The pardoner has his bag of supposed relics and his satchel full of pardons, which he claims to be from Rome, ready to rob a poor widow or a country parson. At the same time he acknowledges that there are parish priests, often impoverished, who are true to their vocation.

Chaucer was the son of a London merchant and worked in the diplomatic field. Another contemporary writer was a cleric in minor orders, William Langland, from Cleobury Mortimer in Shropshire. His *Piers the Plowman* was written and reworked over a period of twenty years from 1370 to 1390. The poem is a series of dreams, but firmly set in the reality of fourteenth-century society, in which the poet sets out from the Malvern Hills in search of the meaning of life. In his first dream he surveys the crowded, noisy plain of the world, in what seems to him a parlous state. In the dreams that follow he is guided on his journey in part by Piers the good ploughman, who is the ideal man or a type of Christ, and through them we are presented with some of the realities of fourteenth-century church life.

As Langland sees it, bishops are ordaining priests who are neither trained nor competent. Many monks spend their time not in the cloister, but managing the land. The friars are eager to help anyone for money, providing easy confession, so that the people take their sins less seriously. The pardoners are making money out of deceiving poor people. Pilgrims move from one holy place to another, collecting their badges, their relics and indulgences, all with little thought. Nevertheless, he comes slowly to appreciate the roles of patience and poverty, and especially of love, and how the Church must, through Piers, plough the field of the world and grow the seed of truth.

To judge from the number of manuscripts surviving, the work was widely read in literate circles. Langland travelled around and spent some time in London. His career in the

Church had been checked by the death of his patrons and, like many minor clergy, he found some employment as a chantry priest, paid to say Masses for the souls of the dead in purgatory.

Parish Church Life

Purgatory was very real for medieval people and they set out to reduce their time there, not only through good deeds and the purchase of indulgences in their lifetime but also by enlisting the prayers of the community after death. Bequests were made to found chantry chapels where priests would say Mass for the dead, which the community would attend. Chantries varied from the simple to the sumptuous, from a separate altar set up in the nave of the parish church to an ornate chapel, such as the Stanbury chapel in Hereford Cathedral, built in the 1470s, with its fan vaulting and a wealth of carving. Chantry priests served in specially founded collegiate churches as well as in parish churches, independently of the incumbent. A very large number of priests in minor orders were employed in this way. Some chantries were perpetual, some temporary, depending on the wealth of the founder. Even people of very modest means could participate through the guilds.

These were local associations; some of them craft guilds, and most of a religious nature. They might be dedicated to the Virgin Mary or to one of the saints, or to a particular aspect of Christian belief; so there might be a Resurrection guild or a Corpus Christi guild. There were many guilds in towns, and usually a few in villages. Their functions ranged from maintaining a collective chantry to supplying candles. Members were expected to be of good character and if they fell on difficult times, they would be helped by the guild. They were expected to attend the funeral of a fellow member. As an act of charity, the guild might pay the burial fees of very poor non-members. They involved themselves in organising processions and sometimes plays, and in repairing and beautifying the parish church. In all they played an important social role in the later Middle Ages.

The Church and its activities dominated community life. The calendar was full of significant days, whether of fast or festival, which impinged on daily life; many of them were non-working days. Virtually everyone was involved, which helped to create the very corporate nature of the medieval Church and gave a sense of unity to society.

There were some seventy fast days, forty of them in Lent, but also Ember Days and the vigils of festivals. There were around forty to fifty feast days – some local and some major obligatory feasts. Holy Week contained the most significant observances, beginning with Palm Sunday and the procession with palms. After the Maundy Thursday Mass the altars were stripped bare and the washing of feet took place, in memory of Jesus' act of washing his disciples' feet at the Last Supper. On Good Friday the people crept to the cross to venerate it. Christ was symbolically buried in an Easter sepulchre in the chancel, in the form of a consecrated wafer, and the venerated cross was wrapped in a cloth. Watch was kept night and day until Easter Sunday when the empty sepulchre became a focal point. This was the only day in the year for many when they received Holy Communion, having previously confessed their sins to a priest. Only afterwards could the Lenten fast be broken.

There is a finely carved Easter sepulchre at the church of All Saints at Hawton in Nottinghamshire, with, in the central part, the figure of Christ rising from the tomb, with the three Marys who have come to anoint his body. Below the Roman soldiers are asleep. There were many much simpler sepulchres, sometimes made of wood.

As well as the major festivals of Easter, Pentecost and Christmas, there was Candlemas, which was forty days after Christmas to remember the presentation of the Child Jesus in the Temple and the purification of the Virgin Mary; it was celebrated by elaborate processions with candles and bell ringing. Trinity Sunday and All Saints' Day were equally important. Sometimes there were plays known as mystery or miracle plays to illustrate the event being celebrated, a tradition that has been revived in many places such as Chester and York. Rogation-tide had its procession too, around the parish boundary, and prayers were said for a good harvest. Saints' days were often marked by feasts and bonfires. New feast days were established: Corpus Christi had been introduced in the thirteenth century, and the Feasts of the Transfiguration and of the Holy Name in the later fifteenth century. New saints' days were added, both local and foreign, from Richard of Chichester to Catherine of Siena. The cult of St Anne, mother of the Virgin Mary, became very popular.

Church and home were linked as the people brought home palms on Palm Sunday and candles from the Candlemas procession. Holy water was taken to the houses of the parish. Households would provide the loaf, which was blessed and distributed to the congregation after Mass, a sign of fellowship and a substitute for Holy Communion.

According to their means, the people contributed to the beautifying of their church, purchasing vestments, vessels, altar frontals and banners; even the poor might provide a candle to place before a favourite saint. Images of saints proliferated, often with their own altars or chapels.

At the very heart of church life was the Eucharist, or

the Mass. There were often several daily celebrations in the parish church, which were less elaborate on weekdays than on Sundays. There was an early Mass for those whose work entailed an early start and chantry Masses at nave altars. Many attended Mass daily. It was seen as a repeated sacrifice, a re-enactment of Christ's crucifixion. An increased number brought increased benefit. From the twelfth century onwards the bread or wafer – the Host – was held high at the consecration and this elevation became the high point of the liturgy. The people had to witness this moment in order to fulfil their obligations and to share in communion with God. For most of them, it was only at Easter that they actually received the bread. This was a far cry from the practice of the early Church: from the regular sharing of bread and wine among believers, remembering the sacrifice of Christ and believing that He was present with them. This belief in the presence of Christ is the common feature of the Eucharist throughout the ages, though it has been differently interpreted at different times. The very early Church did not feel the need to analyse and define how it was so. The doctrine of transubstantiation was how the medieval Church expressed its understanding.

Along with the doctrine came an increasing sense of the mystery and holiness of the Eucharist, and of the reverence due to the elements of bread and wine. The chancel became both a focus and a place apart for the celebration of the mystery, separated from the nave by a screen of wood or stone. Within it there developed architectural features: a piscina for the washing of the vessels used in Holy Communion, and sedilia – stone seats for the clergy involved in the celebration.

While the priest performed his role as a mediator in the sanctuary, the people busied themselves with their own prayers, responding at key moments of the liturgy by kneeling and raising their hands in adoration. In time texts were produced to encourage greater participation, at least by those who were literate. There was the Lay Folk's Mass, not a service book, but containing paraphrases and meditations on the Mass, and there was the Lay Folk's Catechism.

The advent of printing towards the end of the fifteenth century led to a great increase in the amount of material, especially of psalters and books of hours, or primers, which included short offices, penitential psalms, prayers and devotions to the Virgin Mary; they were in Latin, which only a few could have read, but contained familiar prayers, with some simple illustrations to help with understanding. They were valued as sacred possessions; some learnt to read through them, but until such time as literacy became common, people experienced their faith through the drama of the liturgy and its extension in the processions and mystery plays.

Immediately before them and dominating the interior of the church was the figure of Christ on the cross, above the rood screen, with the figures of Mary and John on either side. Most were destroyed in the Reformation. The rood screen itself was often painted with figures of the apostles or the saints, as it is at Ranworth in Norfolk, where in the Lady Chapel are also paintings on the reredos of the three Marys and their children, and of St Margaret, the patron of women in childbirth. Through paintings, images and carvings, the people became familiar with the saints. Few could have been more impressive than the stone figure of St Christopher at Norton Priory, in Runcorn, which is almost three and a half metres high, and dates from around 1400.

Stained-glass windows taught the people about Biblical

characters and events, or reminded them of the Works of Mercy or the seven sacraments: baptism, confirmation, the Eucharist, penance, extreme unction, orders and matrimony. Fonts sometimes provided illustrations of the sacraments too, like that at Walsoken in Cambridgeshire. Even the bosses in the roof vaults might illustrate the Christian story.

Experience of life at the time, of pain, disease and famine, together with the fear of hell and judgement, encouraged most people to observe what the Church required of them and to cherish the hope of heaven, but pagan ways of thinking continued too. At one end of the worshipping spectrum there were elements of superstition, a perception of divine action as magic, constituting a thin line between prayers for protection and charms. In society at large sorcery was still practised. Fonts were locked to prevent misuse of holy water. Astrology had its devotees. At the other end of the spectrum there was a search for a deeper more personal interior life, which found its clearest expression through a number of mystics.

Fourteenth-Century Mystics

There was a long tradition of mysticism in the Church. Common to all mystics was a direct experience of God which brought great joy. It was a state arrived at by the means available to all Christians, through prayer, reading and the sacraments, but in addition through lengthy contemplation.

The fourteenth-century mystics in England were all connected with the solitary life, a part of the monastic tradition that had not withered. Although Latin was still the language of theological writing, they all wrote at least some of their work in English, for the benefit of all their fellow Christians. The titles of their most well-known writings speak for themselves: Richard Rolle's *The Fire of Love*, Walter Hilton's *The Ladder of Perfection* and the anonymous *Cloud of Unknowing*.

Best known of these fourteenth-century mystics is Julian of Norwich, not only for her *Revelations of Divine Love*, the first book to be written in English by a woman, but also by the many Julian groups that her book has inspired: groups formed for the purpose of contemplative prayer.

The Norwich of her day bristled with churches and monasteries. It also had some forty cells for anchorites who committed themselves to an enclosed life of prayer. They lived either close to a monastery or convent under a Rule, or were under the direction of a bishop and lived in a building attached to a church, which might consist of two or three small rooms with a walled garden. The anchorite often had a servant. Julian herself undertook this way of life after a series of visions of the passion of Christ, which she received at the age of thirty when she became very ill. For the next twenty years she meditated on her experience before describing it in detail in her book. It only became generally available in the twentieth century and seems to have had a limited circulation during her lifetime. It is possible the Church of her day did not feel wholly at ease with some of her perceptions, though she never questioned the Church's teaching.

Her insights centre on what she sees as the unlimited love of God and her absolute trust that, ultimately, all will be well. She saw anger as totally incompatible with this love. Long before the days of political correctness, she felt God is as much our Mother as our Father, even then not a new idea. The conclusion of her intense reflections on Christ's passion was to see it as an expression of boundless love for humanity. Her writing is full of optimism, encapsulated in her call to live joyfully because of His love; this in spite of a background to her life of plague and war, poverty and bad harvests, and the Peasants' Revolt in which Norwich was involved.

Her cell at St Julian's church, from which she took her name as an anchoress, was pulled down during the Reformation, but rebuilt when the church itself was restored after the bombing in 1942. Here she had lived for forty years. The cell then had two windows, one looking into the church, so that she could share in the Mass, and another on to the street, through which she could counsel those who sought her advice, part of her role as an anchoress.

One of those who came to see her was Margery Kempe of King's Lynn, a mother of fourteen children. She too received a number of visions and in later life went on several pilgrimages. In her *Book of Margery Kempe*, she wrote about her journeys and her mystical experiences – and of her visit to Mother Julian.

John Wycliffe and the Lollards

A different voice was making itself heard in Oxford, where the philosopher and theologian John Wycliffe was teaching and writing. Fourteenth-century Oxford had developed as a centre of study and independent thinking. Wycliffe had become increasingly critical of the Church of his day, particularly of its wealth and worldliness. He questioned the power of the papacy and the existence of the monastic orders; in his view neither had any scriptural basis. He believed it possible to reach a personal faith without the mediation of a priest, and that unworthy priests should be disendowed. He questioned the sale of indulgences, and the extent to which superstition was associated with images and relics, and even with the Mass itself. He disagreed with the doctrine of transubstantiation, believing that Christ was present in the Eucharist in a spiritual sense. It was his teaching on this issue in particular that led to his being judged a heretic. The pope, bishops and later the university condemned his teaching. Wycliffe refused to change his views and was obliged to retire to his rectory at Lutterworth in 1382, where he worked as a parish priest until he died two years later.

His views had spread beyond Oxford through his followers there and through his writing. One of his great achievements was to give the Bible a prime position. In his opinion, it was the sole authority for doctrine, all truth was to be found in it, and it should be available to everyone, in the vernacular, and not received only secondhand, as interpreted by the pope, councils and clergy. He inspired some of his followers at Oxford to undertake translations of the Latin Bible into English, first Nicholas of Hereford, then John Purvey. Many manuscripts of these translations have survived, even though it was dangerous to own them in the years following his death.

His death was not the end of the matter. A council of the universal Church at Constance in 1415 condemned his doctrines, but his views continued to have influence. There were, in particular, groups of quite humble followers who met to study the Bible in English and to keep alive his teaching. They became known as Lollards, though the term came to be used of all critics of the Church.

Itinerant preachers had become quite common in Wycliffe's lifetime, not only preaching powerfully against the wealth of the Church, and aspects of its organisation and practice, but also against excessive taxation. Such preaching was seen as a threat both to orthodoxy and to society in general. Richard II had all Lollards expelled from Oxford, and the Government took repressive measures; from 1381 Parliament legislated for the arrest of these preachers.

This was the year of the Peasants' Uprising, centred in the south-east. Some priests and friars as well as a few Lollard preachers were involved in the rebellion – they sympathised with the peasants' demands for freedom from serfdom, and for justice in wages and taxation. John Ball, a priest who had been imprisoned for his strong views on social equality, was set free by the rebels and was present when the archbishop of Canterbury, Sudbury, who was also chancellor and so representative of the unpopular government, was beheaded by them. John Ball met with the same fate himself later in the year.

In 1401 the Lollard William Sawtrey was burnt for heresy, even before an Act was passed to bring in the death penalty for heretics. It had the desired effect in that some Lollards recanted, but many continued to propagate their views through preaching and conventicles – small group meetings.

Lollards were not all of one mind. Nor did their views always coincide with Wycliffe's, although they were seen as his followers. The need for a personal faith, the pre-eminence of the Bible and its availability in English were common ground. So was their view of the papacy and the religious orders as unbiblical. They were agreed in condemning indulgences. Over the matter of transubstantiation, Wycliffe had been concerned that the doctrine encouraged superstition, but Lollards generally came to see the Eucharist simply as an act of commemoration. They were much more condemnatory in their attitude to images than Wycliffe, even going so far as to destroy them. Sections of the movement developed ideas about the redistribution of the wealth of the Church. There was some opposition to tithes and to fasting; some even came to see church buildings as irrelevant. Women were among their preachers and some Lollards saw the possibility of women priests.

Wycliffe had opened minds and encouraged questioning, but in an academic way. The Lollards went much further in their very vocal and active defiance of the status quo.

In 1414 Sir John Oldcastle, a Lollard leader from Herefordshire, planned a rebellion. It was foiled and after some time in hiding, Sir John was executed. There were heresy trials in Norwich and in 1428 the authorities took action against the Lollards in Kent, Essex and Suffolk. William White, who had been very influential in eastern England, was burnt, along with others. In the same year Wycliffe's body was exhumed and burnt as a heretic. Another rebellion was planned in 1431, but it too was foiled.

There followed the burning of Lollard books in London. The Lollards had produced their own Bible; they wrote and copied sermons and tracts, and wrote books. The growth of literacy and the greater availability of reading matter helped their cause and also profoundly challenged the Church.

The movement was particularly strong in London and Essex, in the Midlands and in parts of the north. Its success was limited by the fact that, as it developed, there were no followers of social standing and influence. It had become dominated by craftsmen and artisans in the towns, and was more radical. To some extent it had been discredited by extremists. In the face of the strong stance taken by the authorities, the movement went underground for some decades.

The Pre-Reformation Church in the Celtic Countries

While the practice of the faith was much the same everywhere, in the Celtic countries the degree to which the Church flourished depended on factors such as poverty and aggression from outside, as well as internal conflicts.

In Scotland, from the reign of Edward I up till 1560 there was often war with England, as the country fought to remain independent. During that time an alliance with France played a significant role. While the period of the Great Schism lasted, Scotland supported the pope at Avignon, though in the fifteenth century its Parliament tried to protect the freedom of the Scottish Church and to reduce papal appointments and fees.

In the parish churches standards were often low, especially in the Highlands and Islands. They suffered from poverty, from shared clergy and from the appropriations of tithes by monasteries and cathedrals. When James II's widow founded Trinity College, Edinburgh, in 1460, she used the revenues of fourteen parish churches under her patronage to do so. The dire effects of such appropriations on parish churches were checked to some extent by an Act of Parliament in 1471.

A number of collegiate churches were created; some were chantries, some private chapels of the wealthy and most were relatively small, apart from St Giles, Edinburgh.

In the monasteries, life had become much easier than intended, but some houses, where abbots had enforced stricter discipline, were in good shape. There was even some major reconstruction at earlier-established houses up till the sixteenth century – at the Cluniac houses of Paisley and Crossraguel, at Iona and at Inchcolm, where much that can be seen is probably fifteenth century. A new Charterhouse was founded by James I at Perth in 1429, the only Carthusian house in Scotland.

Attacks by the English in the Scottish Border country in the fifteenth century and again in the 1540s caused a great deal of damage to monasteries, which it became difficult to make good. One of the problems was that, as time went by, many monasteries were no longer directed by abbots or priors, but by commendators, who were often appointed by the king as a reward for service. Some were not even in orders, but took orders after appointment, never intending to become monks.

The friars were still active, and a few friaries were set up in the fourteenth and fifteenth centuries, along with houses for orders of nuns associated with them. At Haddington, the birthplace of John Knox, the parish church of St Mary, the longest in Scotland, was built. Its most famous son would give the church a significant role in the course of the Reformation.

Some bishops of the time made their mark: Bishop Forman of Moray encouraged the friars to preach in the Highland area of his diocese; Bishop Elphinstone of Aberdeen edited the *Aberdeen Breviary*, one of the first books to be printed in 1510; this was to become the official prayer book of the country. It was partly through the initiative of bishops that universities were founded in Scotland. St Andrew's received its charter as a university in 1411. In 1412 Stirling University was founded, followed by Glasgow in 1451 and Aberdeen in 1495. This constituted a great advance educationally, an experience not shared by either Wales or Ireland.

In 1472 the current pope was persuaded by the bishop of St Andrew's to make his see an archbishopric. In response the king and Parliament ensured that Glasgow also became a metropolitan see in 1492.

The century had also brought a new challenge, partly through Lollard influence. Questioning voices, suggesting the need for reform in the Church, were making themselves heard – and meeting with swift action by the authorities. The first to go to the stake was an English priest in Perth in 1406. A Czech reformer met the same fate in 1433. In the meantime an anti-Lollard oath had been introduced as the movement for reform gathered momentum in Scotland.

In Ireland the Church functioned as best it could against a difficult social and political background. In 1315 Robert the Bruce, encouraged by his victory over the English at Bannockburn, sent his brother Edward to Ireland with an army, ostensibly to establish solidarity between the Scots and the Irish, and so liberate them from the English. They stayed for three years. The result was more factions, exacerbated by a famine. The campaign ended with Edward's death. A lot of damage was done, from which the Church did not escape.

The Black Death followed in 1348, with repeated outbreaks. The population was greatly reduced, particularly in towns, where the friars were badly affected. Many who were ill-qualified were admitted to a depleted priesthood. The monasteries were in a bad state; appropriations of parish churches brought them some income, but were of no help to the parish churches. There was very little building of churches; fortified-castle building was more in tune with the spirit of the time in the complex culture that was Ireland.

The fifteenth century brought some light into the general situation when there was a movement for reform among the friars. The Franciscan Order had split into two: the Observant Friars claimed to be faithful to the Rule of St Francis in returning to the original poverty of the order, and separated from the less strict Conventuals. The movement began in the north and west of Ireland. Forty new foundations were established in Tuam and twenty-five in Armagh. It spread to the south and east, where eighteen houses were founded in Cashel and four in Dublin. Older houses also adopted the reform, which went even further in the formation of a Third Order Regular of lay associates who had a particular concern for education.

There are many now-ruined friaries to remind us of this new lease of life in the Irish Church, and glimpses in them of the development of an Irish Gothic style. Kilconnel friary in Galway was founded in 1414 and actually remained in use until the seventeenth century. The ruins are sufficiently well preserved to give us an idea of the original: a narrow tower, windows with fine tracery, and cloisters. The friary at Quin in County Clare has similar features; it was built in 1402 within the remains of an Anglo-Norman castle and continued to house friars until the early nineteenth century. The continued use of many friaries long after the dissolution of the monasteries suggests the influence of the friars was felt in the Irish Church for centuries after.

One of the relatively few parish churches to survive from the later medieval period is that of St Nicholas in Galway, founded in 1320. It has three naves and a fine west doorway. It is claimed that Christopher Columbus attended Mass here before setting out on one of his voyages. The largest medieval parish church to survive is St Mary's, Youghal, in County Cork, built in the fifteenth century on an earlier foundation as a collegiate church. The transept contains one of the few chantries to survive in Ireland.

Pilgrimage was as popular among the people as ever, both to traditional sites such as Croagh Patrick and Lough Derg, to healing wells, and also to venues that had acquired statues or other attractions to draw the pilgrim. There was a popular statue of St Molaise on Inishmurray and one of St Maelruan at Crossabeg in County Wexford, the object of a cult which continued for many centuries.

In the parishes, associations of lay people were formed using books of piety, many in Irish. Clergy were using Archbishop Peckham's tract on the catechism for teaching purposes; the friars were also involved in teaching. Religious drama was developing in the miracle plays held in church or churchyard, especially at festival times, and was encouraged by guilds. The guilds of St Anne and St George, founded in Dublin in the early fifteenth century, were very active.

The movement for reform in the Church, which was gathering momentum in England, and touched Wales and Scotland, had further to travel to Ireland. Lollard influence there was slight before the sixteenth century.

In Wales, after Edward I's conquest, the Church there was very much subject to the interests of the English throne. All four dioceses had received a grant which made St David's, at least, a more desirable see. Its bishop from 1328 to 1347 was Henry Gower, one of a minority of Welshmen to achieve preferment. He was an enthusiastic builder and we can still enjoy the work of his masons, not only in the cathedral of St David's, with its enlarged nave and the fine stone screen separating it from the choir, but also in the still-impressive ruins of the Bishop's Palace next to the cathedral, with its arcaded parapet and rose window still visible. However, such expenditure on buildings was rare in fourteenth-century Wales.

Levels of learning were steadily improving through some scholarly bishops and also through the friars. Two important Welsh manuscripts belong to the early part of the century: the White Book of Rhydderch, a mixture of religious works and romances, and the *Book of the Anchorite of Llandewi Brefi*, a collection of religious and philosophical writings. Passages of Scripture, prayers and hymns were being translated into Welsh. Other writings appeared, including works of devotion and instruction manuals to help clergy. The writing of poetry continued, some in secular vein, sometimes critical of the Church.

The middle of the century saw the onslaught of the plague, first in 1348 and in recurring epidemics, exacerbating already poor economic conditions, and reflected in neglected church buildings and depleted clergy numbers. Many appropriations of parish churches were made for their tithes, sometimes by English monasteries.

The Lollards were making their presence felt in the Marches, where Oxford scholars John Aston and Nicholas Hereford were active, and William Swinderby, a priest and powerful preacher, was expressing his views about indulgences and the pope. Another Lollard, Walter Brut, a Welsh layman with anti-clerical views, was associated with him. Both Swinderby and Brut would be tried as heretics by the bishop's court in Hereford. Their activities may well have had an unsettling effect on the border areas.

When Owain Glyndwr instigated a rebellion against English rule, the people, including many clergy, rallied to his call. Glyndwr was no rough upstart, but a descendant of princely families in Wales. He had been educated in England and had served there in the army. When the earl of Ruthin took possession of part of his estate in what would become Denbighshire, his campaign started – firstly against the earl and the English communities in the area. In 1400 he declared himself Prince of Wales and by 1404 his position was strong enough to summon a Welsh Parliament at Machynlleth. His aim was an independent Wales with a separate province of the Church within it, presided over by Welsh bishops with Welsh clergy, its possessions restored. He also wanted two universities for Wales. For more than a decade the movement had remarkable success. Then Glyndwr disappears from history, along with all hope for Welsh independence.

The uprising caused much devastation; lawlessness was widespread. As for the Church, great physical damage had been done to cathedrals, parish churches and religious houses, and patterns of worship had been disrupted.

Yet Wales made a remarkable recovery. Slowly trade resumed, some families prospered and became patrons of the Church. Buildings were repaired and extended. Denbighshire, where the uprising had started, blossomed over the next century as churches were extended by doubling the nave, an unusual feature of the area, and embellished with fine carved woodwork in rood screens, images and roofs.

The Church of St Collen at Llangollen has a superbly carved roof with choirs of angels, one of a number in the area, including those of St Marcella at Denbigh and St Giles at Wrexham. St Dyfnog's Church at Llanrhaeadr has in addition a large and very fine Tree of Jesse window, dated 1533. A path leads up from the church to the well of the sixth-century St Dyfnog, which continued to be a popular place of pilgrimage; the gifts of the pilgrims may well have paid for the beautification of the church.

At Brecon the rebuilding of the old Benedictine priory continued. There, the rood was said to have healing properties. The church became known as the Church of the Holy Rood and a place of pilgrimage. Pilgrims, kings among them, had never ceased making the journey to Holywell, some to give thanks, some in search of healing. At the end of the fifteenth century an octagonal chapel with an elaborate canopy was built directly over St Winifred's well, and its popularity continued.

Stone sculptures from the time survive: a figure of Christ from Mochdre in the Kerry Hills, now in the National Museum; another of Christ bound for scourging at Bangor Cathedral; and there is the remarkable fifteenth-century carving, in oak, of the figure of Jesse at St Mary's Priory in Abergavenny. The long-established monastery at Llantwit Major had been extended over the centuries and had acquired several medieval treasures, among them a fine mural depicting St Mary Magdalene, and a representation of St Christopher.

In the south-east, at Partrishowe, a small church stands above the ancient well of the Celtic saint Issui. An earlier chapel adjoins the church to the west, and may have been used as an anchorite's cell at one time. The church contains a beautifully carved fifteenth-century rood screen and loft, though the rood figures are lost. A figure of Time remains painted on the wall: a skeleton with scythe, spade and hourglass. There are fragments of other wall paintings. The font is thought to date back to pre-Norman times. To step inside the church is to feel transported back in time. Archbishop Baldwin and Gerald of Wales came this way on their tour of Wales in 1188; tradition has it that Archbishop Baldwin preached the Third Crusade from the cross outside the church.

The monasteries in Wales were declining; some accepted the help of nobles as patrons, some began leasing out their land to lay people. Life for the monks was becoming more relaxed. The friars too were less active. Many bishops offered little spiritual leadership: they were often appointed as rewards for service in other spheres, in turn appointing family members, increasing secularisation in the Church. There were few centres of learning, and in the parishes the clergy were often untrained and very poor.

However, there were signs of improvement in English-Welsh relations. In the later fifteenth century, the government of Wales passed into the hands of a Council of the Marches based in the town of Ludlow. Welsh bishops and judges, along with a few lawyers and landowners, were among its members. Wales now had a voice in a government that was closer to home. The year 1485 brought Henry Tudor to the throne. He was partly of Welsh descent, a fact which engendered a measure of loyalty to the English throne hitherto unknown.

Church Building in Fifteenth-Century England

The town of Ludlow, which had developed around the Norman-built castle, had flourished through its wool and cloth trade, and through its royal connections after the castle passed into the control of the Crown in 1461. This was when the parish church of St Laurence was largely rebuilt, part of a great wave of building and rebuilding throughout England in the century before the Reformation.

Like many another church built at the time, the tower of Ludlow's St Laurence announces its presence for some distance around, and its interior is spacious and lofty. In the fifteenth century the nave would have been dominated by a large cross above the rood screen; beyond it the beauty of the chancel in its roof, its stonework and its elaborately carved stalls; down to the detail of the poppy heads on the bench ends and the misericords, some with their earthy depictions of medieval life.

There are other reminders of the time: indications of chantry chapels in the nave in the remaining piscinas around the walls for the washing of the sacred vessels; and the stained-glass windows in the chancel for the instruction of the laity, illustrating the suffering of St Laurence and some of the Ten Commandments. The Palmers' Guild of the town – a guild of pilgrims – had prospered and gave generously to the church. The Chapel of St John became their special chapel, with its Palmers' window, another depicting the Annunciation, and two apostles' windows. A large Tree of Jesse window adorns the Lady Chapel.

Quite apart from the church of St Laurence, the town had five small chapels, two in the castle and three on the outskirts. One of these was on a bridge and was used at one time by a hermit. The town also had an Augustinian and a Carmelite friary; two hospitals, of which one was for lepers; and two outdoor crosses, of which one is termed a weeping cross, for penitents – in all, an indication of the high profile of the Church in a small but important town in the late medieval period.

The Perpendicular style that St Laurence's church illustrates had evolved from the Early Gothic through a stage known as Decorated Gothic, which was an innovative period with greater ornamentation, rich carving, pinnacles, parapets and more elaborate window tracery. At the church of St Mary Redcliffe in Bristol all the stages of Gothic architecture mingle to make what Queen Elizabeth I described as the fairest parish church in England.

Many fine parish churches in the Perpendicular style

owed their existence to the wealth created from wool. In the south, great church towers became a defining feature of the landscape in this wool-rich area, from the wonder of the Boston stump in the east, inland via giants of churches such as Long Melford and Lavenham, to the Cotswolds with its many wool churches from Burford to Cirencester, and on to the fine towers of Somerset. Imposing church towers were not confined to these areas. The style spread westwards into Devon at Widecombe and Hartland, and to St Austell and Probus in Cornwall, and eastwards into Kent to the towering churches of Maidstone and Tenterden. Everywhere they are an abiding reminder in our more secular times of the presence of the Church.

We can travel north from the Cotswolds via great churches built in the same period at Stratford and Warwick, the impressive towers at Market Harborough and Newark-on-Trent, to one of the jewels in the Gothic crown at Beverley in Yorkshire. Today's Beverley Minster was begun around 1220 and completed around 1420, so incorporates all three stages of Gothic architecture, united inside by a continuous vault. Outside, the west front and twin towers are strikingly symmetrical. The minster has many carvings of musicians, a feature it shares with Beverley's other notable church, St Mary's. Yorkshire, like East Anglia and the Cotswolds, was renowned for its wool, with much of its wealth concentrated in its abbeys.

These Gothic churches are flooded with light from large expanses of windows. At Melton Mowbray, a set of forty-eight windows form the clerestory, running the length of the nave and transepts, creating a band of light around the church. In places medieval stained glass has survived in some quantity. The church of St Mary at Fairford in Gloucestershire was built at the end of the fifteenth century. It has a complete set of twenty-eight windows telling the story of the Christian faith: at the east end is the life of Christ; in the nave are prophets, apostles and martyrs; and at the west end is a Christ in Majesty and the Day of Judgement. Fine screens, choir stalls and misericords complete the church.

Everywhere the interiors of churches were embellished in countless ways by the skills of medieval craftsmen – in rood screens and lofts, in choir stalls and misericords, and in the new benches and pulpits. Many churches featured spectacular roofs of carved or painted panels, or hammerbeam roofs, sometimes adorned with hosts of angels, as in the church of St Wendreda in March, Cambridgeshire. One of the glories of the period is the fan vaulting, extensive at Sherborne Abbey and reaching its finest expression in the late fifteenth century at St George's Chapel, Windsor; and in the early sixteenth century in Henry VII's Chapel at Westminster and in King's College, Cambridge.

In the cathedrals a great deal of work continued up to the Reformation. It was at St Peter's Abbey in Gloucester, now the cathedral, that early experiments in the Perpendicular style were made in the course of rebuilding. At Exeter in the fourteenth century the cathedral acquired the longest continuous stone vault of all the cathedrals.

In some places ingenious solutions were found to problems: the collapse of the tower at Ely led to the construction of its stone octagon with a wooden lantern above it, and at Wells, where ominous cracks indicated the tower was too heavy, inverted arches were installed beneath it, which give a unique aspect to the nave.

From the thirteenth to the fifteenth century work continued at York; the minster acquired its present design, and the great east and west windows were installed. Great changes were made at Canterbury, where the Norman nave was replaced in the Perpendicular style; the Bell Harry tower was built, with its fan-vaulted lantern; and a carved stone screen, with steps leading up to it, separated the nave from the choir.

It may be in this amazing outburst of creativity in the church building of the later Middle Ages that the seeds were sown for the popular perception of the Church as buildings rather than its people.

In a society where the Church was at the heart of community life, it was natural that accumulated wealth should be used on church buildings, ostensibly to the glory of God. It is also clear that the wealthy made use of them to make a statement about themselves, their success and status, and to ensure what they saw as a worthy burial in the form of elaborate tombs and memorials, an art form in itself. The installation of benches or pews led to the system of pew-letting, and was another opportunity for the rich to assert their importance. An inversion of basic Christian principles, which set no store by power, wealth and status, was becoming very apparent.

While the building frenzy gave the appearance of a flourishing Church, what was actually happening within the Church, in terms of both belief and practice, gave many cause for questioning. A number of events on the Continent brought their concerns into sharper focus.

New Influences from the Continent

Fourteenth-century Italy had seen the advent of the Renaissance – a renewal of interest in Roman and Greek civilisation in its many aspects: art, politics, philosophy and languages. Its scholars became known as humanists. It spread to northern Europe and reached England towards the end of the fifteenth century. John Colet and Thomas More were among notable Christian humanists. John Colet was an Oxford-based scholar, who gave a series of influential lectures there on St Paul's epistles, advocating a return to the discipline and practice of the early Church. As dean of St Paul's for the last fifteen years of his life, he was in a position of influence. His friend, Thomas More, whose house was a meeting place for the intellectuals of the time, was a lawyer and theologian. He engaged positively with the Renaissance, but did not share the views of Church reformers on the Continent. More was aware of the abuses and failures within the Church, and gently satirised them in his book *Utopia*. He was disturbed as he saw the authority of the Church threatened; an authority that he saw as springing from its centuries-old tradition and the decisions of General Councils. In the face of Protestant activists, he feared anarchy and schism, and believed it right to deal summarily with those seen as heretics. He would also be prepared to stand up for what he believed against the king – as Thomas Becket had done.

In the middle of the fifteenth century, as the new learning of the Renaissance was spreading, came the invention of printing in Germany and in 1476 the first English printing press was set up in Westminster. New ideas could now be spread more quickly and the demand for reading material better satisfied.

Another influence on contemporary thinking came from Holland through a movement known as the "*Devotio Moderna*", a revival in spirituality accompanied by the social involvement of groups of clergy and laity, of men and women. Out of this came a significant community called the "Brethren of the Common Life". They founded other communities that ran their own schools and later their own printing press. Some of their students were outstanding: Thomas à Kempis, author of the *Imitation of Christ*, a devotional classic that is still widely read, was one of them. Erasmus of Rotterdam was another.

Erasmus, who started his career as an Augustinian canon and was ordained a priest, changed course. He gained an international reputation as a very erudite humanist and writer of satire, which he directed mainly at the Church, at monasticism and university teachers (schoolmen as they were called), and their speculations. He was very impatient of superstition and relics, as he was of pilgrimages and indulgences. He wanted a simpler church life and he exposed to ridicule things that he felt needed reform. His amusing style made his books very popular. What also made a great impact was his own edition, in 1516, of the Greek New Testament, using Greek manuscripts, which he published with a fresh Latin translation. He wanted the Bible to be available ultimately to everyone in their own language, including, as he put it, the farm labourer and the weaver. He helped prepare the way for the Reformation; through visits to England his views became well known. He was even drawn into public debate with Luther, but he did not become a Protestant. He was very pro-peace in matters of religion, an attitude that made him settle, in the end, for the stability of church tradition.

The Renaissance had inspired many humanist scholars with a fresh interest in the original Hebrew and Greek texts of the Bible. Up till that time the Latin Vulgate, largely the work of the fourth-century St Jerome, had been the accepted version of the Church. The invention of printing was a further impetus to the work of translation: reformers were inspired to attempt translations into European languages. Luther's German Bible was a significant landmark.

In England it was William Tyndale who earned for himself the title of "father of the English Bible". A Gloucestershire man who studied at both Oxford and Cambridge, he was convinced of the need to bring the Scriptures within everyone's reach and made it his life's task.

Circumstances were not auspicious. Since 1407 English bishops had forbidden any new translation of the Bible to be made without their sanction and had also forbidden the use of the versions Wycliffe had encouraged. In 1520 a group known as the seven godly martyrs of Coventry were condemned for teaching children and family the Lord's Prayer and the Ten Commandments in English. The only support Tyndale found for his banned project came from merchants, but the enterprise proved hazardous: he feared arrest and the loss of his manuscripts, and in 1524 left England for Germany. In the following year his New Testament from the Greek was ready and printing started at Cologne, but he was being watched and had to flee, this time to Worms, where the task was completed in 1526. Further editions were printed in Holland and copies, concealed in cargoes, began to reach England, where they met with strong disapproval from senior bishops and others, including Thomas More. Many copies were burnt. Tyndale spent the rest of his life in Antwerp, where he set about translating the Old Testament from the Hebrew. He also wrote works that showed the extent of his views on Church reform, many coinciding with those of Luther, and his concern with the implications of the Christian faith for daily living. In 1535 he was arrested in Brussels and imprisoned. In the following year he was strangled and burnt at the stake, at little more than forty years of age, his last words: "Lord, open the king of England's eyes". He had not been able to complete his translation of the Old Testament, but the first five books and the book of Jonah had been printed, and further work remained in manuscript. His legacy has remained to this day. His translation formed the basis of subsequent English Bibles, including the Authorised Version. He had an unrivalled sensitivity to language and rhythm; many of his memorable turns of phrase passed into common use, to the great enrichment of the English language.

While the Renaissance and humanist influence, together with the invention of printing and work in Bible translation all contributed to preparing the way for change, it was the role of Martin Luther that proved to be the catalyst that led to actual reform.

Martin Luther

Luther was an Augustinian friar and priest – that much he had in common with the young Erasmus, but Luther was no humanist. He went through a long spiritual crisis, when strict observance of traditional church practice and ritual failed to satisfy him. From his study of the Bible he emerged with a conclusion that became basic to his thinking: that man is justified, or reconciled to God, through faith alone and the grace of God. It was emphatically not achievable through good works and man's own efforts, as much of the teaching of the medieval Church implied, but was a gift from God, through Christ. Good works flowed from it, but did not lead to it.

After his initial public invitation to debate the question of indulgences, his views gathered support and the movement for reform was launched. It was not Luther's intention to divide the Church, but to reform it from within. His stand was Bible-based and he found no Biblical support for the primacy of papal authority. He stood firm against the pope, who excommunicated him, and against the Emperor, who outlawed him.

Elements in the reforms Luther inspired were at the heart of the Reformation as it unfolded: the centrality and authority of the Bible, made available to everyone; the doctrine of justification by faith; and the affirmation of the priesthood of all believers. In his new view of the Church, each individual had access to God through Christ, and the priest was no longer a mediator. The gradual abandonment of Latin in worship for the use of the vernacular had started in earnest. The hymns Luther wrote encouraged further congregational involvement and were an aid to understanding. The new emphasis was on understanding and the individual's thoughtful response, rather than on the routine observances required by the institutional Church.

A major concern of the Reformation centred on the interpretation of the Eucharist. Luther no longer saw it as a repeated sacrifice, which seemed to call into question the sufficiency of Christ's sacrifice. Sacrificial language was removed from the liturgy; there were no more private Masses, and the people received both bread and wine. In other respects Luther's interpretation was conservative: he believed in the real presence of Christ, defining the mystery as consubstantiation, in which the bread and wine remained after consecration, coexisting with the body and blood of Christ. His view was far removed from that of Zwingli, the leading reformer in Zurich, for whom the Eucharist was simply an act of commemoration. Attempts were made to reconcile these two views in the hope of presenting a united Protestant front. Luther and Zwingli, together with other reformers, met to discuss the matter, but Luther was not to be dissuaded from his view.

There were other changes. Because Luther found no scriptural support for priestly celibacy or for monastic vows, priests were free to marry, and monks and nuns were freed from their vows if they wished.

Luther caused great division in his own country and his influence on other countries was immense. In England there were different reactions to events in Germany. Groups met to read and discuss his banned books; they had been burnt publicly in 1521. One particularly active group at Cambridge influenced the future reforming bishops Latimer, Ridley and Matthew Parker. Thomas More became involved in debate with Luther on the subject of the seven sacraments of the medieval Church, which Luther eventually reduced to two: baptism and the Eucharist. Henry VIII himself had joined the debate and gave his name to a paper refuting Luther's views on the subject, for which the pope gave him the title of "Defender of the Faith", ironic in view of the events that were to follow.

Germany was not the only country to wield influence in matters of Church reform. The movement was active in Switzerland. After the disagreement between Luther and Zwingli, the influence of Switzerland tended to increase. There cantons became divided and battles ensued. In one of them Zwingli was killed. His successor at Zurich was Henry Bullinger, who would conduct a vast correspondence with eminent people all over Europe, including Henry VIII, Edward VI and Elizabeth I and her advisers during his forty-four years at Zurich. A tolerant and conciliatory man, he was the major figure in the Swiss Reformation until the rise of Calvin at Geneva.

England had an opportunity to observe and reflect on

what was happening on the Continent before she actually embarked on her own Reformation. In the event it would prove to be quite distinctive both in its initial motivation and in the end result.

IX

REFORMATION

The Church Under Henry VIII

The Reformation in Germany began with the religious convictions of a once-obscure friar of humble stock. In England it was launched by the personal desires of the king. When Henry VIII wished to divorce his first wife, Catherine of Aragon, a dispensation was needed from the pope as head of the Church. Cardinal Wolsey failed to achieve the divorce and left the political scene in disgrace. His immense wealth and power as cardinal and chancellor had alienated many from the papacy.

Henry was able to move the situation forward when he appointed Thomas Cranmer as archbishop of Canterbury. He could not have foreseen how significant the appointment would prove to be. Cranmer, a Cambridge man and a priest, already had Lutheran sympathies, unlike the king; he had even secretly married the daughter of a German reformer. He also believed in royal supremacy over the Church, and saw it always as his duty to serve the king well. He declared Henry's first marriage to his brother's widow invalid; within days Henry's marriage to Anne Boleyn was announced. The pope, predictably, excommunicated the king and declared his divorce and remarriage void. By the Act of Supremacy of 1534 Henry declared himself "Supreme Head on Earth of the English Church", and assumed the functions and rights of the papacy in England. An Act of Succession made the children of Anne Boleyn heirs to the throne.

Some men of principle, such as Thomas More and John Fisher, a former bishop of Rochester, refused to take the oath accepting the new arrangements. Both were executed, to general consternation. There were others who met the same fate, Carthusian monks among them.

By this time one of Wolsey's protégés, Thomas Cromwell, had moved centre stage. Like Cranmer he favoured royal supremacy over the Church. By 1535 the king had made him vicar-general, with major responsibility in matters relating to the Church. Cromwell would introduce statutes in Parliament that allowed the king greater control over new legislation and over the clergy. He was, in fact, one of the architects of the English Reformation in its early stages. In 1536 he organised a visitation of the monasteries – an opportunity to assess their value. They had fallen in popular esteem and were an obvious source of revenue for the king. In the same year the smaller monasteries were dissolved by Act of Parliament. Only in the north was there any large organised protest, known as the Pilgrimage of Grace. It was quickly suppressed and two hundred of those involved were hanged.

Three years later the greater monasteries met the same fate. The friaries too were suppressed, not for their wealth but because they were seen as having close links with the papacy. The king had exercised his power as head of the

Church to the great benefit of the treasury: the monasteries represented around one-sixth of the country's wealth. A great deal of monastic property would pass into the hands of nobles and gentry. A small proportion of the money raised went to educational purposes: a few colleges and schools, and a few professorships at Oxford and Cambridge. A great deal was lost, as auctions were held, and libraries and treasures dispersed, often irretrievably, or destroyed, though some books found their way to colleges and the king himself acquired a large library.

At Gloucester and Bristol, and at four other major religious houses – Chester and Peterborough, Oxford and Westminster – new bishoprics were founded and the buildings preserved. In some places where the nave of a monastery church had been used by local parishioners for worship, as at Shrewsbury Abbey, that practice continued and the parish became responsible for its upkeep. In some cases the townspeople bought the local abbey church, as they did at Tewkesbury. Cathedrals that had been monastic, such as Canterbury and Durham, became secular chapters of canons.

Monasteries had traditionally provided social services such as hospitals, almshouses and schools, and many buildings could have continued to be put to good use. In the event, the Government had ordered them to be demolished. Most were ravaged and left as blots on the landscape, an unedifying spectacle and an ignominious end. By 1540, Cromwell too was seen to have outlived his usefulness and was beheaded, charged with heresy and treason.

While all this ruthless destruction was taking place, more positive action had been taken towards bringing the Bible to the people, something Cromwell, along with

Cranmer, favoured and promoted. After the near obsession on the Church's part with preventing an English Bible falling into lay hands, at the risk of being misinterpreted, there had been some change of attitude. Sympathy with reform had been gaining ground at court and among some bishops.

Tyndale's work of translation had been continued by Miles Coverdale, who published a complete English Bible in Zurich in 1535, based on Tyndale's version, where it was available. Coverdale's translation of the psalms has continued in use through the centuries in the Book of Common Prayer. He had dedicated his Bible to the king, and Cranmer advised the king to allow its publication. Other versions followed and in 1538 there was a proclamation that a Bible – the Great Bible, a revision of Coverdale's – should be placed in every parish church and made available for everyone to read, though not for use in services. In 1543 a reversion of policy allowed only certain social groups to read it: clergy, nobles, gentry and merchants.

The remainder of Henry's reign was characterised by this vacillation between a very tentative promotion of reform and a return to traditional Catholicism, with which the king seems to have been well content in his personal practice. The Ten Articles of Faith of 1536 made some concessions. They recognised just three sacraments: baptism, the Eucharist and penance, rather than the seven of the medieval Church; and also the importance of Bible teaching.

Many feast days were abolished, to general resentment, and between 1538 and 1540 Henry turned his attention to the much-loved shrines. Many major ones were demolished, including that of Thomas Becket, its treasures appropriated by the king, and Becket's name, an unwanted memory, removed from the church calendar. An attack was launched against the abuse of images, and many were removed or destroyed. Lights were allowed only before the rood and the Easter sepulchre.

In 1539 the Six Articles of Faith replaced the Ten Articles of Faith of 1536 and reaffirmed traditional Catholic belief and practice; they imposed penalties for denying transubstantiation, and rehabilitated private Masses, confession, communion in one kind and the celibacy of the clergy. One might imagine Cranmer's wife appearing discreetly at home, or disappearing abroad according to the vagaries of the royal mood. Cranmer actually opposed the Six Articles in the House of Lords – and, remarkably, survived; two bishops resigned. From time to time there was some persecution of Protestants, of those denying transubstantiation and of those supporting Lutheranism. Many books were burnt.

Henry VIII died in 1547. He had made the Church subject to the Crown in Parliament and stripped it of a great deal of its wealth. His greatest concession to reform had been to make an English Bible more available. Most significant for the future, he had allowed his son, Edward, to be educated by tutors who favoured reform. That would become the dominant concern of the young king's reign.

Church Reform Under Edward VI
Edward VI was only nine when he became king in 1547, so government passed into the hands of the Privy Council, led for the first three years by the duke of Somerset, the king's protector and brother of Edward's mother, Jane Seymour. He and many members of the Privy Council were in favour of Church reform.

Parliament repealed Henry's Six Articles and the

laws for trying heretics; there was freedom to print and to circulate the Scriptures, clergy were free to marry, the chalice was restored to the laity, and any remaining images were to be removed from churches. Processions were banned, together with accessories to ceremonies – candles, palms and ashes. A poor box was installed in each church, and the people encouraged to give the money previously spent on images, lights and pilgrimages to those in need.

A new Act was passed to suppress the chantries and guild chapels, which numbered more than two thousand: the doctrine of purgatory, which gave the chantries their reason for being, was quite unacceptable to the reformers. This change was much more keenly felt in local communities than the loss of the monasteries had been. Some chantries that had functioned as schools became grammar schools bearing the king's name; others were lost. Colleges at Oxford and Cambridge that had been chantry foundations were spared, as were some large collegiate schools such as Eton. As with the monasteries, many people of rank and wealth benefited from the spoils of the Church.

Alongside these changes came liturgical reform under the masterly hand of Archbishop Cranmer. He was in a powerful position when Edward came to the throne, not only as archbishop of Canterbury but also as executor of Henry VIII's will and godfather of Edward. His survival against the ever-changing scenario under Henry had been astonishing, but he was above all a scholar and had devoted most of his time to study and writing. He had not been involved in any political intrigue; though others plotted his downfall, the king never ceased to trust him. Cranmer, for his part, had had the canniness to move slowly in matters of change in the Church.

In the new circumstances he wasted no time in

preparing for a new liturgy: he introduced a Book of Homilies to help improve preaching and which explained Reformation thinking; the Epistle and Gospel were to be read in English; a set of devotions, also in English, was introduced into the Latin Mass; and some ceremonies were abolished. These moves climaxed in the first Book of Common Prayer (the Prayer Book), which was the work of a commission of thirteen, led by Cranmer. It was approved by Parliament in 1549 by an Act of Uniformity, making it the only legal form of worship, with penalties for not conforming to it. Bishops were ordered to destroy all Latin service books. The new Prayer Book was based on the Sarum rite, the Salisbury version of the Roman rite that was the most widely used in the country. With Cranmer's wide knowledge, many influences were brought to bear on it, from the early Christian Fathers through to Luther and other Continental reformers.

It had a mixed reception: for the reformers it did not go far enough; for conservative Catholics it went too far. While it kept the structure of the Latin Mass, prayers for the dead and the reserved sacrament, it offered some change in doctrine – the idea of a repeated sacrifice was replaced by an emphasis on the "full, perfect and sufficient sacrifice of Christ". It retained some of the words and signs of the old rite, especially in the prayer of consecration, with some ceremonial and vestments. A lectionary of continuous reading of the Bible was introduced and a new catechism. In 1550 an Ordinal clarified the duty of clergy. No longer was the priest charged to "offer sacrifice and celebrate Mass for the living and the dead", but to "preach the Word and administer the sacraments". Following the lead of Bishop Ridley of London, the Privy Council ordered all altars to be removed from churches and replaced by wooden tables, which could be moved into the nave for celebrations of Holy Communion.

Two rebellions followed the publication of the Prayer Book. In Devon and Cornwall protestors banded together from all over the two counties and marched to Exeter, where they camped outside the city and held it under siege. They demanded that the Mass be restored and the new liturgy, which they described as a "Christmas game" be abandoned, along with all the other reforms under Edward. They wanted a return to old beliefs and ways, which had formed the fabric of their community life. The uprising was short-lived; confronted by a professional army, the rebels were defeated and routed. Many were killed as they returned home. Some four thousand died, and a few priests were executed as an example.

In the same summer there were uprisings of a different flavour in the Midlands and the Home Counties, but concentrated in the east of the country. Those involved included many Protestants; they hoped to exact some social reform from Protector Somerset. Economic conditions were bad, exacerbated by enclosures of land. Many reformers, including Somerset, had social concerns; he had set up an Enclosure Commission in 1548 to inquire into the situation. The term "commonwealth" was widely used. Erasmus, More and Cromwell had provided some precedent for views concerning the common good in society. Bishops Ridley, Latimer and Cranmer were associated with this thinking. Closer acquaintance with the Bible had inspired views on justice and equality at many levels of society. Somerset hesitated to crush a movement for which he had some sympathy. The duke of Northumberland had no such qualms: the uprising was suppressed, Somerset was demoted and later beheaded for treason, and Northumberland emerged as his successor. Indifferent to social reform and not widely trusted, he proved to be even more intent on moving the reform of the Church forward. The king was now twelve years of age, intelligent, well educated, keen to reform the Church and participating more in government.

In 1551 the draft of a second, more radical Prayer Book to replace the first was discussed. Cranmer had consulted widely. A number of reformers had come to England from the Continent. Martin Bucer, a leader from Strasbourg, and the Italian Peter Martyr both had some influence on the redrafting and on Cranmer's rethinking of Eucharistic doctrine, as did John Knox, who would be the prime mover for reform in Scotland. Most significant in the new Prayer Book were the words used at the giving of Holy Communion, "Take and eat this in remembrance that Christ died for thee and feed on him in thy heart by faith with thanksgiving". It presented the Eucharist as an act of commemoration in which the believing recipient received Christ in a spiritual sense through the bread and wine, a significant change in interpretation.

The 1552 Prayer Book proved to be an enduring legacy to posterity. Cranmer's respect for traditional language and structures perpetuated something of the essence of the liturgy to which people were accustomed. His gift for language and his restrained style made the Prayer Book a great literary work as well as a sensitive vehicle for worship. Through its regular use, congregations absorbed the tenets of Protestant faith and the English language was greatly enriched as its phraseology passed into common usage.

The compilation of forty-two Articles of Faith of 1553 completed Cranmer's work. They made clear what the Church of England believed and what it had abandoned from the past. The influence of Continental reformers was apparent, especially that of Martin Luther and of John Calvin.

By 1552 the Frenchman John Calvin had established a theocratic regime in Geneva, believing as he did that the state and Church should work closely together. The Church he inspired became known as the Reformed Church and was quite separate from the Lutheran Church, with a more reformed liturgy and a greater concern for church structures and discipline. While sharing Luther's view on justification by faith, he emphasised the sovereignty of God. Incorporated into his teaching was a belief in double predestination: that God had foreordained some to be saved and others to be condemned, a hard and always controversial teaching. He insisted too on very high standards of morality in Geneva. His ideas spread far beyond that city through his book known as the Institutes, which was the textbook of theology in the Reformed Church for many centuries following. Here, Calvinist doctrine would prove particularly influential in nonconformist circles.

While the second Prayer Book was being prepared, Calvin's influence was felt in England partly through the Polish reformer John a Lasco, whose thinking was similar to Calvin's in some respects. Lasco led a congregation in London of some five thousand Protestant exiles from the Continent. It was a free, independent church where Lasco was supported in his role as superintendent by elders and deacons, as in the Genevan Church. It had its own creed and catechism, its own order of worship, and provided another example of a reformed Church in action. Cranmer chose not simply to follow one model; he considered closely the views of all the leading reformers and all the developments in Europe before the English version of a reformed Church emerged. He had hoped to create a pan-European link between the Protestant Churches of all the European countries, but this did not materialise.

By the end of Edward's reign in 1553 England was far from being a Protestant country, but the new ways were establishing themselves, particularly in the south and south-east around London, and in the areas where the Lollards had been a strong influence. The new English liturgy had replaced the familiar Latin Mass. Congregations were involved to a much greater degree and were receiving more instruction. Churches looked very different, with no images, shrines or lights, with Bible texts on newly white-washed walls and the king's arms where the rood had been. The clergy too looked different: the simple surplice had replaced the old vestments. The social function of the parish church had been greatly reduced in the absence of the guilds; even the church-ales, a main source of revenue, were banned.

Edward's reign had been short, but of great significance, both at the time and subsequently, for its effects on national life. For some it stood for the destruction of the traditional Church. For others it had been a time of excitement, of liberation from the past, a new freedom to think for oneself in matters of faith and a new climate of debate.

With the untimely death of Edward in 1553 at the age of fifteen, all that had been achieved by the reformers seemed threatened at the prospect of the Roman Catholic Mary's accession. The attempt to avert it by making the Protestant Lady Jane Grey Edward's successor was very short-lived: support for Mary, both in Parliament and the country, had been grossly underestimated and ensured that it was, indeed, Mary who succeeded to the throne.

Reversal Under Queen Mary

Queen Mary was the daughter of Catherine of Aragon. Much of her life after her mother's divorce had been one of humiliation, but she had refused to renounce her Catholic faith, even under pressure.

Her prime aim as queen was to restore Roman Catholicism. Bishops who had been removed from their sees under Edward were reinstated. Bishop Gardiner of Winchester became her trusted chancellor. Reforming bishops were imprisoned. Her half-sister Elizabeth, successor-in-waiting, spent some time in the Tower of London, but was later released. Refugees from the Continent left England for Protestant cities in Germany and Switzerland, together with many English Protestants including clergy who had married. There their convictions would be fuelled by their experience of Continental Protestantism, which would bear fruit on their return to England in friendlier times.

Mary chose to marry Philip of Spain, against the advice of Parliament. She hoped for a child to ensure a Catholic succession. The marriage was not popular among her subjects and even prompted a rebellion in the south-east.

All the measures for Church reform taken under Edward were repealed by Act of Parliament. A new papal legate, Cardinal Reginald Pole, arrived in England. He absolved Parliament and the Convocation, the ruling body of the Church, for their schism. The authority of the papacy was restored, though welcomed, it seems, by relatively few, and Pole became archbishop of Canterbury. The old liturgy was restored, and Bishop Bonner of London ordered the restoration to churches of Catholic features that had been removed and, in many cases, destroyed in Edward's reign

– roods, crucifixes, altars and vestments. Some treasured objects came out of hiding.

Laws against heresy were reinstated and in 1555 the burning of some three hundred Protestant heretics began. Many showed great courage. Among them were numbers of clergy, but also many of quite humble status, including women. Five were former bishops. Latimer and Ridley died together, Latimer's words of encouragement to his fellow bishop proved to be prophetic: "We shall this day light such a candle by God's grace in England as I trust shall never be put out". Bishop Hooper of Gloucester and Bishop Ferrar of St David's were also burnt at the stake. Cranmer, after being subjected to prolonged interrogation, recanted his Protestant beliefs. His support for royal supremacy over the Church had been severely tested. His recantation would not save his life, and when he was finally led to his death, he publicly renounced his recantation and offered the hand that had signed it first to the flames. The courage of the martyrs was counterproductive for Mary's cause. The extension of the persecution to all classes gave rise to some anger among the people. In the midst of conspiracies and disappointment at having produced no heir, Mary died in 1558 and Elizabeth I came to the throne, the third of Henry VIII's children to reign.

The Elizabethan Settlement

When Elizabeth became queen she faced many challenges, not least that of holding together a country divided in its view of the Church. Whatever her personal convictions or preferences in matters of religion, her aim was a national Church that would be as inclusive as possible. Many of her subjects were still Roman Catholic; among the Protestants, some would have been content to return to the settlement achieved under Edward, yet others, mostly former exiles returned from German and Swiss cities, would want further reform. The queen chose Matthew Parker, a moderate and scholarly man, to be archbishop of Canterbury.

The repeal of Queen Mary's legislation was the starting point for change. In 1559 Parliament passed an Act of Supremacy and Elizabeth became Supreme Governor of the Church of England, a more discreet title than her father's "Supreme Head", and one that implied trusteeship. By an Act of Uniformity, the Prayer Book of 1552 was reissued with a few changes. The most important was that at the administration of Holy Communion the traditional formula of the 1549 edition should precede that of 1552: the use of both allowed a wide interpretation of Eucharistic doctrine. Both were retained in the 1662 version. The use of the Prayer Book was compulsory as was attendance at church on Sundays, in the hope of reversing the absenteeism of both Edward's reign and Mary's. Between two and three hundred priests resigned or were deprived of their charge, but most continued in their parishes, content to use English in worship and to have the freedom to marry; some served through all the changes of four reigns, from Henry to Elizabeth.

For a time things moved slowly; by retaining some of the old ritual Elizabeth hoped to mollify the Catholic wing. In 1562 Bishop John Jewel of Salisbury wrote his *Apology*, a defence of the Church of England, which he saw as truly Catholic, based on Scripture and the early Church. In 1563 the Articles of Faith were revised and reduced to the 39 Articles that still stand. The established Church was in place, with bishops still in their traditional role, the liturgy, structures and the Articles of Faith very largely as they had been under Edward. Many of the more moderate of the returned exiles, such as Jewel, supported the Elizabethan Settlement; some of them became bishops. An official version of the Bible, called the Bishops' Bible, was issued in 1568, but did not prove anything like as popular as the Genevan Bible that the exiles had produced, in which, for the first time, the text was divided into numbered verses. The Book of Psalms by Sternhold and Hopkins encouraged the already established use of metrical psalms. Hymns were allowed at the beginning and end of Matins and Evensong.

Church music flourished during Elizabeth's reign. Thomas Tallis served as organist and composer in the Chapel Royal during four successive reigns. Providing settings for the liturgy during that time was a challenging task as it alternated between the Latin Mass and the English Prayer Book. He was joined by another outstanding musician, William Byrd, and together they enriched the tradition of church music with motets, anthems and settings for the metrical psalms. Both were Roman Catholic and remained so, their talents allowed to flourish within the comparative privacy of the Chapel Royal.

During the course of the 1560s, more radical voices made themselves heard. For them reform had not gone far enough. The ex-Genevans wanted to put into practice in the English Church what they had experienced in Geneva – a Presbyterian form of church government, less ritual than they found in the Prayer Book, no vestments, no kneeling to receive Holy Communion, everything to be subject to the authority of Scripture, and metrical psalms, but not hymns because they were not scriptural. Increasingly the Calvinists were becoming known as Puritans though the words were not synonymous: not all Calvinists were Puritans and not all Puritans were Calvinists.

In 1569 there was a Catholic rebellion in the north. It was

quickly put down and four hundred and fifty rebels were executed. In the following year the pope excommunicated Elizabeth, freeing her subjects from their allegiance to her. As a result some persecution of Catholics began and the Mass was forbidden.

Goaded by the Catholic rebellion, which they saw as the result of concessions, the Puritans submitted two admonitions to Parliament, where there were many who wanted a completely reformed Church and Prayer Book. The second admonition proposed that bishops should be abolished and replaced by the more democratic Presbyterian system. The queen would not hear of it. The debate continued between Thomas Cartwright, who was the Puritan leader, and John Whitgift, both Cambridge scholars. It was more than a debate about church structures. For Whitgift, the Church was for preaching and the sacraments, while Cartwright saw it as a sacred society that should impose its own discipline on its members and be quite separate from the state. It should be much more proactive in the reform of Church and society, fulfilling its covenant obligations to God; Calvinists made much of the idea of a covenant between God and His people.

When Archbishop Parker died in 1575 the queen appointed Edmund Grindal to replace him, seemingly unaware of his Puritan sympathies. By this time the Puritans were very active in the provinces. The family Bible reading that they encouraged was becoming common. They were also founding lectureships, engaging their speakers to preach in schools, halls and even in parish churches on Sunday afternoons. There were open-air Puritan gatherings called prophesyings. The queen ordered Grindal to suppress them; when he refused, he was suspended for a while from some of his duties.

At his death in 1583, John Whitgift replaced him. He was no Puritan and very concerned at their prevalence, in the court, among the merchant classes and, even more alarmingly, in the Church itself. Groups of ministers in particular areas were meeting together like presbyterial synods. A General Assembly appeared to be meeting secretly. They were not aiming at a separate Church, but to reform the national Church from within: bishops were under threat, work was going forward on an alternative liturgy, on a Book of Discipline and on a Directory of Presbyterial Government, to establish elders in parish churches and local presbyteries of ministers, with one at national level. A quarter of clergy – some five hundred – signed their acceptance of it. Earlier in the decade Robert Browne had set up an independent congregation at Norwich, based on a church covenant. There were other independent congregations in London. This was the beginning of the English Congregationalist movement.

With Spain threatening it was difficult for Elizabeth and her Government to take forceful measures against the Puritans; their support and their wealth might be needed. The defeat of the Spanish Armada in 1588 changed that. England was now secure so action could be taken. An Oath of Loyalty to Queen Elizabeth I and to the Church of England was introduced, along with a Court of High Commission, which sent many to prison. A new Act against Puritans and Separatists meant exile, transportation or death for refusing to go to the established Church. Three prominent Puritans were executed. Browne and other Separatists fled to the Netherlands for a time. Puritanism went underground and became more extreme.

In the last decade of the sixteenth century the Church of England found its most able defender in Richard Hooker and his treatise on the *Laws of Ecclesiastical Polity*. He was a protégé of John Jewel, who in 1562 had produced his defence of the Church of England, which Hooker developed further. For most of Hooker's career he was a much-loved parish priest, and also a gifted theologian with a generous spirit – even those of a different church affiliation might, as he put it, "touch the hem of Christ's garment".

Five books of Hooker's treatise were published during his lifetime, which provided an answer to Puritan views. While for Puritans only what was commanded in Scripture was lawful in the Church, Hooker took a much wider view, claiming the Church to be evolving and Church structures to be open to change under the guidance of the Holy Spirit. Nor did he see the Bible as a set of rules to cover every circumstance. He saw the Church of England as based on Scripture, tradition and reason, three elements broadly mirrored in the evangelical, catholic and liberal views within the present Church of England. The fifth book offers a theological commentary on the Prayer Book which, in his view, contained all that was needful for guidance in the Christian life. He holds a respected place in the history of Anglicanism.

By the 1590s, the Church of England seemed secure, but Puritan opposition had only been temporarily suppressed, and it was quite unacceptable to faithful Roman Catholics, now a minority of the population.

Reformation in the Roman Catholic Church

As the Protestant Reformation had developed through the course of the sixteenth century, so too a Reformation had been taking place in the Roman Catholic Church on the Continent, which would have its effect on this side of the English Channel. In Spain in the 1530s, a group formed around Ignatius Loyola, which would become the Society of Jesus. By developing education to the highest level, the Jesuits became a leading force of resistance to Protestant thinking in Europe and one of the most powerful weapons of the Catholic Reformation.

The century produced a number of outstanding and influential Spanish mystics, such as St Teresa of Avila and St John of the Cross, who not only wrote powerfully on the spiritual life but were also actively involved in reform. The negative side of the Reformation was already manifest in the Spanish Inquisition, which was in place at the end of the fifteenth century, intent on stamping out heresy, and very active against Jews and Muslims.

In Italy new monastic orders had been founded with a view to revitalising the Church. In the 1530s, the papacy itself became involved in reform, on the one hand giving its approval to the Society of Jesus and their missionary work, and on the other setting up the Congregation of the Inquisition in Rome, a high court for heresy trials.

There had, for some time, been a widespread desire for the Church to have a General Council, which eventually began in 1545 at Trent, south of the Alps. It met intermittently over a period of twenty years, interrupted by plagues and battles. While there was some desire for reconciliation with Protestants, most of the participants wanted simply to redefine Roman Catholicism. The result was a very conservative statement of doctrine and discipline, reaffirming transubstantiation, the status of the Virgin Mary, maintaining the seven sacraments of the medieval Church, celibacy for the clergy and Latin as the language of the Mass. Very significant for the future, it acknowledged the need for a better trained and educated clergy: a seminary was proposed for every diocese.

While it was intended to be a council of the universal Church, the representatives at Trent had been mostly Italian. The conclusions of the council were most effective in Italy, but they encouraged reform throughout the Catholic Church and its findings stood for four centuries.

What impact did the Catholic Reformation have on faithful Roman Catholics in England? The law under Elizabeth required all her subjects to attend the services of the Church of England. This many Roman Catholics did while also worshipping in secret according to the Roman rite. Many wanted to be loyal to their church and to their queen. Those who refused to attend the Church of England would become known as recusants. While it is impossible to tell the extent of surviving Roman Catholicism in the country at large, it was still well represented in the north and the south-west at least. William Allen, a Lancastrian and an Oxford fellow, renounced his post to devote himself to training Roman Catholic priests on the Continent for work in England, in order to preserve the Roman Catholic faith in the country. The first seminary he founded, in 1568, was at Douai in northern France. The English College there was quick to expand. The first ordinations took place in Brussels in 1573, and within five years, fifty-two priests had returned to England to an uncertain future. The first to be martyred was Cuthbert Mayne, who was executed at Launceston in Cornwall in 1577, one of the forty martyrs of England and Wales canonised in 1970 by Pope Paul VI.

The Douai Bible, used by English-speaking Roman Catholics for three centuries, was produced by the scholars at the English College, a necessary tool for the priests' training. In 1579 William Allen was invited by the pope to found another English seminary in Rome, followed by others in Valladolid and Seville, before his death in 1594.

A supply of priests for the English Mission was assured. It had, meanwhile, become even more dangerous work. There was talk in Rome and in England of deposing Elizabeth.

In 1568 Mary Queen of Scots had fled Scotland for England. Her presence proved to be a rallying point for plots against Elizabeth, her cousin, in the hope of restoring Roman Catholicism. Mary was not only Roman Catholic but also a granddaughter of Henry VII. The Catholic rebellion in the north followed and was viciously suppressed, while at the same time the pope issued a Bull excommunicating Elizabeth and leaving her subjects free to act against her. This put Roman Catholics in the difficult situation of having to choose between queen and Church. It also increased a fear of Roman Catholics in the population at large. In 1587 Elizabeth reluctantly agreed to the execution of Mary and Parliament introduced legislation against Roman Catholics, while the Catholic Philip II of Spain resolved on a political solution by an invasion of England.

The defeat of the Spanish Armada in 1588 created a strong national feeling and Roman Catholics were even more marginalised. The willingness of families to risk their lives by sheltering Roman Catholic priests, often in elaborately constructed priest holes, was crucial. Many met the same fate as Margaret Clitherow in York, condemned to death in 1586 after several imprisonments, for using her home for the celebration of Mass and for the education of children. From 1577 up to the end of Elizabeth's reign in 1603, of the four hundred and fifty priests trained abroad, one hundred and twenty-three would be executed, along with some sixty people accused of assisting them. Edward Campion was one of a number of Jesuits to meet his fate in this way. First ordained as a deacon in the Church of

England, he was later received into the Roman Catholic Church at Douai and became a Jesuit. Having returned to England to work, he was discovered in hiding and imprisoned. Refusing to recant he was executed in 1581, declaring himself no traitor and praying for the queen – another of the forty martyrs canonised in 1970.

In the latter part of the sixteenth century another Jesuit, Robert Bellarmine, who was involved in the training of English priests in Rome, did for the Catholic Church what Richard Hooker had done for the Church of England when he wrote his *Disputations against the Heretics of our Time*, a thorough and powerful defence of every aspect of Catholic teaching.

The English seminary in Douai was only the beginning of an English presence there. It had made an incalculable contribution to the survival of a relatively small but doggedly faithful minority of Roman Catholics in England, and is remembered there today through the William Allen Association, formed as recently as 1995.

Wales

The response of the Celtic countries to the Reformation was unique in each case. Since Wales had been annexed to England in 1536, the legislation that brought changes to the Church in England applied to Wales. The Church there, with ill-trained clergy and bishops who were often absentees, was not flourishing. The country was poor and sparsely populated, many living in comparative isolation. New ideas may have filtered through to the population in the few towns and ports, and along the border with England where the Lollards had been active. A small number of students who went from Wales to Oxford and Cambridge would have been exposed to the ideas of the Renaissance, of humanism and of Luther. Any impetus to reform the Church would have been confined to a small minority, and the printing of books, which would have helped the process, was slow to get under way: it was expensive and for a limited market.

The Tudor Henry VIII enjoyed a degree of popularity in Wales because of his Welsh descent. His break with the papacy and the dissolution of the monasteries were accepted. Many local people benefited by the acquisition of monastic land, which confirmed their loyalty to the king. The class of minor gentry was increasing.

At the once-great Cistercian abbeys at Neath and Margam, which had made a good recovery in the fifteenth century, there were very few monks. At their dissolution Margam Abbey survived because it was used for parish worship; Neath Abbey became a ruin. In Carmarthen, then the largest town in Wales, with an estimated population of two thousand, few tears were shed at the dissolution of the monasteries. There had been a great deal of ill-feeling and rivalry between the New and the Old Town, where the monks enjoyed privileges over trading and taxes. The Augustinian priory and the Franciscan friary were dissolved.

For twelve years of the latter part of Henry's reign, William Barlow was bishop of St David's and was keen to reform the Church through education. He wanted to establish grammar schools for the education of clergy and laity, such as the one he founded at Brecon, where there were regular lectures in divinity. He saw Carmarthen as much better placed than St David's to play a leading role in the Welsh Church and wanted to move the bishopric there, but the canons were opposed and St David's, with its medieval associations, continued in place.

There were other Welsh voices supporting reform in Henry's reign: the Cambridge humanist and writer, Richard Whitford, wanted a purer Church, but like Thomas More, who was a friend of his, could not approve Henry's actions. Sir John Price of Brecon, a commissioner for the dissolution of the monasteries and a humanist, published the first book to be printed in Welsh in 1546, a primer containing the basics of the faith in the native language – the Creed, the Lord's Prayer and the Ten Commandments.

Soon after Edward's accession William Barlow was succeeded at St David's by Robert Ferrar, also a reformer, but a controversial figure who, in Mary's reign, would be burnt in the market place at Carmarthen as a warning to others who might have reforming ideas. Another Welshman, William Thomas, who had been clerk to the Privy Council in Edward's reign, was also executed.

The more radical reforms of Edward's reign had brought changes to the customary life of the Church in Wales with the removal of guilds and chantries, and the provision of a new liturgy, but for most people the English Prayer Book was no more intelligible than the Latin Mass had been. Reversal under Mary would no doubt have been welcomed, apart from efforts to impose clerical celibacy, long resisted in Wales. The accession of Elizabeth inspired enough fear to send some Roman Catholics into exile and probably caused little more than confusion among those who remained. Yet out of the confusion, the Reformation became meaningful and relevant to Wales, because the queen and her Government recognised the Welsh language as the key to communicating new ideas. An Act of Parliament of 1563 required a Welsh translation of the Bible and Prayer Book to be prepared for use in worship. This proved to be good news for Protestant and Catholic alike – good for the Church, for the language, for literature and for the Welsh sense of nationhood.

The first translation of the New Testament into Welsh appeared in 1567. A preface entitled "Letter to the Welsh Nation" welcomed the Reformation as a return not only to the early Church but to the early British Church. It was accompanied by a translation of the Prayer Book.

This was followed in 1588 by a translation of the whole Bible into Welsh by William Morgan – a landmark event in the life of Wales. A Cambridge man ordained twenty years earlier, he had set himself a formidable task while a parish priest. The translation is rated as comparable with Tyndale's English translation in its felicity of expression and immense influence on the national culture. The Privy Council ordered copies of both Bible and Prayer Book to be provided in every parish church.

In 1595 William Morgan became bishop of Llandaff and during his time there published an improved edition of the Welsh Book of Common Prayer, another event of profound significance for Protestant worship in subsequent centuries.

Not everyone welcomed the development of Welsh as the language of worship. There had been a degree of anglicisation among the expanded gentry class and among the clergy. Others felt it desirable, in the name of unity, that English should be the language of Protestantism.

Both Protestants and Roman Catholics fought for reform and for the allegiance of their compatriots, but those who actively promoted the Catholic Reformation in Wales were often exiles trained abroad, who did not appreciate the importance of the Welsh language. Yet Roman Catholics persisted in their loyalty; there was a very small number in the diocese of Bangor, rather more in the south-west, but particularly in Flintshire and Montgomeryshire and most of all in the diocese of Llandaff. Only sporadically did the Government take action against individuals on religious grounds. It seems most people went discreetly with the flow in successive reigns.

Towards the end of the sixteenth century a number of bishops in both north and south were providing leadership and oversight. The establishment in 1571 of Jesus College, Oxford, promised a greater supply of educated clergy as it increasingly became a college for Welsh students. Along with these signs of hope the degree of acceptance of the Elizabethan Settlement was growing, but without the Welsh Bible and Prayer Book the Church in Wales would not, at that stage, have become part of the established Church in any significant sense.

Ireland

The Reformation in Ireland followed a quite different path, although the situation there had much in common with that in Wales in its poverty; in its sparse, largely rural population; and in its general acceptance of church life as it was in the late Middle Ages.

Ireland in the fifteenth century had achieved a degree of independence from England, but, in the 1530s, Henry VII and Henry VIII had tried to increase English authority in the country. When Henry VIII declared himself head of the Church, the Church in Ireland was included and legislation was passed in 1536 by the Irish Parliament. It became an offence to support papal authority and high treason to refer to the king as a heretic. When it came to the dissolution of the monasteries, it was a patchy process; many persisted into the seventeenth century, some friaries even longer. Little else was changed in Henry VIII's reign.

The more radical reforms under Edward caused resentment. There had been no movement for reform in Ireland to prepare the way. Lollard influence had been negligible. Humanist ideas and Lutheranism may have percolated to the few towns. In theory, the clergy accepted the first Prayer Book of 1549, but made the new liturgy as like the traditional Mass as possible. The more Protestant second Prayer Book presented a problem: few clergy could teach the principles of the Reformation. The reforming Archbishop Browne of Dublin, appointed in 1535, found it difficult to win acceptance for the new thinking when he introduced the use of the Prayer Book to the cathedral. The English Protestant John Bale became bishop of Ossory and met with little cooperation in his diocese. The Observant Franciscan friars made their opposition clear.

Many activities continued as before, including the guilds, since their funds had not been appropriated by the Crown as they had been in England. Chantry priests continued Catholic worship, for a while in guild chapels until driven to resorting to private homes. With the Irish Sea as a delaying factor, the reforms barely had time to take effect when Mary succeeded to the throne and normality could be restored, but her reign was even shorter than Edward's and the reality of Protestantism returned with Elizabeth.

The Acts of Supremacy and Uniformity took effect in Ireland in 1560. In 1564 an ecclesiastical Court of High Commission was set up in Dublin. While most bishops took the oath of allegiance, to keep their position, the bishops of Kildare and Meath refused. There were penalties for not using the Prayer Book in public worship, and crucially, it was forbidden to translate it into Irish. There were fines for not attending church, but no consistent effort to enforce the Elizabethan Settlement. The Government depended on proclamations and fines, and ultimately on force. Periods of toleration alternated with action.

Among the native Irish, the Catholic Church was held in great respect, in spite of the inadequacies of the clergy, which allowed ignorance and superstition to flourish. The reverence for holy places and people had not waned. The friars were highly regarded. There may have been a measure of outward conformity, but the Mass remained.

The Catholic Reformation, in the meantime, was beginning to take effect. Priests were completing their training at the new seminaries on the Continent. A few Jesuit priests came to Ireland and inspired some young Irishmen to join the Society of Jesus. The Jesuits were active in education, which would provide the priests of the future, a need now difficult to achieve in Ireland, which would be more fully addressed by the founding of thirty colleges in Europe for educating in the Catholic faith. A number were also going to Continental universities for higher education. Many Catholics left Ireland for Spain and the Netherlands, then in Spanish hands.

By the 1580s, many people were defecting from attendance at the parish church. A decade later baptisms and marriages were taking place in the home. There were minor rebellions led by individuals. Many risked everything by allowing their homes to be used for teaching and for celebrating the Mass. It was in the 1590s that Pope Clement VIII decided to appoint Irish priests as vicars apostolic to exercise the functions of bishops, since the historic sees were now occupied by bishops conforming to Protestantism.

Meanwhile the established Church in Ireland was realising the need to provide training for its own priests and in 1592 Trinity College Dublin was founded. For faithful Roman Catholics, the road to training for the priesthood was a much harder one and much more dangerous. Nevertheless, they persisted and helped to create in Ireland a unique situation among the Celtic countries in that the majority of the population remained Roman Catholic. The attempt of the Elizabethan Government to impose the acceptance of Protestant doctrine and liturgy without reference to the native language and culture had built in a high degree of failure, and the Roman Catholic Church was becoming increasingly identified with the Irish sense of nationhood.

Scotland

The course of the Reformation in Scotland reflects a doughty spirit of independence. After the death of James V in 1542, his daughter Mary, then a mere baby, became queen of the Scots, which placed her mother, Mary of Guise, in a powerful position as regent. The French alliance was in good heart.

One of the early Church reformers in Scotland, George Wishart, preached reformed doctrines at great personal risk. His impact on John Knox, a farmer's son from Haddington, would be lifelong. Knox became a passionate advocate of the Protestant cause, fiercely anti-papist, and, through his gift as a preacher, enormously influential. When, in 1546, Wishart was taken into custody at Edinburgh Castle, then burnt at the stake, Protestants invaded the castle and took their revenge by murdering the archbishop of St Andrew's, Cardinal Beaton, who was responsible for Wishart's death. The castle was recaptured with the help of French forces and many, including Knox, were taken captive, spending two years as galley slaves.

On his release he returned to England where he was for a time chaplain to Edward VI and had some influence on the redrafting of the first Prayer Book. He refused a bishopric because he did not approve of bishops. The accession of Mary Tudor drove him into exile on the Continent, and he spent time at Frankfurt and Geneva ministering to English exiles. The church Calvin had established at Geneva he described as the "most perfect school of Christ... since the days of the apostles". It was his inspiration.

In the meantime Reformation ideas were spreading, particularly in the Lowlands. In 1557 some pro-reform lords entered into a covenant "to establish the most blessed word of God and his congregation". They became known as the Lords of the Congregation, and had substantial influence as a political party. They had the support of English troops and of John Knox when he returned to Scotland in 1559. It was a year in which the situation gathered momentum, though not without some civil disturbances. At Perth, Knox interrupted the Mass at the Church of St John and preached a fiery sermon against popery. A riot ensued – the church was destroyed as well as the friaries in the town. Such disorder was cut short by the death of Mary of Guise and the departure of French troops. English troops too were withdrawn.

With the death of the regent and the absence of Mary Queen of Scots in France, where she had married the dauphin, the Scottish Parliament seized the moment – a defining moment for the Reformation in Scotland – and declared the country Protestant: the Mass was forbidden, all papal claims rejected and a very Calvinistic Confession of Faith adopted, which Knox and others had drafted.

Knox was also largely responsible for the *Book of Discipline*, which covered every aspect of church life, following the model of the Church Calvin had established in Geneva. It established that ministers should be elected by the people, along with elders and deacons. The country was to be divided into ten areas supervised by ten superintendents, also elected, with a role very like that of bishops, which was particularly necessary in areas where there was no reforming bishop. At the heart of the new arrangements was the vital role of the local congregation. The reformed Church in Scotland was rooted in the people, who had the responsibility of choosing worthy men as ministers, who would in turn be accountable to the people. The development of local and regional presbyteries followed.

These moves by Parliament in 1560 lacked only the queen's ratification to become law. They would be followed in 1564 by the introduction of the *Book of Common Order*, known as Knox's liturgy or, popularly, as the Psalm Book, which was adopted by the General Assembly. It offered a simpler liturgy than the English Prayer Book and was very Bible-based. It showed the influence of the German and Swiss cities where Knox had spent his time in exile.

These three elements, the *Confession of Faith*, the *Book of Discipline* and the *Book of Common Order*, were the foundation of the Reformation in Scotland. They bore the indelible mark of John Knox, the outstanding churchman of his time and an enduring influence on the Scottish Church subsequently.

In the meantime Mary Queen of Scots, now a widow, had returned to Edinburgh and the Roman Catholic Mass returned to Holyrood Palace. It enraged Knox, who repeatedly entered into disputes in his audiences with the queen and preached against this Roman Catholic revival from the pulpit of St Giles where he was now minister.

Mary's subsequent marriages to Darnley and Bothwell, and the intrigues and even murder associated with them led to her being deposed in 1567, leaving her son James, then one year old, as king. He was proclaimed king at the Church of the Holy Rude in Stirling; the preacher was John Knox. The young king would be brought up as a Protestant. The earl of Moray, acting as regent during the king's minority, held a parliament which made the 1560 measures legal. Knox worked closely with him until Moray's murder in 1570. His successor as regent was the earl of Morton, a man of very different views. He wanted the Scottish Church to be episcopal like the Church of England, and subject to the Crown.

In 1572 John Knox died. The reformed Scottish Church was in place, distinctly Calvinistic in its theology. His successor, Andrew Melville, who had spent time in Geneva, made its organisation fully Presbyterian through the second *Book of Discipline*, with assemblies at every level: local, regional and national. It gave parity of status to the offices of pastor, minister and bishop, and made clear its wish to eliminate bishops as traditionally understood from the system.

The Government responded with the so-called "Black Acts" of 1584, reasserting the supremacy of the king, the role of bishops and of Parliament. There were those who wanted conformity with the Church in England. The result was a period of uncertainty in the Scottish Church when the episcopal and presbyterial systems were in contention, though without impairing the wish for a national Church and a desire to reach a compromise.

In 1592 an Act of Parliament largely resolved the matter and Presbyterianism became the norm, but the Crown preserved its right to convene the General Assembly, leaving open the possibility of reintroducing bishops, while allowing ministers to take up vacant bishoprics and to sit in Parliament.

Reformation had been achieved in Scotland with relatively little persecution, rebellion or damage to churches. It had set its face against the apostolic succession of bishops, and against ceremony and vestments. The emphasis on the Bible and on access to it was central. The Geneva Bible became the Bible of the Scottish Reformation, placed in every church and systematically read. The sermon assumed much greater importance and printed sermons became popular reading material. In 1564 the first Scottish psalter of metrical psalms appeared – the only musical element in the service, in line with Calvin's view that only what was Biblical should be used in public worship. There was no instrumental music. A strict discipline was exerted over the moral lives of Church members through the kirk sessions, when ministers and elders heard offenders confess and repent of their misdemeanours during the service. In many places communion tokens were issued to confirm the holder's fitness to receive Holy Communion. Instead of receiving it at the altar rail, the participants sat around a table. It was the intention that services of Holy Communion should be more frequent, but it was a difficult transition for people who were used to receiving it once a year.

As for the monastic communities, they died a slow death, as they were no longer able to celebrate Mass and lead the life traditional to them. Through an Act of Annexation in 1587 the land of bishoprics and abbeys passed to the Crown. Some monastic church buildings continued to be used for parish worship. Others were abandoned and fell into ruin, though some, such as Iona Abbey, were restored at a later date.

The Reformation brought improvements to education in schools and universities, but Scottish Gaelic proved to be one of its casualties. The use of the Geneva Bible and a liturgy in English were major factors in its decline.

Reformation had begun in the Lowlands and spread to the Highlands, but small Catholic minorities remained in the north-east, the south-west, and in the Highlands and Islands. The continuing Reformation in Scotland would centre on the question of bishops and on the relationship to the English Church, since, from 1603 on the death of Queen Elizabeth I, Scotland and England had but one ruler when James VI of Scotland became also James I of England.

Conclusion

With the death of Elizabeth in 1603, a new stage of the lengthy and complex process of Reformation was about to begin. It had made remarkable progress in the sixteenth century against the background of a medieval church tradition that was deeply embedded in society. It had started as a minority interest, which, although concentrated among scholars and senior churchmen, had its representatives at all levels of society in England, at least, thanks to the influence of Wycliffe and the Lollards. Less edifyingly it won the support of many in the upper classes who benefited from the dispersal of church lands. The fact that this was a European movement gave a strengthened purpose to its supporters, many of whom gained first-hand and valuable experience of the Protestant Church in action through their exile on the Continent.

At the heart of the Reformation's progress were the availability of an English Bible to the laity and the spread of literacy. The new liturgy was establishing itself in the hearts and minds of the worshippers, now participating rather than spectating. Printed books offered a new resource. Among them John Foxe's *Book of Martyrs* was encouraged reading. In 1571 the Convocation decreed that it should be placed in all cathedrals, and many parish churches also acquired a copy of it. John Foxe had conceived the idea of writing a history of England's Protestant martyrs while in exile on the Continent in Queen Mary's reign. It was based on letters, witnesses' accounts, and on local and church records. Through its graphic stories of the experiences of martyrs, he aimed to vindicate the Protestant Reformation and expose the errors of the Roman Church. It went through four editions in his lifetime.

Some of his accounts involved women. The Reformation was, in fact, raising the profile of women, through both Protestant and Roman Catholic female martyrs. The influential Calvin in Geneva had recognised their potential: women had, in fact, been active in the Church there before his arrival. The public perception of women, of their ability and spirituality, was slowly changing.

Similarly, the people's view of the Reformation had changed with the succession of four monarchs, each with a very different agenda for the Church, and changed slowly in its favour. After the self-serving changes under the still-Catholic Henry came the genuine church reforms under the young Edward and his protectors. Queen Mary's reign showed the impossibility of putting the clock back and its persecution arguably did more to further the Protestant cause than to weaken it. This was a situation that Elizabeth exploited by aiming to establish as inclusive a Church as possible. That was reassuring initially, but in practice it foundered in the face of two determined minorities, one irreconcilable and the other intent on further reform.

In principle the Protestant Reformation was established in England, Wales and Scotland; only in Ireland had it failed to make an impact on the majority. But nowhere had the Reformation yet run its full course and the minorities of Elizabeth's reign would constitute a problematic legacy for her Stuart successors.

X

AN UNFINISHED REFORMATION

Stuart Rule

James I came to England in 1603 with high hopes. He had ruled Scotland as James VI for twenty years with some success in spite of quarrelsome lords and a Presbyterian Church hostile to royal authority. England must have looked like the promised land: it was wealthier, more orderly in its relationships between king and nobles, and the monarch was head of a Church that had retained its bishops. That fitted better with his view of kingship as being a God-given right to rule Church and state, and of bishops as a protection for that authority.

He was idealistic and took as his motto "*Beati Pacifici*" – blessed are the peacemakers. He hoped to unite his kingdoms, but Scotland and England remained two kingdoms with their separate Churches differently organised. At the beginning of his reign James gave an impression of greater tolerance in matters of faith. The Puritans seized the moment to present him with a petition of a thousand signatures, the Millenary Petition, asking him to complete the Reformation and do away with all that remained of Roman Catholicism – the sign of the cross, bowing at the name of Jesus, confirmation, kneeling to receive Holy Communion and surplices; they were discreet enough not to ask, yet, for the removal of bishops.

The result was a conference at Hampton Court in 1604. The king, bishops and deans, together with the Privy Council, assembled with just four carefully chosen moderate Puritans. Their demands received short shrift. The king took the opportunity to make clear his support for an Episcopal Church. The Puritans achieved little, but towards the end of the conference their spokesman, Dr John Reynolds, dean of Lincoln, made a suggestion that pleased the king: that there should be one translation of the Bible to be used by everyone. James seized on the idea: it would be a symbol of the unity that was his ambition for his people.

The work would be a highly organised joint enterprise on which some fifty scholars, with bishops among them, would be engaged; they would be working in six groups – two at Westminster, two at Oxford and two at Cambridge – with each group allocated a section of the Bible. The work of each group would be checked by the others, and the translation would receive its final form through a final meeting of representatives from each group. The scholars would make use of previous versions, from Tyndale's to the official Bishops' Bible of Elizabeth's reign. Moderate Puritans would be among the translators, but no extremists. Archbishop Bancroft of Canterbury busied himself with the arrangements, when an event occurred that shattered the peace and optimism of the new reign.

Roman Catholics had become disaffected by the king's

attitude. The early impression of tolerance had given way to a calculated distancing of himself from them. A small group of extremists reacted. The Gunpowder Plot, which aimed at replacing king and government by blowing up Parliament at its opening, was uncovered at the eleventh hour in November 1605. In the aftermath of the discovery, there was an inevitable backlash for Roman Catholics in general. They were required to take an oath of allegiance to the Crown; without it they could not hold public office of any kind. Roman Catholic priests and Jesuits were banished. Sermons on the plot became an annual event and perpetuated the story of the survival of Protestant England.

At the other end of the religious spectrum, groups of Separatists continued to meet in conventicles. At Scrooby, on the border of Lincolnshire and Nottinghamshire, they were repeatedly harassed by the authorities, and even arrested. In the summer of 1607, some fifty of them resolved to leave England for the Low Countries and greater religious freedom. For some, their ultimate destination would be the New World when the *Mayflower* sailed from Plymouth in 1620. Their leader, William Bradford, a Lincolnshire man, would become governor of Plymouth, Massachusetts.

Within the main body of the established Church there were signs of a return to some of the ceremonial that had been ousted by the Reformation. It was as if the Reformation was now sufficiently firm to allow the retrieval, from pre-Reformation days, of aspects of church life that some found valuable. The trend can be seen in the life of Lancelot Andrewes, one of the outstanding churchmen of the time. As dean of Westminster he had been involved in the coronation of James. He was a devoted Royalist, at the centre of national life and a regular preacher at the court. He became, in turn, bishop of Chichester, Ely and Winchester, and later dean of the Chapel Royal. He had served his apprenticeship in the Church in Elizabeth's reign. He knew Richard Hooker and shared something of his outlook: both valued tradition, but were not uncritical of it, and both were concerned for the integrity of the Church of England. Andrewes was alienated by aspects of Calvinism and by the rigid approach of many Puritans. He saw some of their concerns as being of secondary importance. For him the apostolic faith of the early Christians, a gospel that embraced everyone, was what mattered most. In the practice of faith the sacraments were central. His own chapel was richly furnished in a way not countenanced by Reformation purists; he defended the use of incense as a return to the practice of the ancient Church. His approach restored something of a sense of mystery and beauty that had been lost in the Reformation's emphasis on the Word, on preaching and the intellect. Andrewes was a great scholar and linguist with a reputation both as a man of prayer and as an inspired preacher. Collections of his sermons and private prayers were published after his death. In them the Bible, the early Church Fathers and Reformation thinking all merge. His approach would influence succeeding generations. It was a part of the poet T.S. Eliot's journey of faith. To the twentieth-century Russian Orthodox theologian Lossky, the breadth and depth of his teaching has much to offer to the ecumenical movement of our time. Andrewes' skill with words was brought to bear on the first five books of the Old Testament as he was director of the first Westminster group of translators. His was a major role in the translation as a whole.

The art of preaching had made a spectacular if patchy recovery during the Reformation. The poet John Donne, as dean of St Paul's, was, like Andrewes, much acclaimed as an inspired preacher. Donne was from a Roman Catholic family; he had changed allegiance, but kept something of the Catholic ethos. He preached regularly at the courts of both James I and Charles I.

In 1611, the new Bible, known as both the King James Bible and the Authorised Version, was published. Its language was rich and sonorous, its tone measured and dignified – qualities that made it well suited to being read aloud. By reference to previous translations it had preserved a degree of continuity. Tyndale's translation had to a large extent survived, sometimes filled out and made more fluid. Yet the new translation was not immediately a wild success. The Genevan Bible continued in its popularity, so much so that in 1616 its publication was forbidden.

The rest of James' rule was a story of poor relationships – with Parliament; with the Puritans, whom he offended by his support for games and dancing on Sundays; and with the Church in Scotland, by trying to impose bishops and to restore practices it had abandoned. Plantations of Protestant Scots and English in Ireland would prove to be a dubious policy with lasting repercussions. For the Church, the most notable legacy from the reign of James I was the Bible that bears his name, which would not come into its own until 1660, with the restoration of the monarchy after the Civil War.

His son Charles I was welcomed at his accession in 1625, but the welcome was short-lived. In common with his father, he held firmly to a belief in the divine right of kings; it made him disastrously autocratic in his dealings with Parliament. Also like his father, he had taken a Roman Catholic wife, so there was a suspicion that he was well disposed to Roman Catholicism. Charles was, in fact, a faithful member of the Church of England, in favour of bishops and a degree of ceremonial. A movement against Calvinism had developed among its clergy and that was quite congenial to the king. The Dutchman Arminius had gained support for his opposition to the Calvinist doctrine of predestination. He insisted that salvation was for all, not just for the elect, and that man had the free will to choose whether to accept it. His more liberal view would influence the development of Protestant theology in Britain, as in Europe generally.

In England the anti-Calvinist party was led by William Laud, who had been influenced by Lancelot Andrewes. He was keen to promote a return of ceremonial and ritual, a restoration of art, organs and music, and altars fixed in the chancel and even fenced off by rails – all in the face of strong opposition from the Puritans, who saw preaching being demoted in favour of the sacraments and Protestantism being undermined. Laud and other churchmen of like mind became known as the Caroline Divines, intent on recovering the purity of the early Church in a Church of England separate from Rome and distinct from the Continental reformed Church. Laud was an ardent Royalist, and after several bishoprics, in 1633 he was appointed archbishop of Canterbury. In that role he dealt harshly with any opposition to his views and made himself increasingly unpopular.

While preaching continued to hold a significant place in the Reformation Church at large, the emphasis that Andrewes had given to prayer and the sacraments, reinforced by Laud, could be seen in the lives of other churchmen. Nicolas Ferrar withdrew from public life to found a unique community for some thirty members of his family at Little Gidding near Huntingdon, where they lived a highly disciplined life of prayer using the Prayer Book. For some the church at Little Gidding savoured of a return to papist ways and the community would not survive Puritan attacks in the 1640s.

Ferrar's friend, the poet George Herbert, also retired from public life and became ordained. During his incumbency at Leighton Bromswold in Huntingdonshire, he had the derelict church reordered; it became an example of a church of the period, with a new tower and nave, and Jacobean woodwork. It kept the movable communion table of the Elizabethan era, but had two pulpits of equal height each side of the chancel arch, one for preaching and the other for prayer, like the church at Little Gidding. This was an arrangement seen as a statement about the relative place of preaching in the liturgy, not to be valued more than prayer. George Herbert was one of the early devotional poets of the Church of England, one in a long tradition of poet priests. Some of his poems in the collection called *The Temple* became hymns of continuing popularity, such as "The God of love my shepherd is". He drew inspiration from the Bible and his own experience to produce poems of apparent simplicity and great sincerity, which appealed to his contemporaries. In the fraught times of the Civil War that would follow, he was widely read by people of different religious and political affiliations. In the rural parish of Bemerton near Salisbury, where he spent the last three years of his life, he wrote his *Country Parson*, in which he defined what he felt country people needed from their priest after a period of great upheaval in the Church: a reassuring balance between the new and the familiar, between reform and tradition, and a sensitivity to the material conditions of their daily life. It was published twenty years later in 1652 and widely read.

In Ferrar and Herbert, as in Andrewes and Donne, can be seen the growth of a distinctive tradition in the Church of England. After a century when Protestant fervour had castigated Rome and portrayed the pope as anti-Christ in language of startling vehemence, a practice that continued unabated, they show a capacity to hold together something of Protestantism and Catholicism, which would lead to a perception of the Church of England as both Catholic and reformed, a *via media*, but a middle way that was also a very broad way, linking at its extremes with Roman Catholicism on the one hand and with evangelical nonconformity on the other.

For the moment the Christian Church in seventeenth-century England was no longer split simply between Protestants and Roman Catholics. A struggle was taking place among the Protestants. Broadly speaking, on one side were the king and many nobles, together with the Laudian party, who were supporting the established Church in a more Catholic or High Church tradition, on the other side was Parliament, along with many of the lower gentry and the merchant class, where the Puritans predominated. When the king, encouraged by Laud, attempted to impose his will on the Scottish Church, the move proved ominous for both. After his coronation in Edinburgh in 1638, with full English ceremonial, which to the Scots smacked of popery, Charles tried to make the Scottish Church subject to Canterbury and to impose the use of a Scottish version of the Prayer Book. When this was first used in the Church of St Giles, Edinburgh, the immediate result was a near riot. The longer-term result was embodied in the Scottish National Covenant, which insisted on preserving Presbyterianism in Scotland. By 1639 the Covenanters had gathered together a large army in the Scottish Lowlands ready to invade England and even hoping to impose Presbyterianism south of the border.

To face the threat of invasion by the Scots, the king needed funds, which only Parliament could grant. After eleven years of personal rule with a council of ministers chosen by himself, he was forced to call a Parliament, but Parliament was not prepared to grant him money before it had settled its grievances against him. The confrontation between king and Parliament had been brought to a head by the Scottish threat. This was followed in 1641 by a rebellion in Ireland by Roman Catholics against Protestants. When the king came to Parliament to prosecute five of his most active opponents, he found they had fled. In their pursuit the king was mobbed and soon after left London. In 1642 the country slid into Civil War, a war of principles sparked off by a constitutional crisis, but with a strong element of religious conflict.

As for Archbishop Laud, his continued high-handedness led to his impeachment by Parliament and imprisonment in the Tower of London in 1641. Four years later he was beheaded, accused of acting against Parliament and trying to restore Roman Catholicism. He had always refuted accusations of being a papist and maintained that the Church of England was closer than any other Church to that of the early centuries.

Civil War

The first period of the war lasted from 1642 until 1646; the second from 1648 to 1649. Royalists and Parliamentarians, or Cavaliers and Roundheads as they came to be known, confronted each other in many battles and sieges. It was deeply divisive; sometimes members of the same family fought against each other. It took a heavy toll among the civilian population as well as among the soldiers. Disease, famine and destitution were widespread. Plunder and vandalism accompanied the fighting. Church buildings were among the casualties, with the fabric defaced, images and stained-glass windows destroyed, Archbishop Laud's altar rails ripped out, and crosses discarded. Many churches were used as soldiers' quarters and as stabling for the horses of the cavalry. Petitions were sent to Parliament by the populace, pleading for an end to the war; ordinary people in the central southern counties and in the Welsh borders tried to restore order in their areas by forming a Peaceable Army. Cromwell did not allow it to survive for long.

In 1643, to settle matters in the Church, Parliament convened the Westminster Assembly. Three-quarters of its members were churchmen of different persuasions; the rest were notable laymen, such as Pym, master of Parliament. The Presbyterians were most heavily represented, but also those from independent churches and Episcopalians, though out of loyalty to the king, these did not often attend. When an alliance was made by Parliament with the Scots, and the Scottish League Covenant was adopted, Scottish representatives were added to their number. The declared intention of this covenant was to oppose "popery and prelacy... and whatsoever shall be found contrary to sound doctrine". Most clergy signed the covenant and became Presbyterian ministers, but an estimated two to three thousand out of some ten thousand clergy lost their livings.

The Westminster Assembly met frequently during the whole period of the Civil War and hotly debated issues such as the sacraments and the Church courts. As a result of their labours they proposed a Directory of Public

Worship to replace the Prayer Book as from 1645. In 1646 bishops were abolished and in 1648 the 39 Articles were replaced by a Confession of Faith. All would be adopted by the Presbyterian Church in Scotland for the long term. In England they were only temporarily accepted and never fully enforced, but for the moment the national Church was officially Presbyterian.

Throughout the Civil War, the role of Oliver Cromwell became ever more prominent. In 1640 he was Member of Parliament for Cambridge, so was involved in the crucial phase of the struggle between king and Parliament from the beginning. At the start of the Civil War he was a colonel in the Parliamentary Army, and by 1645 had helped create the New Model Army and become an army commander. The driving force of his whole career was the conviction that throughout he was doing the will of God. He came to the conclusion that the removal of the king was necessary for the nation to move forward. In 1649 King Charles I was tried, condemned as a tyrant and traitor, and beheaded. In the eyes of some, the king was a martyr. Cromwell was one of the signatories of the death warrant – a fact that alienated some of his former supporters.

The Commonwealth

The country was now a republic. The House of Lords was abolished and by 1653 Cromwell held the title of "Lord Protector of the Commonwealth". During his time in office there was a degree of religious toleration, which did not, of course, include Roman Catholics or those churchmen who remained in favour of bishops, some of whom chose exile, others became private chaplains or tutors, and yet others used the pen to express their views. There were clergy who conformed outwardly while choosing to be ordained secretly by bishops who otherwise kept a low profile. There were some who continued to use the banned Prayer Book; some even learnt to say its funeral and baptismal services off by heart so that they could use them while appearing to pray extempore. Ironically, the situation of those faithful to the Church of England was very like that of the recusant Roman Catholics. The diarist, John Evelyn, records how he invited an Anglican priest to his home to preach to his family and celebrate Holy Communion in the library. It seems the use of the Prayer Book was tolerated in a few London chapels. It was at one of these that Evelyn and his wife attended a service of Holy Communion on Christmas Day in 1657, surrounded by soldiers pointing their muskets at the offending congregation – the celebration of Christmas had been banned, along with other feast days. Daily life had assumed a certain drabness as many of the pleasures of the laity were curbed in an attempt to improve moral standards: alehouses and theatres were closed, gambling discouraged, maypole dancing and cock fighting forbidden, and strict Sunday observance required.

In the course of the seventeenth century Protestants had become more diversified, partly as a result of Archbishop Laud's attempt to impose his own view of the Church on everyone. Nor was Presbyterianism popular. Groups had formed that repudiated the notion of a large institutional Church; some were opposed to certain practices. This was true of the Baptists, who were strongly opposed to infant baptism, favouring adult baptism by immersion. They were divided into two groups; the stricter Particular Baptists were Calvinist, the General Baptists were Arminian, and opposed to the doctrine of predestination.

The Congregationalists who grew out of the Separatist Churches of Elizabeth's reign had greatly increased in number. Each congregation was independent and autonomous. In 1658 representatives of one hundred and twenty of their churches met together at a conference that issued a document, known as the Savoy Declaration, asking for recognition of their form of church government alongside that of the Presbyterians. Some congregations met in castles at Chester, Bristol and Dover. In Exeter Cathedral a brick wall was built to separate the Presbyterians and Congregationalists. They had also become known as Independents. Cromwell himself was more inclined to the Independents than to the somewhat intransigent Presbyterians with their more complex church structures. They were numerous in his New Model Army, in which many officers were preachers; others led prayers among the soldiers.

His policy of toleration did not extend to the groups of Quakers who had spread throughout Britain and Ireland, largely through the influence of George Fox. They were seen as very radical: they rejected both the sacraments and ordained ministers, as well as set forms of worship. Through their refusal to take oaths, to pay tithes and to do military service, they appeared as a threat to society. Many, including Fox, spent time in prison; some hundreds of their number died there.

Jews, on the other hand, who had been expelled from the country at the end of the thirteenth century, were now legally readmitted.

At Cromwell's death in 1658 his son Richard succeeded him, but did not prove to be a strong enough leader. He resigned his position in 1660: the way was open for a return to the monarchy.

Restoration of the Monarchy

With the return of the monarchy came the end of Presbyterianism as the order of the national Church. The parish system was still in place, as were many of the clergy; bishops resumed their role, church buildings were repaired and the church calendar again governed the course of the year. Now it would include a day to remember the death of Charles I. In 1662 a revised version of the Prayer Book was made obligatory, and some two thousand Presbyterian ministers who could not accept it or the requirement to be re-ordained, lost their livings. Many good churchmen were lost to the established Church.

Puritanism had not prevailed. It had started off in the mainstream of the Reformation and had belonged within the Church of England. It had brought attitudes and habits that were in themselves worthy – a disciplined life and a strong work ethic. Yet their suspicious attitude towards pleasure, and their literal reading and following of Scripture were alienating to many.

The court of Charles II was, by contrast, immoral and extravagant. In matters of faith the king was privately inclined to Roman Catholicism, but he conformed outwardly to the Church of England and made life difficult for Dissenters. Unauthorised worship was banned. The Five-Mile Act prevented ministers of dissenting groups from working in towns, where their congregations were mostly based. Later, in an attempt to help Roman Catholics, the king issued a Declaration of Indulgence to allow public worship for them and for Dissenters. Dissenters were sufficiently encouraged to establish congregations, but a year later, in 1673, Parliament responded with the Test Act, which required both an oath of allegiance to the Crown and regular communion in the Church of England of anyone wishing to hold office in the state or the army. The sacrament was being used for political purposes, and a very clear division arose in society between those who belonged to the established Church and those outside it.

In spite of the strictures imposed on them, Dissenters persisted, and even flourished, undaunted when Roman Catholic plots, real and imaginary, led to greater persecution. They and clergy in the Church of England tried to raise moral standards by encouraging personal piety. Texts proliferated on the walls of churches. At Stokesay in Shropshire, St John's Church, rebuilt after serious damage in the Civil War, has many examples. Devotional books became popular reading.

More accessible than most writing of the time, and destined to become an international classic, was John Bunyan's *Pilgrim's Progress*, which appeared in 1678, the first of many editions, with a sequel in 1684. It describes the journey through life of the pilgrim Christian, from the City of Destruction to the Heavenly City, and his encounters and experiences on the way. The work recalls William Langland's *Piers the Plowman*, written two hundred years earlier, though life seen as a pilgrimage is a theme common to all ages. Christian's was a spiritual quest as he "walked through the wilderness of the world", and the work is written in language of a directness and simplicity that could engage readers of all conditions. From the first it was a success with ordinary people; only later was it appreciated by the better educated.

Born in 1628 at Elstow in Bedfordshire, John Bunyan was of humble origin, the son of a tinker, or brazier, a mender of brass. He had some schooling and as a boy attended the parish church. As a young man he served for two years in the Parliamentary Army. For a time he went through a spiritual crisis, when he was influenced by the writing of Martin Luther who had suffered a similar experience. Both were men of the people; both came eventually to a passionate personal faith.

After his conversion Bunyan became a member of an independent congregation in Bedford. A few years later he felt called to be a preacher. At the restoration of the monarchy he refused to give up his ministry or to attend the Church of England, so he spent the years between 1660 and 1672 in Bedford Gaol, "imprisoned until conformity". He did some of his writing during this time, including an autobiography, *Grace Abounding to the Chief of Sinners*. He seems to have been allowed to leave prison on occasion, and continued to be actively involved in the Bedford congregation.

For the last eight years of his life he was a free man, and continued as preacher and evangelist, often visiting and preaching in London. His last written work, published after his death in 1688, was a treatise against the Roman Catholic Church, *Anti-Christ and her Ruin*, occasioned by what he saw as the threat of a return to Roman Catholicism under James II.

From the same period emerged another literary classic, Milton's *Paradise Lost*, which is an account of the fall of man, and its sequel *Paradise Regained*. John Milton was a Cambridge scholar who, like John Bunyan, became a Dissenter. He was not only a poet but a controversialist too, critical of clergy, of bishops and their power, and of an established Church. A pro-Commonwealth man and a secretary to Cromwell, he opposed the restoration of the monarchy and was imprisoned briefly post 1660.

Paradise Lost was written between 1658 and 1665. It aimed "to justify the ways of God to man" and paints a picture of the cause of evil in the world and its consequences. An epic poem on a grand scale unlike anything that had gone before it in English, it assured Milton of permanent fame. Through writers such as Bunyan and Milton, the Puritan ethos continued to be conveyed to the reading public. After Milton's death a work of his on Christian doctrine was published, which suggests that some of his views were unorthodox, particularly on the doctrine of the Trinity and creation. It confirms him as a man of independent thought, one of an increasing number.

The Reformation had indeed set men free from the intellectual straitjacket of the medieval Church. It would lead some to scepticism and some to view the Christian faith more critically. The Bible would come under scrutiny; in particular its chronology, its miracles and its prophecies. Theology would also be questioned, notably the doctrine of the Trinity and the doctrine of the Church as an institution. There was a desire to do away with superstition and ignorance; not surprisingly, there was also a desire to leave behind the long period of religious turmoil and dissension.

The Cambridge Platonists were a group of scholars opposed to extreme positions in matters of faith. Influenced by the French philosopher, Descartes, they commended the place of reason as a guide to revelation. The existence of God was not in dispute: they saw evidence of it in creation, but were relatively uninterested in institutional organisation and dogma, which obscured Christianity as a way of life. To pursue that life, they felt the individual needed the freedom to work out his duties and responsibilities, and that required a tolerant society.

A group of writers known as Latitudinarians, who were eminent churchmen and heirs to the Cambridge Platonists, took up the case of reason as guide and interpreter. Cool reason was in; "enthusiasm" was out. Enthusiasm in seventeenth-century terms stood for religious fervour, even fanaticism. The place of morality was secure – it was reasonable and highly desirable in the period of licentiousness that the Restoration had inaugurated. However, revelation was gradually taking second place to reason and an impersonal God was emerging.

Changes in Church Architecture

Two catastrophes marked the reign of Charles II: in 1665 the Great Plague in which at least one-third of the population died, and in 1666 the Great Fire of London. Among the casualties of the fire were some two-thirds of London's churches – a disaster and an opportunity.

There had been very little building of new churches once the Reformation was seriously underway, rather there was simply the adaptation of existing churches to the new Prayer Book liturgy. Chancels had become less important, altars replaced by tables that could be moved into the nave among the people for the service of Holy Communion, and new uses found for chantry chapels, which were often converted into family pews. Few were more elaborate than the Kederminster pew at St Mary's Church in Langley Marish, Slough, which is almost completely enclosed, though the occupants could see the pulpit through lattice grilles. It had a library installed behind it. The new prominence that the sermon had assumed meant that churches became spaces where the preacher needed to be seen and heard for maximum effect. The seventeenth century saw the advent of three-decker pulpits of imposing height for priest, clerk and reader, which ensured the preacher could be seen over the box pews now installed in many churches and rented out to families, creating a new and reliable source of income. Galleries provided further seating – and viewing. Jacobean woodwork featured in pulpits, pews, lecterns and sometimes in decorative screens, as it does in the church of St John, Leeds, one of the few new churches built in the 1630s. The royal coat of arms surmounts the screen, where the rood and loft would have been in the medieval Church; this was the post-Reformation symbol of the unity of Church and state that was made compulsory after 1660.

It was largely due to the timely genius of Christopher Wren that a new St Paul's Cathedral, the first new cathedral since the Reformation, and some fifty parish churches emerged from the ashes of the Great Fire and transformed the London skyline. Wren had been influenced by a visit to Paris and a meeting with the Italian Bernini, a great exponent of the baroque in architecture. He took the opportunity to break with the Gothic style and establish an English version of the classical style: outside were colonnaded porticos surmounted by towers, steeples and spires in a variety of designs; inside were more columns supporting galleries and domes, bright with light through clear glass. St Stephen's, Walbrook, has many of these features with furnishings still from Wren's time.

Ornately carved woodwork of fruit, flowers, urns and cherubs was a feature of the new furnishings. The font at All Hallows by the Tower is the work of Grinley Gibbons, a master of the art. Similar designs appeared in plaster work. The new motifs introduced a more secular note.

While London burgeoned with new building, there were only isolated examples in the provinces. Wren designed the church of St Mary at Ingestre, Staffordshire, with many features common to his London churches, including a fine plasterwork ceiling. At Tunbridge Wells, a church was built in the style of Wren and dedicated to King Charles the Martyr.

The tradition of English church music which had flourished earlier, most notably through Thomas Tallis and William Byrd, continued through musicians such as Orlando Gibbons and his son Christopher, who were organists in turn at Westminster Abbey and the Chapel Royal. They were followed by Henry Purcell, the outstanding composer of church music of his day.

Charles II died in 1685, after being received into the Roman Catholic Church. He was succeeded by his brother James, already a Roman Catholic: the worst fears of most of the population were realised. Through two Declarations of Indulgence, King James II allowed Roman Catholics and Dissenters freedom of worship. Seven bishops, including the archbishop of Canterbury, refused to read these declarations from the pulpit and were sent to the Tower of London, to be tried and later acquitted. The birth of a son to James and the prospect of a Roman Catholic succession were seen as an imminent disaster. When William of Orange, the husband of James' Protestant daughter, Mary, landed in England at the invitation of Parliament, James fled to France, and William and Mary succeeded to the throne in 1689, an event known as the Glorious Revolution. It brought with it a reaffirmation of Protestantism and a Bill of Rights establishing that no Roman Catholic could succeed to the English throne. It brought also a degree of toleration for Dissenters, who were no longer obliged to attend the Church of England, but were still required to take an oath of allegiance. Thousands of Quakers were released from prison.

Following the Toleration Act of 1689, Dissenter

chapels sprang up all over the country, austere in style, a plain rectangle with a dominant pulpit. In these chapels simpler services took place, consisting of Bible reading, prayers, the sermon and hymns. One of the earliest to be built at this time must have been the chapel in Brook Street at Knutsford in Cheshire, now a Unitarian chapel. Then, the congregation would probably have been Presbyterian, since Unitarians, like Roman Catholics, were excluded from the Toleration Act. Not far from it, in the village of Great Warford, a group of Baptists acquired a small barn and cottage in 1712 which became their chapel. At Jordan in Buckinghamshire, a Quaker meeting house was built at the end of the seventeenth century, characteristically simple in style, with benches on a brick floor, in tune with the simplicity of its meetings; there were no ministers, no set liturgy and no sacraments. Here, William Penn, founder of the state of Pennsylvania in the United States, attended the meetings. Another Quaker meeting house at Come-to-Good in Cornwall remains virtually unaltered since 1710. Everywhere, Dissenters were becoming a visible part of community life.

The Effects of Changes in the Church on Individuals' Lives

The impact of developments in the Church in the course of the seventeenth century is best seen in the lives of individuals. Those who chose to become ordained faced many hazards, as the careers of two contemporary churchmen illustrate: Jeremy Taylor and Richard Baxter were both born during the reign of James I, and both were ordained in the Church of England in the 1630s. Jeremy Taylor was a Cambridge scholar and a gifted preacher, whose career was advanced by Archbishop Laud. He served as a chaplain to Charles II and remained unequivocally a Church of England man. Richard Baxter, by contrast, was a largely self-taught Shropshire man, who found himself sympathetic to some of the views of Dissenters. For twenty years, with some interruptions, he ministered within the Church of England with great success at Kidderminster.

With the advent of the Civil War, both men served in the army, Taylor with the Royalist army and Baxter with the Parliamentarians, both for a time as chaplains. Taylor was imprisoned by the Parliamentarians and, on being released, took refuge in Wales. In 1655 he chose to exercise his calling at a London church and fell foul of Cromwell who had him imprisoned for a time in the Tower of London. In 1658 he left England for Ireland, and at the Restoration he became a bishop in the Church of Ireland, but his ministry was blighted by the antagonism of Scottish Presbyterians, and his own harsh attitude to them and to Roman Catholics.

Richard Baxter had favoured a restoration of the monarchy and was actively involved in bringing it about, but when he later refused a bishopric, he was relieved of his position at Kidderminster. He had long since rejected episcopacy. When the Savoy Conference was called in 1661 to review the Prayer Book, he presented a *Reformed Liturgy*, which he had laboured to produce, as a replacement for the Prayer Book, but it was not considered. In all, some two thousand Presbyterian ministers who could not accept the 1662 Prayer Book lost their livings; Baxter, too, left the Church of England.

For the rest of his life he preached in London as a Dissenter, watched by the authorities and imprisoned in his own house for preaching there. He still speaks to congregations through hymns such as "Ye holy angels bright". He lived to see the end of the reign of James II, and welcomed the Toleration Act under William and Mary, which allowed Dissenting ministers to register their place of worship and to preach openly.

There were many other churchmen who had to pay a price for their principles. Thomas Ken was an incumbent at Winchester who stood firmly against the immorality of the age. He earned the respect of Charles II and was made bishop of Bath and Wells. He was one of the seven bishops who refused to read James II's Declaration of Indulgence from the pulpit and were sent to the Tower of London. There was yet another challenge to come: with the accession of William and Mary, clergy were required to take an oath of allegiance to the new king. This Thomas Ken refused to do, since he had already vowed his allegiance to James II. He was not alone: nine bishops and some four hundred priests also refused and were deprived of their livings – another exodus of able churchmen from the established Church. They became known as the Non-Jurors. Thomas Ken lives on in the hymns he wrote; two of them were for the pupils of Winchester College: one to begin the day, "Awake my soul and with the sun thy daily course of duty run", and another to end it, "Glory to thee my God this night". Hymn writing was still in its early stages.

At the turn of the century other hymn writers were emerging. Isaac Watts, one of the founders of English hymnody, did a great deal to overcome resistance among worshippers to accept hymns rather than the established psalm singing. Many of his hymns remain well loved, none more so than "When I survey the wondrous cross".

Philip Doddridge followed in his footsteps. Both he and Watts came from families of Dissenters on the maternal side, who had fled persecution on the Continent; Watts' mother was of Huguenot extraction and Doddridge's from a Prague Lutheran family. Yet for English families too, standing by their convictions was a risky business in the seventeenth century. Watts' father had been twice imprisoned; Doddridge's grandfather had lost his living in 1662. Both men became pastors of Independent congregations after receiving their training at Dissenting Academies: Oxbridge colleges were meant for members of the Church of England. Doddridge saw hymns as a way of teaching and illustrating his sermons. His "Hark the glad sound! The Saviour comes" continues to be a popular Advent hymn.

Even those who had no strong allegiance to the Church faced unexpected challenges. The diarist Samuel Pepys was a tolerant sceptic, though with a remnant of childhood faith that made him observe the conventions of church attendance from time to time. His career at the Admiralty brought him into close contact with King Charles II and his brother James. Rumours about Roman Catholic plots were rife at the time, and there was a great fear of a return to Roman Catholicism when James would become king. Pepys found himself faced with accusations of being a papist and even spent a brief period in the Tower of London. He worked assiduously at his own defence only to find the witnesses brought against him had melted away. His fortunes were later restored, but he could quite easily, like many another similarly accused, have been imprisoned indefinitely, or worse. It is small wonder that he took the precaution of applying to a local vicar for a certificate of regular attendance at church and another proving that his wife had died a Protestant – a small insurance for the future.

The Development of Societies

Pepys' wide interests led him to become a member of the Royal Society, founded in the middle of the seventeenth century to encourage research in the sciences and to provide a forum for debate. Individual scholars of stature were exerting considerable influence on attitudes to religious faith, leading some to atheism. The mathematician and physicist, Sir Isaac Newton, another member of the Royal Society, had a great interest in matters theological. For him, the order and beauty of the world were proof of the existence of God; knowledge and faith were mutually illuminating, but he could not accept the doctrine of the Trinity. The philosopher, John Locke, who did not underestimate the importance of belief, was a strong advocate of toleration, though this was a limited toleration that excluded Roman Catholics and atheists: in his view they were a threat to the state. For him, reason was the key to both natural and revealed religion. He expounded his views in a book entitled *The Reasonableness of Christianity*, which appeared in 1695 and caused some controversy. The Irishman, John Toland, went further in a book he entitled *Christianity not Mysterious*. He dismissed the supernatural in Christianity as of pagan origin. It aroused shock and horror, and the book was burnt in Ireland. Toland's book defines the movement of thought known as Deism, which was developing towards the end of the seventeenth century and that reached its fullest expression in the following century. Essentially it was a belief in natural religion. Many Deists gradually abandoned the idea of a God involved in His Creation and the belief in a life after death. Its most extreme form was reduced to a belief in an impersonal Creator God, a view that was strongly challenged by men such as Joseph Butler in his *Analogy of Religion*, and

William Law, in his *Case for Reason*. Both argue that reason has its limits, and that revelation and faith are necessary. Deism did not have as large a following in England as it did in France and Germany.

While scholars speculated, the Church was deeply concerned about the generally low standards of morality and levels of education. One of its initiatives was the founding of societies. In 1691 Societies for the Reformation of Manners were formed, which aimed at making the justice system more effective in dealing with immorality. At the turn of the century two of the most enduring missionary societies were founded: the Society for the Propagation of Christian Knowledge (SPCK), which encouraged the setting up of charity schools throughout England and Wales, and increased the supply of Bibles at home and abroad; and the Society for the Propagation of the Gospel (SPG), which developed the missionary work abroad that SPCK had begun. Both were founded by Thomas Bray, a parish priest who had already set up some eighty parish libraries to improve the level of education among the clergy. Part of his very active parish ministry was a concern for London prisons, which led to a Government enquiry into prison conditions. A humanitarian interest in disadvantaged groups was growing and philanthropy spreading.

The more tolerant reign of William and Mary came to an end in 1702. Mary's sister Anne succeeded to the throne and restored the fortunes of the High Church party for which William, as a Calvinist Presbyterian, had had little sympathy. A new Act required fifty new churches to be built to serve London and its growing suburbs. Fewer than half that number materialised. The architect Nicholas Hawksmoor, who had been an assistant to Sir Christopher

Wren, designed six of them; two – St George's, Bloomsbury, and Christ Church, Spitalfields – have recently been restored to their former glory. In the same period James Gibbs added two notable churches to the London scene in St Mary's-le-Strand and St Martin-in-the-Fields, which was built by subscription as the parish church of Buckingham Palace, and where George I became churchwarden, an office first established at the beginning of the seventeenth century.

This was not the only encouragement Queen Anne gave to the Church. Through a fund that became known as Queen Anne's Bounty, the stipends of very poor clergy were increased; well over a thousand had been worth less than £10 per year. The fund continued to assist the Church of England up till the twentieth century, when it was merged into the work of the Church Commissioners.

Queen Anne died with no heir and the succession passed to the House of Hanover, through a Protestant descendant of James I. In 1714 George I inaugurated a new chapter in the English monarchy. In this way it was hoped to foil Stuart claims to the throne, a measure justified by the Jacobite risings of 1715 and 1745, both of which failed. From that time onwards, prospects for Roman Catholics gradually improved.

Scotland

Outside England the rule of the Stuarts had impacted in different degrees on the Celtic countries, but, at every turn of events, on Scotland in particular; this was partly because a Scottish king ascended the English throne and because the Scottish people, in opting positively for the Reformation, had chosen a very specific model of church polity in Presbyterianism, which they refused to renounce.

The determination of both James I and Charles I to impose an Episcopal Church resulted in the Scottish National Covenant of 1638, signed by three hundred thousand, which claimed the Church of Scotland to be Presbyterian, and independent of king and state. The subsequent invasion of northern England by a Covenanter Army persuaded the king to cede to their claim. An alliance was formed between the Covenanters and the English Parliament in 1643 – called the Solemn League and Covenant. When Charles surrendered to the Scots in 1646 he hoped to break the alliance, but when the Scots demanded that the English Church be made Presbyterian he refused. He was handed back to the English and to his grisly fate in 1649. In the meantime the Westminster Assembly had produced the Directory of Church Government, the Directory of Public Worship and a Confession of Faith, all accepted temporarily in England, but adopted for the long term by the Church of Scotland.

The execution of Charles I did not meet with widespread approval in Scotland. His son was crowned Charles II at Scone in 1651 and he led an army south, only to be defeated at Worcester by Cromwell's army. He fled abroad and Cromwell effectively ruled Scotland with England until the restoration of the monarchy.

Unfortunately for the Scots, the restored Charles II considered Presbyterianism "not a religion for gentlemen". Bishops returned and attendance at the newly ordered Church became compulsory. The Covenanters took to meeting in conventicles and became a more extreme group, even going so far as to murder the archbishop of St Andrew's. The more moderate majority, chiefly in the Lowlands area, were not prepared to accept an Episcopal Church either. The Test Act of 1681 required all office holders to reject the covenant and a period of persecution followed. When the Roman Catholic James II succeeded his brother in 1685, his attempt to promote religious toleration did not work out in the conditions of Scotland. There was still a minority of faithful Roman Catholics in the Highlands and Islands; in the north-east the Episcopal Church had not lost favour, while Presbyterians were particularly strong in the Lowlands area. Everywhere in seventeenth-century Europe conformity to the state religion was the norm and seen as essential to national unity. Religious minorities were treated harshly. The art of peaceful coexistence had yet to be learnt.

When James was deposed to make way for the Protestant William and Mary, Scotland was prepared to accept their rule provided their national Church was Presbyterian. This was agreed, and many Episcopalians and the more radical Covenanters who did not accept William were forced out of their livings. The Church of Scotland remained Presbyterian and a minority Episcopal Church continued alongside it, under lingering suspicion because of its Stuart sympathies.

In 1707 in Queen Anne's reign came the Act of Union; England and Scotland became Great Britain. Scotland lost her Parliament, but the independence of the Church of Scotland was recognised, as were her legal and education systems. The Act was generally supported in the Lowlands, but continued subsequently to be resented by many Scots. In the north, particularly in the Highlands, there was still a degree of loyalty to the Stuarts. The first Jacobite rebellion of 1715, when the son of the ousted James was declared king, was short-lived: as a Roman Catholic supported by the French, his claim had only limited appeal. The second rising of 1745 was much more successful, as Scots responded to the charismatic Bonnie Prince Charlie, but it ended in defeat at the battle of Culloden. After Culloden every effort was made to destroy the clan system and the culture that went with it.

Wales

In Wales in the early seventeenth century the established Church of England was generally accepted; Roman Catholics were represented by only a small minority and Puritan influence was not as strong as in England, so it was a quieter period in Wales than in Scotland.

In 1620 a revised version of the Welsh Bible was produced by Richard Parry, bishop of St Asaph, and has remained in use, like the English Authorised Version. The foundations of the hymnody, which would flourish in later centuries, were laid by Vicar Prichard, who was later chancellor at St David's, and by Edmund Prys, who wrote versions of the psalms in simple language and metre.

Under the Commonwealth, an Act was passed in 1650 for the Better Propagation and Preaching of the Gospel in Wales. Almost three hundred Anglican clergy were ejected and preachers were appointed. Dissenting groups increased, particularly of Baptists and Presbyterians, but also of Quakers. They would form the basis of future dissent in Wales, though many Quakers and Baptists emigrated to Pennsylvania in the 1680s.

With the Restoration and the Act of Uniformity in 1662, an Episcopal Church of England was re-established, and Dissenters risked fines and prison by persisting. The new Prayer Book of the same year appeared in Welsh two years later.

By the 1670s, there was clearly a variety of views in Wales, yet a degree of cooperation developed between

Anglicans and Dissenters. In 1674 a Welsh Trust was set up by men concerned for the spiritual welfare of the people. Its dual purpose was to establish schools to teach the poor to read and to provide good reading material, all with a view to evangelism. There were new editions of the Bible, the Prayer Book and Prys's Psalms as well as a church catechism. Out of these efforts emerged Welsh pietism, expressed in household devotions and in a concern with morality and education. It embraced both Dissenters and Anglicans.

There was some change in this cooperative approach in the 1680s as Church of England clergy tried to win over Dissenters, but the 1689 Act of Toleration under William and Mary was an encouragement to Dissenters to build their own chapels and license their own preachers. One of the earliest chapels to survive is Maesyronnen, near Glasbury in South Wales. Registered in 1697, it seems to have been in use long before that – its list of ministers begins in 1645. Once a barn, its early furniture remains on the flagstone floor: the pulpit and reading desk, the seat for the deacons, benches, pews and a centrally placed table dated 1728, with benches either side for the taking of Holy Communion. The oldest surviving Quaker meeting house in Wales, The Pales, at Llandegley near Radnor Forest, is thought to date from around 1717 and is still in use.

In the first quarter of the eighteenth century the SPCK took up the mantle of the Welsh Trust and founded around a hundred charity schools in towns and villages in Wales. Elementary education was slowly expanding; there were grammar schools in towns, a Dissenting Academy in Carmarthen and diocesan libraries for clergy. School expansion continued through the remarkable work of Griffith Jones. He came from a family of Dissenters but was ordained into the Church of England. He travelled around as a preacher and set up circulating schools for children and adults, run by travelling teachers. With help from bodies such as the SPCK there were more than three thousand schools at his death in 1761.

All this activity in education, the publishing of Welsh books and the growth of pietism among the committed spelt positive progress for Wales, but this took place against a social background of poverty, low moral standards and increasing scepticism.

Ireland

In predominantly Roman Catholic Ireland, hope had revived at the beginning of the seventeenth century on the death of Elizabeth. Roman Catholics took over the churches and restored Mass in some of the towns, before the Government stepped in and the faithful would yet again look outside the churches for their spiritual sustenance. In 1612 the Government saw fit to make an example of a Roman Catholic bishop and a priest, whom they accused of working against the Government. They were executed in Dublin, martyrs to the large crowd who witnessed the deed.

The main problem for the Roman Catholic Church was to establish structures to ensure a continued ministry to its flock. Continental seminaries were supplying priests who were working – not without some conflict – alongside the friars. The towns were reasonably well served and ministry was spreading in rural areas. Since all tithes went to the established Church of Ireland, Roman Catholic clergy were supported partly by funds from the guilds, which had not been suppressed in Ireland, but also by family, so the clergy depended to a large extent on the laity. Central to ministry were religious instruction and the Mass, held in houses and in the open air. Gradually there was some building of chapels or Mass houses. Catholics paid fees to Protestant clergy, then went to their own clergy for baptism, marriage and funerals. The success of the Roman Catholic Church prompted the Government to close chapels and ban priests in 1629, but it failed to enforce the measure.

There were violent episodes as the century progressed. In 1641, thousands were killed in an uprising in Ulster of the Old Irish against the new immigrants, who were mostly Scottish Presbyterians planted by James I. In 1649, following the execution of Charles I, Cromwell arrived with his army, intent on the conquest of all Ireland in the hope of suppressing support for Charles II. After massacres at Drogheda and Wexford, he left his son-in-law to complete his work. There were pockets of resistance up till 1653 and very great loss of life.

During the Commonwealth period, a great deal of property was transferred from Roman Catholics to those prepared to support the army and to army officers. Land held by Roman Catholics was reduced to little more than one-fifth of what it had been. At the same time, the parish system of the established Church in Ireland was falling into disarray as its ordained priests were hounded, some executed and some deported. About one and a half thousand left the country.

With the restoration of the monarchy in 1660 a proclamation banned meetings of all religious groups except the Church of Ireland, with its bishops now restored. A small proportion of land was restored to Roman Catholics.

In the towns, relations between Old English Catholics and Protestants were improving, when one Titus Oates raised an alarm about an alleged Roman Catholic plot to assassinate Charles II. Many innocent people were arrested. The Roman Catholic archbishop of Armagh, Oliver Plunket, who had worked successfully to raise moral and educational standards in his diocese, was taken to England, tried for treason and executed at Tyburn in 1681. He was canonised in 1975.

More violence was to come when William and Mary replaced James II; the deposed king made for Ireland and tried to re-establish himself there. The unsuccessful siege of Derry and the Battle of the Boyne in 1690, when James was defeated by William of Orange, put paid to his hopes.

The harassment of Roman Catholics continued: as non-communicants in the established Church and by refusing to take the oath of allegiance to the king, they were excluded from Parliament, from the legal profession and from local civic offices. In 1697 Roman Catholic priests were required to leave the country; many complied. For those who remained, an Act of 1704 required them to register themselves and their parishes, and to find two guarantors for their good behaviour. Lay Roman Catholics often had to testify as to where they had last heard Mass and who the celebrant was. Rewards were offered to any who caught a Roman Catholic priest fulfilling his calling. Such action was counterproductive; it increased the people's regard for their priests, and their faithfulness to the Mass and to other devotions – to the Virgin Mary, to the Stations of the Cross and the Rosary. The importance of the native language had been recognised: a translation of the Bible into Irish was now available. Some attention was being given to the need for education through the hedge schools run by itinerant teachers and through some parish schools.

Dublin, which had been for the most part Protestant,

was now a largely Catholic city with a parish system and chapels. In parts of western Ireland there were not enough Protestants to fill the necessary civic offices and a degree of tolerance resulted in these circumstances. With the departure of the Stuarts and the change to the Hanoverian dynasty in 1714, Roman Catholics acquired freedom to worship and hold minor offices; their situation was improving but two centuries of religious differences and brutally suppressed rebellions, deeply etched on the national memory, together with the extreme poverty of the masses, left an explosive legacy.

By the middle of the eighteenth century a society more akin to our own was emerging: increasing travel, expanding trade, the growth of towns and industry, developments in science, a degree of secularisation and more open debate. The Age of Reason, also known as the Enlightenment, spanned the eighteenth century. It took a critical look at established ways of thinking, and in doing so challenged the traditional authority and dominance of the Church.

Persecution, witch-hunts and civil strictures had failed to produce one national Church. The Dissenters had held firm despite all the difficulties put in their way, as had faithful Roman Catholics. The very existence of these minorities – together comprising about a tenth of the population – continued to be a provocation, particularly to High Churchmen. In 1709 one of them, Sacheverell, chose the emotive November 5th to preach a sermon at St Paul's on "The Perils of False Brethren in Church and State". Riots followed, and six Dissenter Chapels in London were attacked and damaged. There were disturbances in other towns and cities.

Such outbursts of violence were rare. For the most part the Church of England displayed little vitality, weary after two centuries of change and debate, wanting to present itself as a Church of moderation, neither as authoritarian as the Roman Catholic Church nor as individualistic as some Protestant sects, and certainly with no taste for fanaticism, otherwise known as "enthusiasm".

In the parishes, clergy were required to provide services of Matins and Evensong on Sundays, and Holy Communion at least at festival times. In the intellectual climate of the day they were more concerned with preaching than with the sacraments, with morality rather than mystery. Some bishops saw little of their sees; they were often politically involved and all were required to sit in the House of Lords. On their brief diocesan visits, confirmation services involved hundreds, even a thousand candidates; the individual laying on of hands was sometimes reduced to a general blessing. The practice among clergy of holding more than one living meant many parishes had no resident clergy.

Among the faithful there were those for whom the routine provision of the Church provided little satisfaction; some formed devotional groups, looking for a deeper spiritual understanding and experience. For others there was not even routine provision by the Church. Population increases in towns and cities exposed an acute shortage of churches, while even in existing churches the practice of renting seats left little room for the poor. Living conditions in the new urban areas cried out for attention.

The established Church seemed unable to harness its considerable resources to meet felt needs. Its governing body, the Convocation, ceased to meet after 1717, so it lost even a forum for discussion. In the event it took the inspired activities of a few individuals to inject a new dynamism into Church life through religious revival.

XI

RIVAL EXPRESSIONS OF CHURCH

The evangelical revival of the eighteenth century was part of a more widespread phenomenon in the Protestant world. One of its earlier manifestations was in 1720s America, where it was known as the Great Awakening. Here the first signs appeared in the 1730s in Wales.

At its heart it maintained the need for an experience of conversion that was life changing. The revival rehabilitated revelation and the supernatural, which rationalism had marginalised. The Bible and its authority were central to it; preachers, for the most part itinerant evangelists who were powerful communicators, stressed man's sinfulness, the reality of hell and the need for repentance. They reached parts of society untouched by the conventional Church: sprawling urban parishes, industrial communities and rural areas, where preachers challenged the individual to respond.

The movement was not dependent on buildings: meetings usually took place in the open air, of necessity given the huge crowds that attended, and were frequently accompanied by emotional scenes, a fact that fuelled a lot of criticism. Nor was it dependent on clergy: lay people became deeply involved and many became lay preachers.

A leading figure in the evangelical revival was John Wesley, from the High Church end of the Church of England, and founder of Methodism. Yet even before his ministry got underway, a spontaneous movement had started in Wales. Its initiator was another High Churchman, Hywel Harris, of Trevecca, near Hay-on-Wye, who, after a conversion experience in 1735, embarked on an itinerant ministry. Later in the same year he met up with a priest from Cardiganshire, Daniel Rowland, whose experience was similar. They worked together as evangelists. Among Harris's converts was William Williams of Pantycelyn, one of Wales' finest hymn writers. He could hardly have foreseen the success of his hymn "Guide me, O thou great Jehovah". Williams was ordained a curate, but was encouraged by another pioneer evangelist, George Whitefield, to persist with an itinerant ministry outside his parishes. It was in the 1740s that the group acquired meeting places for preaching and educating, and formed an association.

George Whitefield meanwhile had started a successful open-air ministry in Bristol. The son of a Gloucestershire innkeeper, he had worked his way through Oxford. There he had met the Wesley brothers, John and Charles, and had become ordained. He was a gifted orator, dramatic and intense, able to sway his hearers powerfully. Whitefield was a Calvinist, a believer in predestination, and, through his visits to Wales, contributed to the establishment of the Calvinistic Methodists as a distinct denomination – the only one to originate in Wales. Although he worked with Wesley for a time, their differences over theology marked the parting of the ways – John Wesley was not a Calvinist, but Arminian in his thinking: salvation for him was open to all, not just to a chosen few. Their differences gave rise to a division in Methodism itself, which became either Wesleyan or Calvinist.

Methodism had its origin in Oxford in the 1720s, where John Wesley and his brother Charles formed a group of like-minded Christians for prayer, Bible study and regular communion. It was nicknamed the Holy Club, and their strictly regulated ways earned its members the name of Methodists. As part of their commitment they also became involved in visiting the local prison and other pastoral work. George Whitefield joined them in the 1730s, by which time John Wesley had been ordained as a priest.

On an unsuccessful mission to the American state of Georgia, John Wesley was deeply challenged in his faith by an encounter with some Moravians, a devout Christian sect that saw personal conversion as essential to becoming a Christian. Wesley felt his life up till that time had been lacking in this respect, but, in 1738, he did undergo an experience that reassured him when he wrote that he "felt his heart strangely warmed" and that "he did trust in Christ and in Christ alone for salvation". His brother Charles had already had a similar experience. For both it was a significant milestone.

It was in Bristol that John Wesley first preached in the open air at the invitation of George Whitefield, an event that confirmed him in his view of "all the world as his parish". His preaching attracted vast crowds of largely ordinary, uneducated people. The hysteria that often accompanied his meetings gave him a reputation as a rabble-rouser in some quarters. Many bishops were hostile to his methods; some clergy were antagonistic; most churches became closed to him. He continued undaunted, travelling the length and breadth of the country on horseback, covering thousands of miles each year. He was not always welcomed; on occasion, he met with hostility and violence. In the wake of his preaching, groups were organised under local leadership. Later they were formed into circuits under the care of travelling preachers – Wesley had a gift for organisation and for him conversion was only the beginning of a new life. A strict discipline was enforced on his converts, who were encouraged to strive after Christian perfection. There was a puritanical side to his ministry, which was strongly opposed not only to drinking and gambling but also to card playing, dancing and the theatre; great stress was laid too on strict Sabbath keeping, attitudes that became part of the Methodist ethos.

The movement he led was quite independent of the established Church, to which Wesley still belonged and that was totally opposed to lay preachers and field preaching. He gradually established meeting houses in Bristol, Newcastle and London. The New Room in Broadmead, Bristol, was built in 1739 – a Georgian chapel with box pews, galleries and a dominant pulpit, where John's brother Charles was minister for a time. Charles made his unique contribution to the movement and to posterity through his prolific hymn writing; some of his hymns are still firm favourites, such as "Love divine, all loves excelling". This was far from being his only contribution. From the beginning he was very involved in preaching and pastoral work, and drew many to Methodism by the warmth of his personality. His gift for friendship and his conciliatory approach to difficult relationships and situations proved a great asset to the movement.

In 1744 John Wesley arranged a conference in Bristol

for his lay preachers and established rules to govern the organisation. The meeting became an annual event and a hundred members were appointed to be in charge of directing the movement. It acquired a legal constitution in 1784. He had always wanted the Methodists to remain a part of the established Church. Towards the end of his life he wrote, "I live and die a member of the Church of England", a position also true of his brother Charles. During his lifetime John Wesley had ruled autocratically, but through his gift for organisation and leadership, the movement had already developed into an independent system, which enabled it to continue after his death in 1791.

The familiar figure on horseback, singing hymns and praying as he journeyed from one preaching venue to the next, was lost to view, though subsequently recalled in a statue near the New Room in Bristol. His legacy was assured. He had been courageous and single-minded, entirely focused on the task he felt had been given to him: to save souls. In later life he had become a much-respected figure. His main influence had been among people unattracted to formal religion. Through him, many found faith, fellowship and self-respect. At his death, they numbered about seventy thousand, but by the middle of the nineteenth century there were close to half a million. He had also inspired an active involvement in social work and philanthropy.

During his lifetime Wesley had shown scant regard for the authority of the established Church. After his death Methodism gradually separated from it and became part of the nonconformist scene. As Wesleyan Methodism settled into a middle-class respectability, numbers broke away to form other groups. The Primitive Methodist

Church, particularly, was concerned with reaching out to agricultural labourers, miners and other industrial workers. Charismatic leaders rose from their own ranks and by the mid-nineteenth century membership had reached around a hundred thousand.

George Whitefield meanwhile had followed a different path, which included many visits to America. He and the Wesleys were Anglican priests who chose to work outside their Church's structures. Other evangelically minded priests of the established Church chose to stay within the system. These men were at first widely scattered. Many had come to see the need for revival from their own experience in a Church that was at a low ebb, lacking both vision and vitality. Among them, Henry Venn exercised a powerful ministry to the workers of his Huddersfield parish; John Newton, a former slave trader, and author of "Amazing Grace" and other hymns, had become an evangelical priest at Olney in Buckinghamshire; and Samuel Taylor of Truro led a revival movement in Cornwall. On the whole, the Anglican evangelicals tended to put less stress on feelings and maintained the practice of their Church's traditions. It was difficult for them to make much headway: many livings were in the gift of patrons, who, for the most part, did not favour evangelical priests. They depended on the exceptional sympathetic patron, such as the wealthy countess of Huntingdon. Alternatively a new church in the growing towns might offer the possibility of a placement. At Cambridge the influential evangelist Charles Simeon set up the Simeon Trust to buy livings for evangelical priests.

However, the evangelical wing of the Church of England did not depend solely on clergy. Towards the end of the eighteenth century, one group of affluent lay Christians was well placed to make an impact on society. They lived and worshipped in Clapham, and became known as the Clapham Sect or "the Saints". They addressed many issues of the day in the name of their faith, the most celebrated of them the anti-slavery campaign that made William Wilberforce a household name. As an MP he became the spokesman in Parliament, but he worked in conjunction with many others for whom it became a life-dominating mission. Quakers were involved from the early days. It gradually became a national campaign, using the press and Parliament, mass meetings and petitions in support of their cause. After a long Parliamentary struggle, traffic in slaves was abolished in 1807 and slavery itself in 1833.

Wilberforce championed other causes, such as the reform of morals through the Proclamation Society. The Clapham Sect was involved in the interdenominational British and Foreign Bible Society, and in setting up the Church Missionary Society. They supported the Religious Tract Society, which aimed at disseminating Christian literature.

Extending education was one of their major concerns. Charity schools, with the support of Anglicans and Dissenters, had achieved some success in providing a basic education. In 1780 Robert Raikes of Gloucester embarked on a new venture when he set up a Sunday school to teach reading and to give religious instruction. In spite of the long hours on the only non-working day for the children who attended, the idea was a great success. As owner of a provincial newspaper, Raikes gave it publicity and Sunday schools were gradually set up throughout the country.

One of the people inspired by Raikes' experiment was Hannah More, a popular writer associated with the Clapham Sect. With her sister she spent some years in the Mendips, where living conditions were very poor and where she was confronted by the Church in one of its weakest aspects: in thirteen neighbouring communities there was not one resident clergyman. Hannah and her sister set up schools and societies where children and adults learnt not only to read but also to spin, which was to alleviate their poverty; all were given religious instruction.

Apart from the evangelicals in the Church of England, there was a group of High Churchmen, known as the Hackney Phalanx, who recognised the need for new churches and schools, and supported the Church Building Society and the National Society to fund church schools, which was set up in 1811.

While there were signs of revival within the Church of England and Methodism gained ground, the old Dissenting churches seemed to have lost something of their initial vigour. Quaker numbers had halved since the seventeenth century, partly due to emigration. Some Presbyterians were becoming Unitarians, a sect that developed in the course of the seventeenth century, which rejected the doctrine of the Trinity and the divinity of Christ. It became an official denomination in 1773. Although at first Dissenters were inclined to view Methodist practices with distrust, new breakaway groups with an evangelical flavour formed gradually from among their ranks. The result was a great variety of Protestant groups by the end of the eighteenth century and a renewed confidence among Dissenters. One expression of this confidence was the setting up of missionary societies. Another was the building of more and larger chapels, some of them more ambitious architecturally than the earlier modest and unobtrusive ones. The Octagon Chapel in Norwich was built in 1756 for Presbyterians. It has classical features – a portico and columns outside, and more columns and galleries inside.

It served as a model for many other chapels. Methodism continued to expand. Before the end of the century, the building began of Bethesda Chapel in Hanley, Stoke-on-Trent, where there was no parish church. It would seat three thousand people – nonconformity had faith in its future.

For Roman Catholics the situation had taken a turn for the better during the course of the eighteenth century. As the century moved to its close, a series of Catholic Relief Acts were gradually lifting the disabilities they lived under, allowing them to acquire property for chapels and schools. After the first of these Acts in 1778, there were public protests culminating in the Gordon Riots of 1780, when a large demonstration led by Lord George Gordon marched to Parliament, attacking Catholic houses as they went, to demand the repeal of the Act. It had to be dispersed by soldiers, and almost three hundred demonstrators died. Anti-Roman-Catholic feeling was still well and truly alive, but such public protest was intermittent.

By the beginning of the nineteenth century there was deep concern over the established Church. In 1832 Thomas Arnold, headmaster of Rugby School, expressed the opinion of many that no human power could save the Church of England in the state it was in at that time. It was seen to be failing in many ways: not coping with the movement of the population to industrial areas, not providing adequate pastoral care, its services were uninspiring and its churches neglected. Almost half the clergy were non-resident in their parishes.

With the example of the French Revolution still fresh, there was some fear of social unrest. Given the role the established Church was seen to have in preserving social order, Parliament was moved to take an interest in its reform. It began by voting to provide one and a half million pounds for church building. Many felt it was also time to address the grievances of Dissenters and Roman Catholics to ensure their loyalty, and Parliament began the process of dismantling the disabilities they still lived under. In 1828 the Test and Corporation Acts were abolished. The Catholic Emancipation Act followed in 1829. All were now free to play an active part in society, both locally and in Parliament. In 1832 the Great Reform Act gave the vote to more, largely middle-class, people. Civil registration of births, marriages and deaths was allowed; marriage could now be celebrated in licensed chapels – a new degree of toleration and equality was being achieved.

Another major initiative was the setting up of the Ecclesiastical Commission in 1835 for the better management of the resources of the Church of England. Some reorganisation of parish boundaries made way for new parishes, two new bishoprics were established at Manchester and Ripon, pluralities were significantly reduced and the income level of the poorest clergy was raised. Clergy attitudes were changing; the number of services and parish activities was increasing, and lay people were more involved. There was greater supervision in dioceses. The future of the Church of England looked rather more secure after this period of reform, which coincided with the accession of Queen Victoria to the throne in 1837.

In Wales meanwhile, nonconformity was rapidly becoming the dominant form of Christianity. The Calvinist Methodists, the largest denomination, had spread from South to North Wales, where Bala became a significant centre. It was not until 1811 that they seceded formally from the established Church, with their own ordained ministers and licensed buildings. It was presbyterian in organisation, and since Presbyterians were traditionally Calvinist, it also became the Presbyterian Church in Wales. The Baptists and Congregationalists had also increased in number as a result of the revival movement.

Many new chapels were built, often in discreet rural places since there was still the possibility of violence against nonconformists. They were small and simple in style externally, and equally unadorned inside, providing an appropriate setting for uncomplicated services of Bible reading, extempore prayers and powerful sermons, accompanied by the fervent hymn singing characteristic of Welsh congregations. Pentre Llifior, near Berriew, is one of a number of Wesleyan Methodist chapels built along the border with England – it is a small, rectangular building of red brick, built in 1798, with a Georgian interior of box pews and a gallery; opposite it was a stable for the ponies that brought worshippers, sometimes over long distances, to the denomination of their choosing. Preachers too were well travelled. At the National History Museum of Wales in Cardiff is a small Unitarian barn chapel of 1777, Capel Penrhiew, moved from its original site in south Cardigan where Unitarianism was strong. Nonconformity flourished and everywhere the chapels had a powerful impact on the local communities that had given them birth, through preaching, mid-week meetings and Sunday schools, and not least through the high moral standards expected of members.

By contrast, the established Church in Wales was seen by many as the province of landowners and industrial managers, often English speaking. Its bishops were seen as political appointees, some of whom did not even set foot in their diocese. Some attempt was made to address the training of clergy by the establishment of St David's College at Lampeter. The Ecclesiastical Commission of 1836 gave some impetus to the building of churches and schools, and to reorganisation in industrial areas to prepare the way for new parishes with residential clergy.

The Roman Catholics in Wales continued to be a small minority, but numbers were slowly increasing through the arrival of Irish immigrants.

In Scotland, where the cause of Dissent had already won the day in the form of the Presbyterian Church, the evangelical revival was slower to make its mark. The Enlightenment had found a home in eighteenth-century Edinburgh, where there was a flourishing intellectual life with a cosmopolitan flavour, which fed into Scottish life and culture.

In the Church of Scotland the Moderates were dominant; their tone rational and their sermons moralising. There were a few evangelicals, some in Edinburgh churches, such as John Erskine, who were popular among the people. The Presbyterian Church did not approve of itinerant preachers. John Wesley's twenty-two visits to Scotland met with only limited success, though a few Methodist chapels were founded. The church of St John, in Arbroath, was opened by John Wesley himself in 1772, built in the octagonal style that he favoured. The brothers James and Robert Haldane were native itinerant preachers and philanthropists who made their mark throughout Scotland, expanding the Scottish school system, organising the Society for the Propagation of the Gospel at Home and setting up colleges to train evangelists.

While not an especially active period in church building, the eighteenth century put its stamp on some new churches. The church of St Andrew and St George in

Edinburgh's New Town, with its elegant spire and classical façade, is one example. At Tynet, in Moray, St Ninian's tells a different story: the Roman Catholic church was built to look like an unobtrusive sheepcote at a time when its members were not yet free to practise their faith.

By the early nineteenth century Thomas Chalmers was working as an evangelical minister in Glasgow, very involved with the poor and encouraging the building of new churches to meet the needs of a growing population; two hundred were built in four years. He was to play a dramatic role in the story of the Church of Scotland. He became an academic at St Andrew's and Edinburgh, and moderator of the Church where evangelicals were beginning to predominate.

In 1843 he led a major exodus from the Church, an event known as the Great Disruption. About one-third of its members and ministers were involved, and they formed what became known as the Free Church. They left on a matter of principle over the question of patronage: patrons were imposing their choice of ministers on churches. Those who left were defending the independence of the Church as a spiritual community and were prepared to give up the privileges of an established Church to preserve that freedom. They aimed to create a parallel Church, relying entirely on their own resources. In four years they set up some seven hundred congregations in their own church buildings and almost six hundred schools; four colleges to train its ministers soon followed – a remarkable achievement.

Those who remained in the Church of Scotland were mostly Moderates, with a sprinkling of evangelicals and some liberally minded churchmen, which led to a degree of questioning – about Darwinism, about Biblical criticism and even about the deeply entrenched Calvinism. Only slowly did theological debate open up in the course of the nineteenth century, eventually allowing some diversity of views, rather than deposing individuals for questioning Calvinist doctrine. One of these was John McLeod Campbell, removed from his post as minister in Row, Strathclyde. He continued to minister to an independent congregation in Glasgow. Another was Edward Irving, who founded the Catholic Apostolic Church, a forerunner of the Pentecostal Church.

The growth of the industrial population in the Lowlands area led to church building by all the denominations, though Scottish congregations did not depend on buildings when occasion demanded. The first service of the Free Church took place in a tent. Sometimes portable pulpits were used by preachers to address crowds in the open air, perhaps during a mission or at the twice-yearly gatherings in the Highlands and Islands for Holy Communion, which served people from a large area. These were great occasions lasting several days.

Services centred on the Word: the Bible was read systematically, and preached on powerfully and at length, preferably without notes, just as extempore prayer was preferred to formal or read prayers. The congregations could expect to be severely dealt with when they lapsed from the high standards required, whether the sin was Sabbath breaking, drunkenness or simply absence.

Unaccompanied metrical psalms continued to hold pride of place in the singing, led by a precentor. Gradually, some hymns were being accepted as the century progressed and the first Scottish Presbyterian hymn book appeared in 1786. We owe to Scottish hymn writers such favourites as "O worship the King, all glorious above" and "We plough the fields and scatter". The use of musical instruments had been totally discouraged in the Scottish Reformation. Only slowly would they become part of worship again in the later nineteenth century.

In the Highlands people were experiencing the pain of the Clearances, as they were forcibly moved out of their homes for the land to be exploited for sheep rearing. In 1824 Thomas Telford was engaged by the Government to design and build thirty-two churches and manses in the Highlands and Islands; the parish church on the island of Iona is one of them. Many Roman Catholic communities had survived in this part of the country. Their numbers were being augmented by an influx of Irish immigrants to the industrial Lowlands and in particular to Glasgow.

The minority Episcopalian Church, which had suffered for its Jacobite sympathies, had benefited from an Act of Toleration passed in 1712 and numbers began to increase in the Lowlands. It was moving towards greater conformity with the Church of England. Recognising its relatively small size, the number of its dioceses was reduced to seven and its chief bishop became known as primus rather than archbishop.

In Ireland in the late eighteenth century, where the majority were Roman Catholics, unrest had already given rise to the formation of local groups with grievances, both Protestant and Catholic. The uprising of 1798 led to the Parliamentary Union of Great Britain and Ireland in 1800. All the British Isles were now ruled from London.

As for the Roman Catholic Church, the legislation of the later eighteenth century, culminating in the Catholic Emancipation Act of 1829, had allowed Roman Catholics religious freedom. It triggered a massive programme of expansion and reorganisation. In 1795 Maynooth College was founded for the training of priests. A wave of new church building began and there was a revival of monastic orders. There was also a rapid increase in the number of schools, in which nuns and the Christian Brethren played a significant role. In 1831 National Schools were set up, in theory non-sectarian, though very largely attended by Roman Catholic children, given their greater numbers. Missions were sent to small towns and rural areas. Ceremonies, such as marriage and baptism, confession and funeral services were gradually transferred from homes to the churches. The parish system was now free to develop. Catholics bought their own cemeteries, and began their own registration of baptisms and marriages – their sense of identity was reinforced. Irish Catholicism was being transformed.

Among the Protestant minority, John Wesley's visits to Ireland, though initially of limited success, were beginning to bear fruit as evangelism spread. They would in time become the third largest Protestant group. Meanwhile the established Church in Ireland had received some stimulus from the evangelical revival in England, but in 1833 the Government introduced the Irish Churches Act, which realistically recognised the limited numbers of members of the established Church in Ireland and their distribution in the population. It proposed to redraw the boundaries of bishoprics and to reduce the number of bishops by ten. The revenue gained would be given to poor livings. The Government could have had little idea of the repercussions that would follow in the wake of the Act.

The Oxford Movement

For some in the Church of England the Irish Churches Act was a step too far by the Government. In their view, the

Church should be free to order its own life as a spiritual community without interference. The same principle had brought about the Disruption in the Church of Scotland.

In response, John Keble, an Oxford professor, delivered a sermon entitled "National Apostasy" from the University pulpit, later seen as the beginning of the Oxford Movement. At the outset it was very much a university affair – a number of academics had become deeply concerned that the Church of England was both in decline and under threat, partly through Government reforms granting toleration to Dissenters and Roman Catholics. With a Parliament no longer dominated by Anglicans, disestablishment was a real fear. From among these concerned academics, John Henry Newman, vicar of St Mary's, Oxford, and Edward Bouverie Pusey, professor of Hebrew, would become, with Keble, the leaders of the movement.

Keble's sermon was followed by a series of tracts that raised questions about the nature of the Church, its authority, its ministry and its sacraments. As a result, those involved in the movement became known as Tractarians. Newman's sermons at St Mary's and a series of his lectures were published, and helped spread their ideas.

They set out to defend the integrity of the Church of England, a middle course between Roman Catholicism and Protestantism, and to revitalise it in the tradition of men like Richard Hooker, a tradition that had been maintained to some extent by High Churchmen.

They had a deep concern for the historical Church and the Catholic tradition in a way that was entirely in keeping with the 39 Articles and the Prayer Book, but they saw some aspects of the Reformation in a critical light. Their greatest inspiration lay in the writings of the Early Fathers and in the primitive Church. They set out to demonstrate that the authority of the Church of England lay in the fact that it was Catholic – a branch of the Church universal, and continuous with the primitive Church. This continuity they saw as bound up with the apostolic succession through the early Church and the Roman Catholic Church, which gave it an authoritative ministry instituted by Christ when he appointed the apostles. The ordination of clergy by bishops in the apostolic succession guaranteed the validity of the sacraments and safeguarded doctrine.

In worship they wanted to recover a sense of the corporate dimension of the Church, by contrast with the Protestant emphasis on the individual. They emphasised the importance of the sacraments, currently underrated in favour of preaching. Baptism and the Eucharist were for them special means of grace, and they encouraged more frequent celebrations of Holy Communion, a radical and permanent change in Church practice, which in time led to the regular Parish Communion.

In daily life the pursuit of holiness was for them an integral part of Christian life – an ongoing process requiring commitment and self-discipline. Practices that had fallen into disuse were reinstated: confession was recommended and fasting before Holy Communion; religious communities reappeared. Those who subscribed to this approach became known at this time as Anglo-Catholics.

The reaction of many to the movement was hostile. Protestantism was strong and criticism not welcome; anti-Roman-Catholic feeling was running high so soon after the Emancipation Act and the Tractarians were seen as Romanists, or "covert papists". Then in 1841 came Tract 90, in which Newman asserted that the 39 Articles of the Church of England were capable of a Catholic interpretation, and that they condemned only abuses that had arisen in the Roman Catholic Church. For those who saw the movement as veering towards Rome, this was the last straw. Even many of his fellow Anglo-Catholics disagreed. The bishop of Oxford forbade the continuation of the tracts.

Newman gradually withdrew from active participation. He had begun to question whether the Church of England was indeed a real Church. He had been brought up in the evangelical part of the established Church, but his spiritual journey led him to Rome in 1845. He was not alone in changing his allegiance; for the first time since the Reformation, the numbers of converts to Roman Catholicism were significant. In his autobiographical *Apologia pro Vita Sua* and in an essay on the development of Christian doctrine, which suggested that each age will interpret the faith for its time, he defended his stance. His legacy as a thinker remains, and also hymns such as "Lead, kindly Light" and "Praise to the Holiest in the Height". He joined the Oratory of St Philip Neri, founded during the Catholic Reformation, and established a branch in Birmingham. After his departure Pusey became the leader of the movement and continued actively to promote it. Keble served for thirty years as a much-loved parish priest at Hursley in Hampshire.

The movement spread into the parishes, and entered a second phase in which ceremony and ritual revived from medieval Church practice became characteristic features: vestments, crucifixes, incense, candles, genuflexion and the use of holy water. Those who promoted them became known as Ritualists. Serious efforts were made through legislation to curtail these practices. Five priests were brought to court and received short sentences.

In the same period their sense of social responsibility led some Tractarian priests to become deeply involved in slum areas, where, in lives of devotion and self-sacrifice, they inspired great respect and affection. Father Lowder was a typical example: when he set up St George's Mission in the East End of London there were no communicants and no school. He gathered a team around him and together they provided pastoral care and teaching, inspiring worship and social activities. After twenty-five years, there were four hundred and fifty communicants and eight hundred children in school. Work in the slums would soon be shared by women. Some ninety new Anglican communities came into being in the latter half of the nineteenth century for the ten thousand women who saw the life as their vocation.

The Oxford Movement was not congenial to many in the Church of England and it was strongly opposed by the evangelicals. It did, however, influence many aspects of church life. It offered a renewed devotional depth to worship and set high standards of discipleship. It contributed to the self-understanding of the Church of England and extended its breadth in a Catholic direction, which, in time, would feed into the ecumenical movement. Its leading personalities had stimulated thought within and beyond the bounds of their own Church.

In Cambridgeshire the Camden Society, founded in 1839, formed a counterpart to the Oxford Movement. Founded for the study of ecclesiastical art, it inspired a great deal of interest in church architecture and, in particular, in a renewal of the medieval Gothic style as an appropriate setting for Anglo-Catholic worship.

Enormous churches were built, for the most part richly decorated with carving in wood and stone, with painted ceilings and murals, and stained-glass windows.

The altar was once more the central focus, often raised on steps in the chancel, where the decoration was richest and where choir stalls were restored for robed choirs. The church of All Saints in Margaret Street, London, is an early example from the 1840s. In Bournemouth, St Peter's and St Stephen's are both in the Gothic style. St Peter's is full of colour and decoration, and its south chapel is dedicated to John Keble, who worshipped there in his retirement. St Stephen's by contrast is more austere. Many others were built in the same style: St Agnes's, Sefton Park, Liverpool, and St George's, Stockport, among them.

The partnership between William Morris and other artists and craftsmen, formed in 1861, made a significant contribution to the interior decoration of churches. The church of All Saints at Selsey in Gloucestershire displays their work in stained glass in a series of windows telling the Christian story in the medieval tradition. The Arts and Crafts movement, from around 1875, continued the revival of decorative art and superb craftsmanship, seen in its many aspects at Holy Trinity Church in Sloane Street, Chelsea.

It was a period that produced many great architects, who were often commissioned by individuals to build new churches: sometimes by aristocrats, as in the case of St Mary's Church at Climber in Nottinghamshire, and sometimes by wealthy clergymen, as at Highnam in Gloucestershire. There was also a great deal of Victorian restoration of churches, some of which was ruthless until it was eventually curbed.

Both the Oxford Movement and the evangelicals had contributed to renewal in the Church of England. There were other factors which helped the process. Bishops were less politically involved and a greater sense of vocation was developing among the clergy, helped by schemes of theological training. The order of deaconesses was restored and lay readers were trained to assist the clergy. The diocese became a stronger local unit. The Convocations of Canterbury and York were revived. The Church was becoming stronger in relation to the state. It was also making its presence felt more effectively in industrial areas.

Roman Catholic Emancipation

Meanwhile the Roman Catholic Church had made great progress. The Catholic Relief Acts of the late eighteenth century had allowed chapels to function as long as they were registered. However, it was still a Church that lacked the support of parish and diocesan structures. The Relief Acts had also allowed Catholic schools. Before the end of the century, Jesuits had returned from Belgium to found what was to become one of the largest Roman Catholic schools in England at Stonyhurst in Lancashire. Douai College in northern France, which had been closed by the French Revolution, founded St Edmund's near Ware in London and Ushaw College in Durham. English Benedictines returned from France to found schools at Downside near Bath, and at Ampleforth in Yorkshire. Even before 1829, the Roman Catholic Church was making progress.

English Catholics were concentrated mainly in Lancashire and the north-east, in the West Midlands and Hampshire; they kept a low profile socially, their worship was sober and they were not overtly pro-Rome. They were soon to be outnumbered: the potato famine in Ireland in the 1840s brought a large influx of Catholic immigrants to industrial areas and cities, and particularly to Liverpool and Manchester. In terms of faith they had more in common with Continental Catholicism in that their worship was more colourful and demonstrative, with images and processions, and they were more Rome-orientated. They were also mostly very poor, with little education, and a threat to the English labour force. That fed into already-existing prejudice and hostility. Anti-Catholic publications fanned the flames, intensifying popular perceptions of Roman Catholics as having a suspect dual loyalty to the Crown and the pope, and as being idolatrous in the practice of their faith. Various Catholic publications also emerged. The situation was full of tensions, expressed periodically in anti-Catholic riots during the course of the nineteenth century.

The number of converts to Roman Catholicism through the Oxford Movement encouraged some leading Roman Catholics to believe England might be on the verge of becoming Roman Catholic again. In 1850 a major initiative was taken to restore the hierarchy. The vicars apostolic became bishops, with Cardinal Wiseman at their head as archbishop of Westminster. The move caused a great furore and became known as the Papal Aggression.

Cardinal Wiseman had spent twenty-two years at the English College in Rome, so had little first-hand experience of English Catholicism, just as English Catholicism had retained limited contact with Rome for three centuries. It had to adjust to his ultramontane approach, looking to Rome for direction and authority. He saw the religious orders as a valuable resource, and new orders for men and women were founded. Itinerant missioners came from new Italian orders to give support.

When the hierarchy was restored, William Ullerthorne was made bishop of Birmingham. From a Yorkshire Catholic family and a descendant of Thomas More, he had become a Benedictine at Downside. At Birmingham he oversaw a great expansion of the Church in all its aspects: in church building, and in the numbers of priests, religious orders, charitable institutions and elementary schools.

As a minority group that had been kept on the margins of society for a long period, Roman Catholics had to undergo a process of assimilation in many areas. Education and the question of separate schools, where children would be nurtured in the Roman Catholic faith, was one of them. Gradually, elementary schools and later secondary schools and training colleges were set up. Ironically, when Oxbridge opened its doors to Roman Catholics in 1856, they were officially forbidden to go there until a Catholic university was established, a decision only reversed in 1895.

Dealing with widespread poverty, particularly among the immigrant communities, was another problem area. Workhouses were seen as being for Protestants. Special Catholic organisations came into being, such as St Vincent de Paul's charity. Over a period of time Catholic children's homes were set up.

As a backcloth to its many-sided activities, the Roman Catholic Church was becoming more visible in the community through its church buildings. Augustus Pugin was among its finest architects. As a member of the Camden Society he had been a passionate advocate for a revival of the Gothic style. In 1845 he became a convert to Roman Catholicism and designed some seventeen Catholic churches, of which St Giles in Cheadle, Staffordshire, is considered one of his outstanding masterpieces, a splendid recreation of a medieval church. His work included the Roman Catholic cathedrals of St George at Southwark and St Chad in Birmingham. Other architects went along with the preference for the Gothic style. The Church of the Holy Name in Manchester's Oxford Road makes a massive statement to the world around it. Some resisted the choice: the Brompton Oratory of 1880 is Italian baroque in style and was commissioned by F.W. Faber, another convert from the Church of England.

In 1865 Cardinal Wiseman died and was succeeded at Westminster by Henry Manning, who, like Newman, had started life in the evangelical wing of the Church of England and participated in the Oxford Movement before his conversion. He became as ultramontane as Wiseman, seeing Rome as the focus of authority in the Church. He was consequently not wholly in tune with the English Catholics.

The pope of the time was Pius IX, a popular figure concerned with revitalising the life of the church and resisting liberalism in all its forms. During his long period in office, some thirty-two years, he approved the dogma of the Immaculate Conception – that the Virgin Mary was free from original sin – a belief with a long and controversial history. His most significant act was to pronounce in favour of papal infallibility at the first Vatican Council of 1869 to 1870; it did not meet with universal approval among Roman Catholics but Manning was a strong supporter.

In his diocese of Westminster he encouraged new seminaries and schools. He worked for social reform and mediated successfully in the dock strike of 1889. His friend and colleague, Herbert Vaughan, for twenty years bishop of Salford, was similarly active in expanding the Church and its schools, and in his pastoral concern for the poor. In 1892 he succeeded Cardinal Manning at Westminster, where he began the building of Westminster Cathedral, imposing in terms of both its size and the height of its squared bell tower, and striking in the alternation of red brick and light limestone. It was completed in eight years.

From time to time there was hope in some quarters of unity between the Churches, even an association for the Promotion of Unity. Vaughan was involved in discussions about Anglican ordinations, but in 1896 Pope Leo XIII unequivocally pronounced them to be invalid, "now and for ever in the future". The road to unity, then very much a minority concern, had reached an impasse.

Newman, after founding the Oratory in Birmingham, was invited to serve as rector of the new Catholic university in Dublin. He stayed until 1858. It seems his views on education were more liberal than those of the bishops and he returned to the Oratory. His writings make clear he was a man of independent thought. He disagreed with Cardinal Manning over several issues and some of his views were seen as suspect in Rome. In his day he was an influential figure in both the Church of England and the Roman Catholic Church, and his spiritual journey has remained a source of great interest. In 1879 he was made a cardinal, his first office in the Church of his adoption.

By 1900 the Roman Catholic Church had made remarkable progress in re-establishing itself in England. Its clergy had trebled in number, as had the number of its church buildings. Given the enormity of its task, its commitment to the socially deprived had been impressive. By 1900 the Modernists had also made their voices heard, among them the historian Lord Acton, and the theologians Baron von Hugel and George Tyrrell. They wanted the Roman Catholic Church to connect more with the world around it. They favoured intellectual inquiry, the application of historical and scientific knowledge to Biblical criticism, and room for the conscience of the individual, all of which led to papal decrees to suppress Biblical criticism and defend the concept of an unchanging tradition.

Social and Intellectual Challenges

There were social and intellectual challenges for all Christians in the nineteenth century. In its early decades the poet and philosopher, Samuel Coleridge was among those who did not see Biblical criticism as a threat: the Bible had the power to inspire faith even when subjected to critical study. Thomas Arnold shared his view. Both wanted the Church of England to be more comprehensive and influential in society. Another liberal thinker, F.D. Maurice, would wield considerable influence as the century progressed. The son of a Unitarian minister who later became ordained in the Church of England, he anticipated, in some measure, the later ecumenical movement in his search for unity between Churches. Some of his views on the atonement, and on the meaning of eternal life and eternal punishment led to his dismissal as professor at King's College for unorthodox beliefs.

In 1848 his Christian principles led to his involvement in the Christian Socialist Movement along with John Ludlow, its founder and organiser, and Charles Kingsley, the novelist and clergyman. The Chartist Movement, which had agitated for better living conditions for workers and an extension of the vote to the working class, had failed. The Christian Socialist Movement took up the challenge at a time when the word "socialist" meant, for many, anti-Christian, or even revolutionary. Underlying the movement were the principles of the fatherhood of God and the brotherhood of man. It aimed to promote cooperation rather than competition. The cooperative workshops they set up encouraged the development of the Cooperative Movement. They achieved some legislation for the Friendly Societies that gave practical support to workers, and in 1854 they established a Workingmen's

College in Great Ormond Street, a pioneer in adult education. As a movement it lasted only six years, but public awareness had been raised. Maurice's ideas on the fellowship of all classes had made their mark and led to increased social commitment within the Church.

In 1877 a group of High Churchmen launched the Guild of St Matthew, under the leadership of a young priest, Stewart Headlam. Its members also worked for social justice over issues such as housing, working conditions and education. A decade or so later, the Christian Social Union, which counted many clergy among its numbers, was founded; its basis being that the Christian faith had to do with the whole of life.

The Settlement Movement followed. Toynbee Hall was set up in a deprived area of London, with the purpose of promoting education, culture and social services. Although religiously motivated, religion was not an intrusive element in the scheme. The approach had a wide appeal and provided a model that different denominations followed.

The Young Men's Christian Association (YMCA) had been started as early as the 1840s with similar aims. It grew into an international, interdenominational movement. Mission churches set themselves up in halls. The Plymouth Brethren, founded by an Anglican in Plymouth in the 1830s had already offered a different model of Church with its small, autonomous groups with no organised ministry.

In 1865 William Booth founded the Salvation Army. There were no ministers and no sacraments; their meetings were held in the open air and their rescue work among the destitute was impressive. A similar organisation grew up in the Church of England when William Carlile founded the Church Army, a body of lay people who worked in the slums of Westminster. It too was evangelistic.

All these initiatives spoke of a determination to reach out to the unchurched, and offer help and opportunities to the underprivileged. Large city chapels were built by all the major nonconformist denominations. One of the largest was the Baptist Metropolitan Tabernacle in South London, built in 1859 to seat five thousand; it was where the evangelical preacher, Charles Spurgeon, drew great crowds. The Congregationalists rebuilt their Westminster Chapel and their City Temple at Holborn. Whitefield's Chapel in Tottenham Court Road was rebuilt on a larger scale. Large mission halls were built: the Wesleyan Mission Hall in the Lozells area of Birmingham had a stage for concerts. Multi-purpose central halls followed at the end of the century, venues for classes and clubs as well as for services.

While the Church, in many guises, responded to the needs of society, it was being presented with other challenges. Darwin's *On the Origin of Species* in 1858 and the later *Descent of Man* in 1871 expounded his theory of evolution: that species evolve through natural selection, without divine intervention. For some Christians this challenged the authority of the Bible in its account of creation, and for some, even the existence of God. Others saw no incompatibility: the creation story of the Bible was for them not a literal account and the idea of evolution could be applied to man's understanding of God developing over time. Geological studies had already prompted questions about the age of the earth.

In 1860 a group of seven theologians, mostly from Oxford, produced a publication called *Essays and Reviews*, which dealt with many of the subjects under discussion: the progressive nature of revelation; the obligation to study the Bible by all available means; and the need to restate some doctrines, among them original sin, the atonement and the question of eternal punishment. The book caused enormous controversy. It was seen as a threat to orthodoxy, its authors seen as traitors, and it was roundly denounced. Two prosecutions followed, later dismissed by a secular court.

Colenso, a Cornishman who had become bishop of Natal, added more fuel to the fire by casting doubt on the date of the first five books of the Bible, the Books of Moses, and whether in fact Moses and Joshua had existed.

A group of three distinguished Cambridge theologians, Hort, Westcott and Lightfoot, responded to the situation by producing a critical text of the New Testament with a series of commentaries. Their contribution rehabilitated the reputation of English scholarship in theology, but their concentration on the New Testament did not resolve current difficulties over the Old Testament.

Almost thirty years after the publication of *Essays and Reviews*, another set of studies, known as the *Lux Mundi*, appeared. The authors were mostly Anglo-Catholics from Oxford, who aimed to relate the Catholic faith to the contemporary world and commend it to others. Its editor was Charles Gore who would soon after establish the Community of the Resurrection. By this time liberal ideas had become more acceptable. There was no furore and before the century ended, one of the contributors to *Essays and Reviews*, Frederick Temple, had survived the censures the book had provoked to become archbishop of Canterbury.

A more rounded approach to faith was re-emerging in the manner of Richard Hooker, viewing the Bible in conjunction with tradition and reason, and also recognising the role of experience as a confirmation of faith. There were those who were able to accept the new thinking without loss of faith. There were those who continued to hold to a literal interpretation of the Bible and traditional doctrines, ignoring the storm around them. Yet others floundered or were shipwrecked. There were many famous doubters – the poet Matthew Arnold, nostalgic for certainty; and the novelist George Eliot, still valuing aspects of Christian teaching. The historian, Thomas Carlyle, held firmly to his belief in God while famously rejecting the Church as an institution together with its theology. Many abandoned belief in miracles and many distrusted dogma. But many initial fears subsided in the belief that the Christian faith was capable of surviving the God-given inquiring mind of man.

By the end of the nineteenth century the church scene had been transformed: the established Church in England no longer had a monopoly, but it had made a quite spectacular recovery in the latter half of the century. The world of nonconformity, meanwhile, had expanded and become more confident. A church/chapel divide had developed in society, embracing two different sets of social values. The old system of dependency and paternalism had left some resentment, and nonconformity pursued the social implications of the Christian gospel. Much working-class political involvement began in the chapels. As class-consciousness grew along with a greater awareness of the inequalities in society, the new point of conflict would be between classes rather than the Churches.

The social gospel had made a great impact – there was ample scope for action. Out of Christian commitment many had addressed social ills, such as the desperate situation of many children, whether abandoned, in prison or working from an early age in appalling conditions. This was the period when Thomas Barnardo founded his children's homes, George Muller his orphanages, and Montjoie Rudolf the Society for Waifs and Strays, which became the Children's Society. It was also when the Quaker Elizabeth Fry worked to improve prison conditions, particularly for young girls, and Josephine Butler addressed the plight of prostitutes and championed the cause of women's rights; while the Earl of Shaftesbury achieved better conditions in factories and mines. There were many other activists.

In all the churches there had been an explosion of church building, not only to supply need, particularly in industrial areas, but also out of rivalry between churches, sometimes regardless of need.

In the meantime the Celtic countries pursued their own path. In Wales, in the 1851 Census, when half the population registered as church attenders, eighty per cent of them were nonconformists. In the chapels there was a strong emphasis on morality, which resulted in the Temperance Movement and in the Welsh Sunday Closing Act. Many new chapels were then built in the centre of communities – this was the beginning of the phenomenon of an extraordinary number of chapels of different denominations in one place, some serving Welsh-speaking and others English-speaking congregations. They were no longer modest in size. One of the largest is Morriston Tabernacle, near Swansea, built in 1872, the architect being a local miner's son. With its high steeple and façade of double pillars with a pediment above, it is an imposing building and the home of a well-known choral tradition.

Roman Catholics had increased in numbers and were building churches. By the end of the century, the Roman Catholic diocese of Menevia included most of Wales, with its centre at the Church of Our Lady of Sorrows at

Wrexham, while Glamorganshire, Monmouthshire and Herefordshire formed a separate diocese, with its centre at the Abbey of Belmont in Hereford.

The established Church had shared in the revival movement and had shown signs of recovery: more Welshmen were becoming bishops, and more clergy were required to speak Welsh in areas where the language predominated. The Oxford Movement had some influence in both north and south Wales, but it was limited. At Lampeter College, founded earlier in the century, its vice-principal, Rowland Williams, had gained some fame as one of the contributors to *Essays and Reviews*. All four cathedrals underwent a much-needed restoration programme. Building projects went ahead in all the dioceses. Llandaff diocese built or rebuilt some one hundred and seventy churches, adding to their clergy and training lay readers, but in spite of its efforts it remained a minority Church in this largely industrial diocese, where nonconformity resonated more significantly with the working population, as it addressed their needs and involved them actively.

A divisive church-versus-chapel culture had developed in Welsh society generally. As the established Church was clearly attracting only a minority, a movement grew for its disestablishment, encouraged by the fact that this had already happened in Ireland in 1869.

In Ireland, in the second half of the nineteenth century, changes took place in the Churches against a background of great poverty and unrest. The famine of 1846 and 1847 had created a situation of desperation for many, and the population had been drastically reduced by deaths and the emigration of some one and a half million people.

The established Church in Ireland was unpopular: the tithes for its upkeep came partly from the Roman Catholic tenant farmer, and most bishops were Englishmen. In 1833 the London government had recognised its minority status, reduced the number of its bishops and reorganised its dioceses. Disestablishment and disendowment followed in 1869. The revival movement had a considerable impact; it had renewed the Church of Ireland's vitality and enabled it to cope with its new situation.

The strength of the Roman Catholic Church in Ireland had been officially recognised. In 1836 it consisted of four provinces and twenty-six dioceses by comparison with the reorganised Church of Ireland with its two provinces and twelve dioceses. It was a Church very much centred on Rome. In 1849, Paul Cullen, who had been director of the Irish College in Rome was sent to be Roman Catholic archbishop of Armagh. He would be a major figure in this period of renewal, concerned with organisation, discipline and training, and later becoming archbishop of Dublin. The national synod he called in 1850 set his ideas in motion. In the century that followed an impressive building programme got under way; twenty-four cathedrals or pro-cathedrals and three thousand churches were built, all through voluntary contributions – gifts, collections and bazaars – and often using direct labour.

There was inevitably an element of local rivalry with the Church of Ireland, particularly in the south of the country and at Armagh in the north, where a Roman Catholic cathedral was built on a hill opposite the long-established and newly restored Church of Ireland cathedral, the tall spires of the new building dwarfing the low outline of the older foundation, both of them dedicated to St Patrick. In Cork the Church of Ireland built a new cathedral with a French flavour (complete with apse, ambulatory and many spires), and another at Kilmore, County Cavan, along with some new city churches. As elsewhere in the British Isles, the competitive spirit played its part in the proliferation of churches.

The expansion of religious communities contributed to the functioning of a now overtly Catholic country. The numbers of nuns had increased from little more than a hundred in 1800 to eight thousand in 1900; they were involved in teaching and social work.

While the Catholic Church became stronger and more confident, the Church of Ireland was far from a spent force. For its size it was wealthy and still had political influence. Together with the other Protestant Churches, it was ill at ease with the growth of its rival. Anti-pope feeling simmered and there were intermittent riots. While at one stage Protestants had contributed to the building of Catholic chapels in Ulster, sectarianism there was increasing. So too was the movement for Home Rule.

In Scotland new voices were making themselves heard in the field of theology, though not without risk. In 1881 William Robertson Smith, a pioneer in Biblical criticism in Scotland, was removed from his professorial chair at the Free Church College in Aberdeen for his attempts to promote greater intellectual freedom in the approach to the Bible. A book by Henry Drummond, called *The Ascent of Man*, helped many to reconcile science, especially the theory of evolution, with the Christian faith. Gradually these scholars gained support and the theological stance of the Presbyterian Church became less inflexible.

Other influences were abroad: a second evangelical revival in the 1850s, and the powerful ministry of the American evangelist Dwight Moody on his visits to Scotland in the 1870s and 1880s. He was accompanied by Ira Sankey, who sang and played the organ. Their missions did much to reinstate the instrument banned by the Reformation, and to increase the popularity of hymns through their own hymn book. There were hymn writers in the mainstream Churches too. Horatio Bonnar's "I heard the voice of Jesus say…" and the blind George Matheson's "O love that will not let me go" have stood the test of time. There were many great preachers during this period and the sermon continued to figure large in the experience of congregations. Church activity was expanding: guilds were formed for young people, and there were missions to remote parishes.

The nineteenth century saw the building of many more churches. The Disruption alone virtually doubled the number of Presbyterian churches, a massive legacy for future generations. Many were in the Gothic style that was part of Scotland's cultural heritage from the Middle Ages. As the century progressed, some architects looked at ways of adapting the traditional style to the needs of nonconformist worship, which were, in essence, an uncluttered preaching space with a very visible pulpit. Edinburgh's Barclay Church of 1864 has a space inside like a theatre with a double gallery. Smaller denominations were also building: the very large and imposing Coats Memorial Baptist Church was opened in Paisley in 1895.

Following emancipation, the number of Roman Catholic churches multiplied from an estimated twenty or so to around four hundred during the course of a century. The Catholic hierarchy was not restored in Scotland until 1878, a generation later than south of the border, and provided two archbishops and two suffragan bishops. In 1886, St Mary's Roman Catholic cathedral in Edinburgh, an extension of the earlier St Mary's Chapel, became the

Metropolitan Cathedral of the new archdiocese of St Andrew's and Edinburgh.

At Govan on the banks of the Clyde, the Church of Scotland built what became known as the "People's Cathedral", St Constantine's or Govan Old Parish Church, within an ancient churchyard site.

In the Episcopal Church too, a period of recovery and renewal was reflected in new building, including seven cathedrals, some of them in the Gothic Revival style that the Oxford Movement had popularised, though St Salvador's Cathedral in Dundee, with its painted interior, was an early example of the Arts and Crafts movement.

The latter part of the nineteenth century saw a positive move towards unity among separated groups. Among the Congregationalists, the Old Independents and the evangelical congregations joined together, augmented later by the Evangelical Union. In 1900 the United Presbyterian Church merged with the Free Church to form the United Free Church of Scotland. Only a small minority of the Free Church – the Wee Frees – held out. This newly discovered strength in unity, the revivals and a fresh appraisal of traditionally held doctrine had addressed both hearts and minds, and brought a new vitality to the Scottish Churches.

The end of the century was closely followed by the death of Queen Victoria. In the sixty-four years of her reign she had presided over an eventful period in church life when a healthier toleration, finally imposed by law, gradually became a reality, and the social and moral implications of Christianity had become more fully recognised. Many Christians had looked to needs beyond their own shores: some nine thousand had gone as missionaries to foreign countries, many of them nonconformists.

The relationship between Church and society was

changing and the role of religion diminishing, undermined partly by greater scientific knowledge and the new critical approach to the Bible, but also by increased optimism about what human beings could achieve.

An estimated thirty to forty per cent of the population still attended Sunday services, but the wave of secularisation was spreading. Its gathering momentum would present a considerable challenge to the Churches of the twentieth century.

XII

UNITY AND COMMUNITY

By the beginning of the twentieth century the Roman Catholic Church had done a great deal to re-establish itself since emancipation in 1829. The Protestants had fragmented even further with the advent of Methodism and of many smaller groups, and nonconformist Churches became known collectively as the Free Churches. The Church of England encompassed a wide spectrum of belief and was in many respects subject to Parliament. Though established, it was also something of an anomaly: it was not a majority Church in terms of church attendance though many non-churchgoers saw themselves as affiliated to it, largely through rites of passage. In Scotland, Ireland and Wales it was clearly a minority; this was a reality acknowledged in Scotland from the sixteenth century, in Ireland at the disestablishment of the Church of Ireland in 1869, and it was soon to be disestablished in Wales.

In a society that had become very class-conscious, the Church of England was seen as dominated by the privileged upper classes, its bishops and other church dignitaries very often the product of public schools and Oxbridge. For most people in the parishes in the early twentieth century, Matins remained the main Sunday service, sometimes preceded or followed by a celebration of Holy Communion. Anglo-Catholic influence was widespread, with its emphasis on the sacraments. Weekly, and even daily, Holy Communion was being encouraged and the word "Eucharist" more widely used. To many churchgoers, used to taking Holy Communion only rarely, this new emphasis was alienating, as was the increasing use of vestments, candles, ritual and Catholic devotions.

The early decades of the century saw the creation of twelve new Anglican dioceses. The foundation stone was laid for a cathedral in the new diocese of Liverpool. At Truro the cathedral was completed and dedicated in 1910. The see had been founded in 1876, with Bishop Benson as its first bishop. It was he who introduced the Festival of Nine Lessons and Carols there in 1880, which King's College, Cambridge, later adopted. It would become a national institution, broadcast every Christmas.

Among the parish churches, the building of one of the masterpieces of the century began at St Mary's, Wellingborough, in Northamptonshire. Built in the Perpendicular Gothic style, the church is rich and spacious feeling, with an open screen between nave and chancel allowing a focus on the altar by the whole congregation. In architectural contrast, the church of St Andrew, Roker, in County Durham, was built in the Arts and Crafts style, with its spectacular interior climaxing in a depiction of the creation story on the chancel ceiling.

The Free Churches reached their peak in the early years of the century. As the population continued to move to industrial centres, many village chapels were forced to close, but in the towns they were well established; they were especially strong in Manchester and Birmingham, while Methodism flourished in Cornwall and the north. Their priorities in worship remained the same – the Bible, preaching, prayer and hymn singing. Services of Holy Communion took place usually once a month and were seen as essentially memorialist, recalling the events at the heart of Christianity. There were fine preachers among them and some made their voices heard in the capital: Hugh Price Hughes of the West London Mission and Sylvester Horne of Whitefield's Tabernacle.

By the twentieth century, colleges for Free Church students had been established at both Oxford and Cambridge. In 1904, Manchester University, which had its origins in Dissent, acquired a faculty of theology. In Birmingham, a federation of colleges for the training of teachers and church workers of different denominations developed at Selly Oak. Newspapers founded by Free Churchmen – the *Manchester Guardian*, the *Methodist Times* and the *British Weekly* – provided vehicles for expressing their views. The Free Churches had become very much part and parcel of society.

One of their strengths during this period lay in their Sunday schools. In 1907 an estimated three million young people attended. Along with the two million who attended those of the Church of England, this represented a powerful influence nationwide. The crusade against drinking and gambling continued, while Sunday remained a very special day in nonconformist circles. Eric Liddell, a Scottish runner, drew public attention to the fact when he refused to run on a Sunday in the Olympic Games in Paris in 1924.

It was in the Free Churches that women first became

ministers, early in the century, a possibility not yet countenanced in the Church of England. The Anglican Maude Royden, frustrated by her own Church, caused a stir, and some censure, when she became a pastoral assistant and a popular preacher at the Congregationalist City Temple. She became the first president of a new Society for the Ministry of Women in the Church and travelled widely promoting women's rights.

The most spectacular event in the Free Churches in the early part of the century took place in Wales in 1904 in the form of a revival – the last of a series, which created an intensely religious climate in the places that experienced it. This particular revival had its beginnings in rural Cardiganshire among the Calvinistic Methodists and gathered momentum under the leadership of a former miner, Evan Roberts. He went from place to place, gathering large crowds, encouraging people to confess their sins and invoking the power of the Holy Spirit. The revival was short-lived – it ended in early 1906 – but it made a powerful impact. Out of it grew two new Pentecostal denominations, with an emphasis on the work of the Holy Spirit. George Jeffreys founded the Elim Four Square movement and Daniel Powell Williams the Apostolic Church. Both had been converted during the revival.

By 1920 there were some two million Roman Catholics in England and Wales. In Scotland they formed around fifteen per cent of the population, with a large concentration in Glasgow. Among their laity were establishment figures – some forty Catholic peers, headed by the duke of Norfolk, president of the Catholic Union. There were several landed families and some converts, particularly through the Oxford Movement, while a large proportion were working-class people, many of Irish extraction, and concentrated in Lancashire, in Liverpool and other northern towns, as well as in London. Pope Pius X encouraged frequent, even daily, communion, to include children from as young as seven or eight; the role of the clergy was dominant. Socially, Roman Catholics were in many respects a people apart; their more relaxed attitudes to drinking, gambling and to strict Sabbath observance were in marked contrast to nonconformist attitudes, and served to emphasise their separateness.

The international nature of the Roman Catholic Church was very apparent. Priests often trained abroad; the English College in Rome prepared many to become bishops. Large numbers of nuns came from the Continent, particularly from France, to teach in convent schools. Papal encyclicals of 1907 condemned modernist teaching, and all priests were required to take an oath "against all liberal interpretation, whether of scripture or history". Building projects continued and the fifteenth duke of Norfolk had two imposing churches built – St Philip's in Arundel and St John's in Norwich, while at Buckfast in Devon the building of a new abbey began on the site of the ruined Cistercian abbey founded in the eleventh century.

For most of the first three decades of the century, from 1903 to 1928, Randall Davidson exercised considerable influence, both nationally and internationally, as archbishop of Canterbury. He was a moderate and cautious man, who tried to hold together the different views within the Church of England and to make it significant in the spiritual life of the nation, particularly during World War I. One of the beacons of light in London during that time was the church of St Martin-in-the-Fields where, under the ministry of the charismatic Dick Sheppard, the doors remained open night and day to servicemen and the homeless, and large congregations came to hear him preach. He had worked among the poor and unemployed in the East End, and had served as a chaplain in the trenches at the Front in the early part of the war. For him, the Church was about the teaching of Christ as found in the Gospels rather than in church dogma.

Post 1918

Great changes in society followed World War I: the growth of the Labour movement and trade unionism, an extension of voting rights, welfare improvements for the unemployed, and compulsory education until the age of fourteen. Christian Socialism was active in many successive groups.

There were changes in the established Church too. In 1919 the Church Enabling Act brought into being the Church Assembly; its main task was to prepare measures for Parliament that concerned the Church. It was also given the administrative power to create new dioceses. The Act made the Church a little less dependent on Parliament.

The year 1919 was also when the Church of England in Wales was disestablished. It was the result of agitation by nonconformists against a minority Church. In 1920 the Church in Wales became a separate independent province of the Anglican Church and Bishop Edwards of St Asaph became its archbishop. There followed the creation of two new bishoprics: the Diocese of Monmouth in 1921, with the church of St Woolo, Newport, as its pro-cathedral; and the Diocese of Swansea and Brecon in 1923, with its cathedral church at Brecon. The newly designated Church was well served from the beginning by effective bishops.

While disestablishment took place in Wales, a more serious situation was developing in Ireland, where unrest reached a peak in 1919 when Sinn Fein declared independence. Two years of violence followed until the union between southern Ireland and the rest of Britain ended in 1922, as did the unity of Ireland. The Irish Free State was overwhelmingly Roman Catholic, but the 1922 constitution granted religious freedom to Protestants. The Government lent a great deal of support to the Roman Catholic Church, where attendance was very high. In the north of Ireland, now separated by partition, a third of the population was Catholic and vulnerable to Protestant power in the allocation of housing and jobs, the seeds of future problems.

In the aftermath of war, the desire for unity would become a persistent feature of church life in the twentieth century. In the latter part of the nineteenth century the Inter-University Christian Union had encouraged interdenominational fellowship among Protestants, and even intercommunion. From 1907 it became known as the Student Christian Movement (SCM) and included about one-fifth of all students in higher education. It would prove to be a powerful influence on many who later became leaders in the Church. It was a key player in bringing about an event seen as foundational to the twentieth-century ecumenical movement – the World Missionary Conference in Edinburgh in 1910.

A succession of ecumenical initiatives followed World War I. At the 1920 Lambeth Conference the archbishop of Canterbury issued an "Appeal to All Christian People" for unity among the Churches.

A different initiative followed in 1921 when conversations were started at Malines in Belgium, this time between Roman Catholic and Anglican theologians. The talks aroused great suspicion in some quarters and they ended in 1926 with no concrete results, but they had encouraged cooperation between the two Churches. At the same time good relations were established with the Orthodox Church, which formally recognised Anglican orders in 1922.

New ecumenical groups followed, and conferences at home and abroad. In 1928 a papal encyclical forbade Roman Catholics to take part in such activities. At Easter of the same year a major international Missionary Council meeting took place in Jerusalem, a successor to the 1910 Edinburgh Conference.

At home, three groups of Methodists decided in 1907 to become the United Methodist Church. The same move towards unity became a reality in 1920s Scotland; this was firstly through the Church of Scotland Act in 1921, which acknowledged the Church's right to govern its own spiritual life and work. This was a preparation for the union of the Church of Scotland and the United Free Church, realised in 1929 – together this represented the great majority of Presbyterians and some four-fifths of Scottish Protestants, a size which justified its view of itself as the national Church.

Some Christians were clearly looking beyond their own affiliations, both nationally and internationally, but the Church was also taking social problems very seriously. In 1918 a commission presented a report entitled "Christianity and Industrial Problems" to the archbishops. It was a foundation document for the Church's attitude to social reform.

In the spirit of this report, Randall Davidson tried to mediate during the General Strike of 1926 through his "Appeal from the Churches" for an end to the strike and for negotiations to follow, an appeal that used the relatively new medium of radio. He had limited support in the Church – many bishops saw his intervention as ill-advised.

This reaction reflected the great unease at mixing politics and religion, but also the fact that those with power and influence had little conception of the realities of daily life for working people, and particularly for the miners, who continued their strike to the point of starvation, or for the many who lived in appalling conditions in the slums.

One priest in the Church who did understand the difficulties the working class laboured under, was the Reverend Studdert Kennedy. As a wartime chaplain at the Front, affectionately known as "Woodbine Willie" because of the cigarettes he distributed, he had won the respect of many soldiers by engaging deeply with their questioning about God and the problem of suffering. He communicated more widely as a writer of popular poetry. After the war he served as a priest in a very poor parish in Worcester, where he had a deep empathy with his parishioners. A gifted preacher, he also travelled the country drawing large crowds. In 1921 he became chief missioner to the Industrial Christian Fellowship. An exhausting schedule led to an early death in 1929 at the age of forty-five. His funeral at Worcester Cathedral was a national event in honour of a very unpretentious national hero, much loved by the working class and by ex-servicemen, and highly valued by his fellow churchmen. William Temple considered him "one of God's greatest gifts" to that generation.

Alongside the social concerns and the ecumenical activity of the early twentieth century, liturgical revision was exercising some minds. The Prayer Book had remained virtually unchanged since 1662. After long deliberation, the new Church Assembly finally presented a revision of the Prayer Book to Parliament in 1927. Opposition came from extremists among evangelicals, who thought it too Roman, and among Anglo-Catholics who thought it not

Catholic enough, and they lobbied MPs to vote against it. The revision was accepted by the House of Lords but narrowly defeated in the House of Commons. With some amendments it was presented again to Parliament in 1928, again to be defeated. The bishops defended the Church's right to order its own worship and, in practice, allowed the use of the variations that the 1928 Prayer Book had sought to introduce.

All the Churches were operating against a background of increasing questioning. The challenges of Darwinism, scientific enquiry and Biblical criticism had created a climate of unbelief among intellectuals and academics. One of their number declared religious belief to be "impossible for modern cultivated man". Writers such as Bernard Shaw and H.G. Wells, and the philosopher Bertrand Russell were well known as atheists. James Frazer's *Golden Bough*, which treated all religions as myth and fantasy, was very popular in the 1920s.

For a while the conventions of churchgoing remained. Some who had abandoned their faith still saw the churches as valuable social institutions. Only slowly did the widespread nature of unbelief become apparent and an acknowledged fact of modern life. In these circumstances the writings of G.K. Chesterton provided a challenge. His books *Orthodoxy* and *The Everlasting Man* made some impact in the 1920s.

Two converts from atheism to Anglicanism would have quite considerable influence. One was T.S. Eliot, the American-born poet who made his home in England and who abandoned the atheism that he found unsatisfying. The other was C.S. Lewis, who had been brought up as a Protestant in Northern Ireland and had become an atheist at an early stage. He was led back to faith partly through the influence of Chesterton.

In William Temple, the Church had an influential leader who both understood the questioning of his time and held very positively to his faith. The son of the former archbishop of Canterbury, Frederick Temple, he became rector of St James's, Piccadilly, and canon of Westminster; both were positions that gave him influence. His appointment as bishop of Manchester in 1921 enabled him to communicate his views more widely, as did his radio broadcasts. He was keen that Christian precepts should influence society at large and, in his own words, thought it "a great mistake to suppose that God was only, or even chiefly, concerned with religion".

His interest in social work and ecumenism stemmed from his time in SCM, and he played a major role in conferences at home and abroad. He had been involved in the Workers' Educational Association from its early days. One of his strengths lay in the fact that he did not identify himself with any particular section of the Church of England. Throughout his career, he was helped and supported by others who had been greatly influenced by SCM: R.H. Tawney, an economic historian at the London School of Economics; J.R. Oldham, a Presbyterian layman and an ecclesiastical statesman of international stature; and William Paton, a Presbyterian minister with a vision for change, both ecumenically and internationally.

All the preoccupations of the early twentieth century – ecumenism, social initiatives, liturgical revision and intellectual challenges – involved especially church leaders, intellectuals and academics. Their views filtered through to congregations. The emphasis on preaching and teaching had shifted over time to greater concern with Jesus' life on earth and its implications for daily living – building the Kingdom of God in the here and now. The birth of radio in the 1920s, under its Scottish director-general, Lord Reith, a Christian of high principles, would play a significant role in the shaping of twentieth-century society. It was used to good effect by men such as William Temple and Dick Sheppard. In 1922 the British Broadcasting Corporation (BBC) began broadcasting weekly church services, and on the first weekday of 1928 it launched the first *Daily Service* from St Martin-in-the-Fields. Radio was only one aspect of change in a society where cars, aeroplanes and the very popular cinema were broadening horizons and opportunities.

In 1928 Randall Davidson was succeeded by Cosmo Lang. Lang had been archbishop of York for twenty years and would be at Canterbury for fourteen years – time for his Anglo-Catholic sympathies to make their mark. The 1930s saw a degree of absorption of Catholic insights into Anglican tradition, aiming to combine the best of both traditions. A liturgical movement on the Continent encouraged the idea of the Mass as the People's Communion; this fed into the move towards the Parish Communion in England.

Cosmo Lang shared his predecessor's deep concern about the social conditions of the working class, particularly pertinent in the decade of the Depression. Some of his younger fellow bishops were moderately radical in social matters: William Temple chaired a commission on unemployment, while Cyril Garbett wrote on the challenge of the slums. George Bell, who later became bishop of Chichester, was committed to ecumenism and international relations. As dean of Canterbury he also renewed the idea of drama in church. John Masefield's *The Coming of Christ* was performed in the cathedral in 1928, and T.S. Eliot's *Murder in the Cathedral* in 1935. Others followed. Initiatives like this connected the Church with a wider public. The 1930s, in fact, saw a new relationship develop between Church and nation.

Among the Free Churches the move towards unity within denominations was still on the agenda, and in 1932 the Wesleyan Methodists and the Primitive Methodists joined with the United Methodist Church. In the country at large, there were already signs of decline. This was true of Sunday schools nationwide. There were also some changes of loyalty taking place in politics and religion. Nonconformity in the Midlands and the south was tending to become more middle class and conservative. Its attitude to drinking and Sunday observance was alienating to some, and there was some movement from the Free Churches into the Church of England, both among lay people and clergy.

Roman Catholics were increasing in number through mixed marriages and conversions. They were also more widespread, and becoming more accepted and integrated into national life, helped by a new and popular archbishop of Westminster in 1935, Arthur Hinsley. With a breadth of experience at home and abroad, he was open to Christians of other affiliations. At Liverpool, Archbishop Downey laid the foundation stone for a new cathedral to be built on a grand scale. In 1938, the new abbey at Buckfast was completed, among its many lovely features were marble mosaic pavements and a striking stained-glass window representing Christ at the Last Supper, which fills the width of the Blessed Sacrament Chapel. It had been a remarkable achievement by a handful of monks under the direction of the German abbot Anscar Vonier. While hitherto concerned with re-establishing and consolidating its own position, the Roman Catholic Church began to see itself as a bastion against the growing scepticism and secularisation of the society around it.

The 1930s saw a significant change in the climate of thought in matters of faith. The preoccupation with the social gospel of liberal Protestantism had proved unsatisfying; there was a hunger for something more, which led to some strengthening of traditional belief and Biblical authority, where the incarnation, the resurrection and the sacraments received due emphasis. There were intellectual Christians encouraging this trend in universities and elsewhere, such as the Congregationalist, C.H. Dodd, who became professor of divinity at Cambridge in 1935, and Charles Williams, a poet and novelist. Frank Morrison produced a popular book entitled *Who Moved the Stone?* There were influences from abroad: the Swiss theologian Karl Barth reclaimed belief in a transcendent God, who could only be known by faith; the American Reinhold Niebuhr wrote on the prophetic role of Christianity in providing a critique of society and its institutions.

On the ecumenical front, Temple, Oldham and Paton were working with others to put into effect their vision of a united, international Church. Two conferences in 1937 resolved on the creation of a World Council of Churches. The decision was a major advance on the ecumenical road, though the plan would be delayed by war.

The decade was fraught with anxieties about Communism, Fascism and Nazism; it was a climate that encouraged an active pacifist movement. There had been some sixteen thousand conscientious objectors during World War I. In the 1930s, the Reverend Dick Sheppard launched a peace movement. Some fifty thousand people responded initially. A mass meeting was held at the Albert Hall in 1935 to form the Peace Pledge Union.

Numbers doubled and some high profile people were involved. As the decade came to a close there would be many resignations.

Among those who remained rock-like in their pacifist commitment was the Reverend George McLeod. A holder of the Military Cross from World War I, he had since renounced all violence. In 1930 he had become minister of a deprived Glasgow parish with high unemployment. Through clubs and a variety of community projects he worked to make the Church relevant to the people. In 1938 he began the foundation of a new kind of community on the island of Iona. The Abbey church there had already been restored for worship in the early 1900s. In 1938 a group of five clergy and five laymen, who were craftsmen, set out to work on restoring the monastic buildings around the church. The work would continue every summer until the task was completed. The sharing of worship and work by clergy and laity was symbolic of what McLeod saw as the oneness of life in the community and the life of the Church. The clergy worked in industrial parishes during the rest of the year. Summer camps on the island for young people from industrial parishes started at an early stage, but it was not until after World War II that McLeod's vision would be fully realised.

A sense of instability on all sides increased as the decade advanced. In 1936 came the abdication of Edward VIII. In the Convocation of Canterbury, Bishop Bell raised concern about the Church in Germany. He was a friend of Dietrich Bonhoeffer, who was in London in 1935 as chaplain to the Lutheran community. Soon after, both Bonhoeffer and Karl Barth were removed from their academic posts in Germany. Another pastor was imprisoned in 1937 – all three were founder members of the Confessing Church, which stood out against Nazism. Awareness of such events increased alarm in some quarters in Britain.

For many parts of the country the 1930s had been a difficult decade, with high unemployment and hunger marches. It ended with the bleak prospect of a second World War – a war that was seen as the product of secular ideologies on the continent of Europe, a perception that allowed some rehabilitation of Christian values. Church leaders were among those who planned for a more just post-war society, with a unity of purpose that crossed denominational boundaries.

The first initiative came from the Roman Catholic Church in August 1940 when Cardinal Hinsley launched the Sword of the Spirit movement; its aim was to promote justice in war and peace. In December of the same year a letter appeared in *The Times* signed by Cardinal Hinsley, Archbishops Lang and Temple, and the moderator of the Free Churches Council. It contained a statement of principles to guide a post-war settlement, and was followed by two public meetings in London on the role of the Church nationally and internationally.

In 1942 Cosmo Lang resigned and William Temple moved from York, where he had been archbishop since 1929, to Canterbury. He lost little time in publishing a short and significant book, addressed to the nation, entitled *Christianity and Social Order*, in which the term "the welfare state" first appeared in writing. Among its themes it considered the balance between the respect due to the individual and the common purpose of society. It also considered the need for certain basic provisions of housing, a living wage and education to allow individuals to make responsible choices. It was widely read and has been reprinted many times.

In the same year he encouraged the setting up of the British Council of Churches: there was a growing realisation of what all Churches had in common.

The war challenged society and the Church over many issues. The more open attitude to Christianity in the 1930s had, to some extent, prepared the way for a fresh consideration of what it stood for. A number of writers helped the process. C.S. Lewis produced *The Screwtape Letters*, *The Problem of Pain* and other accessible books on theology, but was particularly effective through his contributions to radio, later put together under the title *Mere Christianity*. Another radio success was Dorothy L. Sayers' *The Man Born to be King*. It caused some controversy at the time, as a down-to-earth treatment of sacred history, but it broke new ground in communicating the faith.

In 1943 Cardinal Hinsley died. He had done much to improve relations between Roman Catholics and Protestants, and was recognised as a national leader: the first Roman Catholic to be seen as such since the Reformation. The following year William Temple died after only two years as archbishop of Canterbury, but more than twenty-five years of influence on many areas of national life, and was deservedly known as the People's Archbishop. Bishop Bell continued his role as supporter of the German Confessing Church in its struggle against Nazi government and was vociferous in his condemnation of the indiscriminate Allied bombing of German towns – an almost lone and unpopular voice.

Post 1945

The years immediately following the war saw some recovery of church life. A number of significant publications appeared. In 1947, *Letters to Young Churches*, a translation of St Paul's letters into modern English by J.B. Phillips, was well received. As a vicar in South London he was clear that the language of the King James Bible was not understood by his youth club members. A translation of the whole New Testament followed in 1958. This was not the first of the new Bible translations of the twentieth century and many more were to follow. Frank Sheed's *Theology and Sanity* provided a clear account of Roman Catholic doctrine, while Bishop Barnes published his more controversial *Rise of Christianity*, in which he rejected the virgin birth, miracles and the resurrection. These and other books provided food for thought. In the climate created by the Cold War and the threat of nuclear war, many were prepared to reconsider the claims of faith.

Archbishop Fisher, who had succeeded William Temple at Canterbury, was quick to take up again the question of unity between Churches in the post-war years, and appealed to the Free Churches to consider adopting bishops into their systems, to facilitate intercommunion. Church leaders were also looking beyond national boundaries. In 1948 pre-war plans for the World Council of Churches were realised. The war had engendered a keen awareness of international situations where positive action was possible. Aid agencies to developing countries were expanding. Some church leaders became very involved with the anti-apartheid movement and in the Campaign for Nuclear Disarmament (CND).

In the 1950s, a number of great preachers, many from the Free Churches, were making an impact on the London scene and beyond, through broadcasting: Dr Leslie Weatherhead, the Reverend W.E. Sangster and Dr Martyn Lloyd-Jones among them, and the Reverend Donald Soper, whose life almost spanned the twentieth century. A great communicator and open-air orator, he was a familiar figure at London's Tower Hill and Speakers' Corner in Hyde Park for most of his life. The Reverend John Stott exercised an influential ministry as rector of All Souls, Langham Place, and led effective missions to Oxford and Cambridge. The American Dr Billy Graham led a three-month crusade at Harringay in 1954, which drew almost one and a half million people. As the decade came to its end, so did the peak of this preaching era.

Some individual Christians addressed problem areas: Chad Varah, a London curate, began the Samaritans, a confidential telephone service manned by volunteers for people who feel suicidal. Group Captain Cheshire, a convert to Roman Catholicism, set up a home for the chronically sick. Both projects expanded to meet a real need.

Attempts at modernising the worship of the Church of England in 1928 had made an abortive start, but, in 1955, a Liturgical Commission was set up that encouraged parish churches to adopt a Parish Communion around 9.00 am as the main service. This was to be the heart of parish life, to increase awareness of the corporate nature of the communion service – belief had tended to become a rather private matter for the individual – and to encourage greater participation by lay people. As the Parish Communion spread, it brought with it the serious loss of non-communicant church attenders.

By this time Roman Catholics formed a tenth of the population, and were very loyal to the pope – many made the journey to Rome for Holy Year in 1950. This was the year when Pope Pius XII defined the doctrine of the Assumption of the Virgin Mary. He also brought some measure of reform: encyclicals allowed greater freedom in Biblical scholarship, and there was some liturgical reform

– rules for fasting were relaxed and evening mass allowed.

Pope John XXIII took the Roman Catholic Church by surprise in 1959 when he called a second Vatican Council to address the need for change in many areas in the life of the Church, including in worship, teaching and in its relations with other Churches. As part of the preparation for it a Secretariat of Unity was set up in 1960, and in the same year Archbishop Fisher visited Rome. This was the first time an archbishop of Canterbury had done so since the fourteenth century.

At Coventry, where only the tower, the spire and the blackened outer walls of the old cathedral remained after bomb damage, Queen Elizabeth II laid the foundation stone of the new cathedral in 1956. In the six years that followed, great works of art were incorporated into the new building – the *Christ in Glory* tapestry, seventy-nine feet high and placed above the massive altar table; the multi-coloured baptistry window stretching from floor to ceiling, at its base a rough-hewn boulder of a font from a hillside near Bethlehem; and, on an outside wall, the bronze figure of St Michael, victorious over the devil. The juxtaposition of the fourteenth-century shell and the modern building speaks of resurrection and new life. It has become a centre of international reconciliation and a base for the Community of the Cross of Nails, which is part of a network of centres around the world. Twenty young Germans came to Coventry to restore the area for the centre and twenty young British people went to Dresden to rebuild a bombed hospital. Each Friday the Litany of Reconciliation takes place in many languages at the altar in the old cathedral ruins with its cross of charred roof beams, and the words "Father Forgive" inscribed in the wall behind it.

At Llandaff, second only to Coventry in terms of the damage done to cathedrals during the war, restoration was complete by 1960. The restored cathedral's most impressive feature is a massive concrete arch, dominating the nave and supporting a cylindrical organ case, with a figure of Christ at its front, forming a striking contrast in a church essentially medieval in style.

By the 1960s, post-war austerity had given way to a period of greater affluence, to a general optimism and a more radical approach to living. Traditional attitudes towards class, race, gender and sex went into the melting pot. The contraceptive pill transformed patterns of sexual behaviour. More liberal laws were passed over divorce, abortion and homosexuality. For many this was a personal liberation from a straitjacket of expectations on the part of both Church and society, though what looked like a new freedom to many looked to others like licence. The steady decline in church attendance gained momentum and there was a dramatic drop in numbers at Sunday schools, which had been one of the main channels through which Christianity had been passed from one generation to the next.

In 1962 the second Vatican Council (known as Vatican II) opened, with one and a half thousand bishops and heads of religious orders attending, along with a number of theologians. Among those present were also forty non-Catholic observers, whose numbers increased to a hundred by the end of the council in 1965. That seemed to augur well for future relationships. Expectations among Roman Catholics were high.

Vatican II proposed many changes; the most dramatic was to be in worship. The Latin Mass had been unchanged for centuries. By 1967 the whole of the Mass was to be in the local language and the participation of lay people was to be encouraged. A new emphasis on the whole people of God and on collegial ministry stood in contrast to the very authoritarian and hierarchical nature of the Roman Catholic Church hitherto. A new approach to morality was being projected: less a question of observing a strict set of rules and obligations than of taking responsibility for a personal response to issues and situations.

In some respects there was great disappointment among many Roman Catholics: priests were to remain celibate; the ban on contraception remained, reinforced in 1968 by a papal encyclical called "*Humanae Vitae*"; and no progress had been made on the role of women in the Church. Ecumenical plans were vague and the implementation of proposed changes subsequently proved difficult.

In the year following Vatican II, the ecumenical situation was helped by an official visit to Rome by Michael Ramsey, who had been archbishop of Canterbury since 1961. Pope John XXIII had died in 1963 and was succeeded by Pope Paul VI. Together, pope and archbishop led an ecumenical service in St Paul's Church, a Common Declaration was signed and a Joint Commission set up to consider the common ground between the two Churches and the way forward. The Anglican Centre was set up to promote the process.

Michael Ramsey was both a national and an international figure – the first archbishop to travel widely abroad. While a distinguished theologian, he came over as a man of humility who saw himself as a pilgrim on a spiritual journey. A gifted teacher, he was appreciated by students and congregations alike, and by readers of his many books and articles. Open to Christians of other persuasions, he advanced the cause of good relations not only with the Roman Catholic Church but also with the Orthodox Church, whose numbers were expanding with the arrival of immigrants from Eastern Europe and Cyprus, and would in time reach a quarter of a million. He was very supportive of the scheme for Anglican-Methodist reunion and its failure was a source of great disappointment to him. As the 100th archbishop of Canterbury, his authority as a spiritual leader was widely accepted.

Early in the decade the new cathedral at Guildford was consecrated, as was Coventry cathedral. Many Anglican theological colleges were founded and the number of ordinations increased. Yet there were those who felt that the Church of England needed to take a fresh look at itself. New initiatives were taking place, including a disco, a coffee bar and training for worker priests in the diocese of Southwark, and there were a number of challenging books.

None caused more controversy than *Honest to God* by the bishop of Woolwich, John Robinson. Published in 1963, it sold one million copies in three years. He was concerned that the Church was not communicating its message, and needed to change its language and some of its imagery to do so: moving from talk of a God "up there" to a God "out there" was not enough. He quoted others who had influenced his thinking: Paul Tillich had suggested thinking of God as the depth of existence, or "the ground of our being"; Dietrich Bonhoeffer that a society that felt no need of religion was looking for a new, religionless form of Christianity; and Rudolf Bultmann wanted to demythologise New Testament language and use terms meaningful to the modern world to project the faith.

For some *Honest to God* was a blast of fresh air, for others it was close to heresy and deeply disturbing. Archbishop Ramsey responded promptly with a pastoral booklet, called "Image Old and New", to allay fears that the faith was being undermined. Far from dismissing questioning, in it he concedes that religion – "the pious practices" some seemed to wish to dispense with – is only a part of faith. For him God is to be found in the middle of life, in people's needs and relationships, but that times of withdrawal are still necessary for believers to develop a relationship with God and with each other; and, though our language and images are inadequate, they are the means available to express our faith.

In the same decade the Church of England introduced a series of services for experimental use, which would culminate in 1980 in the Alternative Service Book, alternative to the Prayer Book. As a result of this and the modernisation of liturgy in the Roman Catholic Church post Vatican II, both Churches, together with some of the Free Churches, were moving towards a similar form of communion service.

There were fresh approaches in the layout of churches. Some offered worship "in the round", with the altar in a central position, at the heart of the liturgy, surrounded by the people. The new Roman Catholic Metropolitan Cathedral of Christ the King in Liverpool, consecrated in 1967, was designed in this way, reflecting the new thinking on liturgy of Vatican II.

In the Church of England the organisation of ministry changed, with legislation allowing the formation of team ministries, and at the end of the decade the Church Assembly was replaced by the General Synod, with a greater role for lay people.

New Churches grew and flourished among the black immigrant communities: the New Testament Church of God and the Church of God of Prophecy among them. It was particularly through the Charismatic movement that growth came in the Church at large. This new Pentecostal movement affected many in the traditional Churches, both clergy and lay people, and brought a renewed emphasis on the work of the Holy Spirit in the life of believers, and on prayer and healing.

There had already been some growth in the healing ministry in the Church of England. Burrswood, in Sussex, which describes itself as a Christian hospital and place of healing, had been founded in 1948. In the 1960s, Bishop Maddocks of Selby resigned his bishopric and, with his wife, devoted the rest of his ministry to healing, supported by a new group, called the Acorn Christian Healing Trust. Many churches have since made healing an integral part of their ministry.

In the same decade, after many years of planning, a hospice for the chronically sick and terminally ill was opened at Sydenham in Kent in 1967. The inspiration behind it came from Dr Cicely Saunders who, as a nurse and hospital almoner, recognised the need for specialised care to be more widely available. After training as a doctor and engaging the support of influential people, her dream was finally realised: a purpose-built hospital, with a chapel at its heart, where patients and their families could be given the care and support they needed, and where training and research could continue. It was the start of the hospice movement which has since spread widely, partly funded by the National Health Service (NHS) but largely dependent on funds raised by supporters, and greatly valued by local communities.

For some, the 1960s in particular spelt the end of Christendom, of the time when Christianity was the dominant religion, backed up by law and custom. The decade had brought permanent changes to social attitudes. Institutions and organised groups fell increasingly out of favour and churches were among the casualties. There were many closures of churches and chapels; in towns and cities some would be converted into mosques and temples for the needs of the growing immigrant population of other faiths.

Yet there were signs that the Church was both renewing itself and looking for new ways to relate to contemporary society. The Charismatic movement inspired the formation of house churches and prayer groups, which offered more informal worship and a closer fellowship. There continued to be a strong body of evangelical Christians across the denominations. The Keswick Convention, founded in 1875, drew many each year for worship and teaching. In 1979 Spring Harvest began as an evangelical youth event at a holiday camp in North Wales. Almost three thousand came for Bible-based teaching and worship. Its scope widened to include adults and children, and expanded to other venues as numbers rapidly increased. Its intention was to equip people for church work and social involvement.

At a local level, relations between churches were improving, partly through ecumenical Lent groups for shared discussion and through joint services. Roman Catholics were becoming more involved. In 1972 the Congregationalist and Presbyterian Churches joined forces to become the United Reformed Church.

In the late 70s, the working relationship between the Roman Catholic and Anglican bishops of Liverpool, Derek Warlock and David Sheppard, became a symbol of what could be achieved locally by cooperation across the church divide. Liverpool's Anglican cathedral was finally completed in 1978 – it was the largest cathedral in

Britain. Hope Street connected it with the Roman Catholic cathedral, and provided further symbolism and optimism for future ecumenical relations.

David Sheppard had gained experience of inner-city problems during twelve years as warden of the Mayflower Centre in East London. It made him a strong supporter of team ministries and more flexible worship and inspired the book *Built as a City*, which was published in 1974. It considered the role of the Church in inner cities and dealt with problems of housing, education and racial attitudes, as well as building up the worshipping community. It would lead to concerted action in the decade following.

In 1975 the abbot of Ampleforth, Basil Hume, became the Roman Catholic archbishop of Westminster. His consecration was a notable event, attended by the monks of his former community, and was followed by Vespers in Westminster Abbey, sung by Benedictine monks for the first time for more than four centuries. The new archbishop would become a much-respected national figure.

When the Polish archbishop of Warsaw became Pope John Paul II in 1978, hopes were high. He had lived through a difficult period in his native country under Communist rule, which made him very much a man of his time, but his approach to his office looked to the past, to the monarchical model rather than to the collegiality recommended by Vatican II, and he was opposed to much that progressive Roman Catholics were looking for. A strong personality cult grew up around him and crowds flocked to hear him on his extensive travels. In 1982 he came to England – the first visit ever by a pope. His itinerary included Canterbury, where Robert Runcie was then archbishop. What was achieved between the two Churches during his time in office was largely due to the work of the Anglican–Roman

Catholic International Commission (ARCIC), which made a study of aspects of church doctrine with a view to reaching a consensus of understanding.

In the liberated society of the 1980s, a majority had turned its back on organised religion without necessarily giving up all belief. Many were still searching for meaning, as if it was not the message that had been rejected, but the messenger – the institutional Church. Books were published by leading theologians that cast doubt over the central dogmas of the Church. At the same time some prominent people converted to Christianity – the journalist Malcolm Muggeridge and the politician Lord Hailsham among them. No one individual made a wider impact than the man who became the new bishop of Durham in 1984, David Jenkins.

His career had taken him from Oxford University to the World Council of Churches in Geneva for five years, and then to Leeds University as professor of theology. He was committed to opening up the possibility of belief in God to people outside the Church. Though he maintained an unequivocal belief in the incarnation and resurrection of Jesus, he did not feel this necessitated a belief in the virgin birth, or even in the empty tomb, as this was only one element of the proof of resurrection. He felt that the Church should be dynamically involved in the present and looking to the future, rather than defensively guarding the past, its history and tradition. Belief in God meant, for him, being on a spiritual pilgrimage, requiring openness and questioning, and sharing experiences, while being sustained by the worship and sacraments of the Church, and careful, informed reading of the Bible.

In the early days of his episcopate he became deeply involved in the miners' strike of 1984 to 1985. Throughout his time as bishop he was prepared to question political decisions openly, where they adversely affected the vulnerable. The vulnerable warmed to him, as did the doubters and seekers. While he was variously dubbed "the unbelieving bishop" and even "the bishop of blasphemy", there were those who welcomed him as a "bishop for unbelievers", who tried, during his ten-year tenure, to give credibility to the Christian viewpoint in a sceptical age. He stimulated a great deal of interest among people outside the Church and a greater readiness to talk about matters of faith in general.

There were many positive responses from the Churches to the challenges of the times, both within Churches and in the community: new forms of worship; efforts to involve young people and lay people; and a variety of music – new hymns, Taizé chants, worship songs from Iona and some revival of plainchant. Teaching courses to introduce Christianity were launched. The Alpha Course, produced by Holy Trinity Church, Brompton, London, would prove phenomenally successful. Many Christian summer festivals took shape which drew crowds of all ages; they were both purposeful and fun.

Chaplaincy work expanded, from hospitals and schools to further education colleges, but also to prisons, to business and industry, and other sections of community life. The number of retreat houses increased until, by the end of the twentieth century, there were more than two hundred.

Church bodies, such as the Catholic Institute for International Relations, the Catholic Agency For Overseas Development (CAFOD), the British Council of Churches and Christian Aid all tackled problems at home and abroad. The Church of England set up a commission to look into conditions in the cities. Its report "Faith in the Cities" led to the setting up of the Church Urban Fund, which continues to facilitate renewal projects in deprived urban areas, with an annual grant-making budget of £3 million.

On the ecumenical front there were encouraging moments of togetherness. Roman Catholic cardinals attended the enthronement of Robert Runcie as archbishop of Canterbury. Two months later he and Cardinal Basil Hume led a pilgrimage of Catholics and Protestants to the shrine at Walsingham, the first public visit by an archbishop of Canterbury. The medieval shrine, created in the twelfth century, was destroyed during the Reformation but restored in the twentieth century. It has become a popular destination for both Roman Catholic and Anglican pilgrims, attracting some half a million visitors each year. The practice of pilgrimage, often ecumenical, took on a new lease of life in the later twentieth century in many parts of the British Isles.

In 1990 a new ecumenical initiative was launched. The British Council of Churches, which had worked to forward unity for forty years, was dissolved. A new body, Churches Together in Britain and Ireland, included Roman Catholics. Pentecostals, Quakers and the Salvation Army swelled the ranks. Local covenants between churches followed. Some new churches were built for ecumenical use.

For the established Church in the early 1990s, the burning issue was the ordination of women. There had been women readers in the Church of England since 1969. The arguments of those opposed were based on the Bible and tradition: the apostles were male, St Paul had maintained the authority of the man in the home and the Church, it was against the practice of the universal Church, and it threatened the possibility of unity with the Roman

Catholic and Orthodox Churches. Supporters quoted St Paul's own words: "There is neither male nor female… you are all one in Christ". They saw their case as founded on Biblical principles and many women claimed a call to the priesthood. It was not until 1992 that the General Synod voted in favour. It had been a long struggle since the efforts of Maude Royden in the early twentieth century.

The Free Churches had shown a greater willingness to accept the ministry of women. The first woman minister in England had been in the Unitarian Church in Leicester in 1904. Other denominations followed, but women were slow to reach key positions. A notable exception was Pauline Webb, who became vice-president of the Methodist Conference in 1967 and who held office in several capacities in the World Council of Churches in the 1970s.

Another big issue concerned homosexuality. Since the late 1970s there have been debates in the General Synod, reports from the bishops on human sexuality and other publications. On one side of the debate are those who stand by a strict traditional interpretation of a few Biblical texts, while the liberal view contends that knowledge and understanding have moved on. The debate at the 1998 Lambeth Conference of Anglican bishops rejected homosexual practice as "incompatible with Scripture", though a sixth of the bishops present dissented or abstained from the final vote. The consecration of a gay bishop in America in 2003 and the blessing of same-sex unions in Canada intensified the debate. Discussion, reports and publications continue, and different perspectives are brought to bear on the issue, including that of human rights.

Developments in the Celtic countries in the latter

part of the twentieth century were as distinctive as their history would lead one to expect. In Scotland, as society became less dominated by the Churches, tensions between denominations were greatly reduced and there are many instances of cooperation at a local level. The Very Reverend Dr Craig, a Church of Scotland moderator and general secretary of the British Council of Churches, was a notable ecumenist. At St Mary's parish church at Haddington, the restored Lauderdale Aisle, with the Chapel of the Three Kings, became the focus of an annual ecumenical pilgrimage from Whitekirk to Haddington, which is a revival from earlier times drawing some two thousand people. In 2003 the Church of Scotland appointed its first woman moderator.

Much has changed in more populated areas, but places remain in the islands where Holy Communion is a twice-yearly event, lasting five days (three days of preparation beforehand and one day of thanksgiving after), where Gaelic is regularly used in worship, few hymns are sung and unaccompanied psalms still predominate.

The island of Iona and its community have played no small part in a widespread rediscovery of Celtic spirituality, with its sense of the sacredness of place, of the world of nature and its understanding of life as a journey. The abbey welcomes thousands of pilgrims each year, as day visitors and residential guests. Worship at the abbey is non-denominational and inclusive; its liturgy, its worship songs and chants are widely used. The members of the community, who come from diverse Christian traditions and places, renew their commitment each year to a spiritual discipline in their daily lives, to work for peace and justice in the world, and for healing and unity.

In Ireland, life in the north was dominated by the

troubles from the late 1960s until the beginning of a resolution in 1995. It created a complex and challenging situation for the Churches. It led to many courageous efforts by individual Christians and church congregations to rise above sectarian issues in order to bring about reconciliation and an end to violence.

One active player in this process was the Corrymeela Community, near Ballycastle in County Antrim. It was founded in 1965 by a Presbyterian minister, Dr Ray Davey, a former prisoner of war, and is open to all denominations. It became deeply involved in the movement for reconciliation. Its programmes brought together individuals from both religious communities and from different backgrounds, and achieved a greater measure of understanding. Its work on conflict resolution has had an international influence.

While Northern Ireland recovers from thirty years and more of violence, circumstances have changed in the South, where membership of the European Economic Community in 1973 not only brought foreign investment and economic expansion, it also created an increasingly multicultural society, which may, in time, make Catholic-Protestant tensions less significant. Society has become more secularised and old traditions have begun to fade. Even here, in a country where Roman Catholicism has been very much a part of national identity in the past, church allegiance has declined.

In the decades following World War II, the steepest decline in churchgoing in all the British Isles was in industrial Wales. The reduction of heavy industry led to the break-up of close communities and their cultural traditions. Many abandoned their allegiance to the chapels; numbers in Sunday schools decreased rapidly, and Sunday, once strictly observed, ceased to be a day apart. By the 1980s, decline was very clear in all the main denominations; only the Roman Catholics and smaller evangelical churches showed signs of growth. In 1974 many churches entered into a local Covenant for Unity and local ecumenical projects continue.

In the Anglican Church in Wales, more than seventy female deacons were ordained on the first occasion in the six Welsh cathedrals. The need was felt to make changes in its traditional worship, and the early years of the twenty-first century saw the emergence of a new Welsh Prayer Book. A new Welsh Bible was published on St David's Day in 2004, the 200th anniversary of the Bible Society.

There has been some recovery of the practice of pilgrimage to time-honoured venues such as St David's, Bardsey Island and Holywell, and there has been increased interest in ancient churches, which embody something evocative of the country's early Christian heritage.

In 2002 the archbishop of Wales, Dr Rowan Williams, a highly esteemed theologian and a poet-priest in a long tradition, became archbishop of Canterbury; the first Welshman to do so. Poetry has continued to be a well-developed expression of the Christian faith in Wales, like music, both characteristic gifts from Wales to British culture.

Other Faiths

The second half of the twentieth century had brought great changes to the composition of society through immigration. All the Christian Churches found themselves challenged by the presence of other faiths. Among them, Islam has the most adherents in Britain, mostly immigrants and their descendants, but also converts, and there are more than thirteen hundred mosques and prayer centres.

There are large concentrations of Muslims in Leicester and many northern cities, as well as in London. There are also significant numbers of Hindus, Sikhs and Buddhists. The Hindu temple at Neasden in north London has become the largest place of Hindu worship outside India. Churches have adopted many positive approaches to the new situation, based on respect and hospitality.

The Jewish community has been part of our society since the seventeenth century, though it expanded greatly in the twentieth century. The Chief Rabbi from 1991 to 2013, Jonathan Sachs, made a significant contribution to public debate, commending openness to others. The Council of Christians and Jews was founded in 1942 to foster good relations between the two faith bodies. The idea has been expanded in the Three Faiths Forum to include Muslims. St Ethelburga's in London has a centre for reconciliation and peace, and is one of many London venues for interfaith meetings. In 2011 there was a further development when a Hindu–Christian forum was launched. Throughout the country, contacts at a local level among faith leaders and lay people are opening up channels of communication and promoting better understanding, both in terms of what they have in common and what is distinctive in each faith.

Post 2000

As Churches embarked on the new millennium, they were committed to the need for different approaches. Phrases such as "fresh expressions of Church" and "pioneer ministries" indicate the wish to break out of confining structures and traditional ways of presenting the Christian faith, to meet people where they are and in ways they find relevant, whether in pub or club, at work, at school, or on the streets. Since 2003, when Street Pastors started their work, their numbers have grown to some eleven thousand in the United Kingdom.

There has been fresh thinking in the ecumenical movement, with less emphasis on structural unity, with its implicit threat of uniformity, and more on a unity that appreciates the diversity of traditions, and the insights and gifts of each one. This has led to more enthusiasm at grass-roots level and a greater sharing, both in mission and action through community projects. Diversity in worship may well be seen as an asset to the Church's mission, offering ample choice, from the joyful and informal worship of Charismatic churches to the more traditional and formal worship of cathedrals, and the many variations in between.

Cathedrals have developed a many-sided ministry that connects with the secular world at many points. Visitors come in large numbers to explore their cultural heritage, and are made welcome by guides, cafes and well-stocked bookstalls. There are special programmes for schools: themed days, craft activities and musical events. Talks, debates and concerts attract a variety of people. Increasing numbers are drawn to cathedral worship, some to the beauty of the liturgy in splendid surroundings and some content to worship anonymously: perhaps pleased to reconnect with the faith they once held, people who have never really given up on the idea of a spiritual reality behind our existence.

The established Church marked the start of the third millennium with a new service book, *Common Worship*, the culmination of a century's work on the liturgy, and a storehouse of past treasures and new approaches in worship. The Church has continued to engage with two divisive issues; one of these has been allowing female priests to become bishops, a matter resolved in 2014 when the General Synod gave its approval. The first female bishop in the British Isles had already been consecrated in the Church of Ireland earlier that year. Dealing with the other issue of homosexuality is still a work in progress. As the decade continues other gender issues have come to the forefront, among them the matter of same-sex marriage. Traditional teaching is challenged in all the Churches and threatens to divide the worldwide Anglican Communion in all its cultural diversity.

The year 2013 brought changes in Church leaders when Pope Benedict XVI was succeeded by Pope Francis, and Archbishop Rowan Williams by Archbishop Justin Welby. The cooperation already established under their predecessors continues, as does the third phase of the Anglican–Roman Catholic International Commission's dialogue.

Through the voluntary work of thousands of people, all the Churches respond to those in need at home and abroad. With the increasing levels of poverty in recent years, they have been particularly involved in running local food banks and establishing fair credit unions. Homelessness is high on the list of priorities and no group has been more faithfully involved in this work than the Salvation Army. Parish churches act as valued sources of emergency relief and care when public disasters strike. Many Christians are engaged with issues such as people-trafficking, the plight of refugees and asylum seekers, and with global warming. Concern for Third World countries has found expression through the widespread development of the Fairtrade movement, and initiatives such as Jubilee 2000 for debt relief, the Make Poverty History campaign and support for the Millennium Development Goals.

In spite of our largely materialistic culture, interest in

things spiritual is very evident. The large Christian summer festivals, such as Greenbelt, New Wine, Soul Survivor and Spring Harvest attract between twenty and forty thousand people each to varied programmes of music, talks, worship and relaxation. Almost two hundred thousand people attended an Alpha Course in 2007. Its influence continues, particularly among those aged fifteen to thirty-four. Individual churches are recognising the need for Christians to be well informed and able to account for the beliefs they hold at a time when the presence of other faiths has stimulated more open discussion of faith issues, which is further fuelled by the often aggressive contribution of atheists. The well-worn argument of whether God exists or not continues, but only willingness to engage with the life of faith and draw conclusions from the experience can resolve that issue.

The monasteries that played such a crucial role in the Christianisation of the British Isles and that saw a partial recovery through the Oxford Movement, still wield some influence. Some three million viewers chose to watch the TV series *The Monastery* and *The Convent*. Monastic life, through its personal discipline, its prayer life and worship, challenges a hyperactive world. Many people have found it helpful to share the life for short periods or to become associates of communities.

Just as in the early days of the Church when non-believers were drawn by the sincerity and commitment of the first Christians, in our secular times only these same qualities in worship and in daily living are likely to commend the Christian faith: a faith that is more than a moral code and more than social activism, but that has, at its core, a relationship with a power beyond ourselves.

The major renewal project at St Martin-in-the-Fields

is just one eloquent expression of the Church's confidence in its message and in its role in the nation's life. It is repeated in a local context throughout the country, not least in the heroic efforts of small rural congregations to maintain the presence of a church in the community – all in the conviction that what the Church stands for will lead to greater human flourishing in a society where justice, compassion and peace are sovereign, just as its founder taught.

Jesus may appear, in our time, to be a very counter-cultural figure – a man for others, unencumbered by possessions, valuing silence and time apart. Yet He still commands respect from many of the uncommitted, as well as the devotion of those who see Him as the supreme revelation of God. Sustained by the life of the Church in its many aspects, the committed try, however imperfectly, to reflect something of His teaching in their way of life, and to be faithful to the commission He gave his followers some two thousand years ago to bear witness to the whole world.

SELECTED BIBLIOGRAPHY

General Sources

Aston, M., *Monasteries* (Batsford 1993)

Chadwick, Henry, *The Early Church* (Penguin 1984)

Chadwick, Nora, *The Celts* (Penguin 1979)

Collingwood, R.G, and Myres, J.N.L., *Roman Britain and the English Settlements*, Oxford History of England (Clarendon Press 1937)

Jones, C., Wainwright, G. & Yarnold, E. (eds), *The Study of Liturgy* (SPCK 1989)

Laing, Lloyd, *Celtic Britain* (Granada 1981)

Latourette, K.S., *A History of Christianity* (Eyre & Spottiswood 1955)

Moorman, J.R.H., *History of the Church in England* (A & C Black 1967)

Orme, N., *Unity and Variety: A History of the Church in Devon and Cornwall* (Exeter University Press 1992)

Piggott, Stuart, *The Druids* (Penguin 1978)

Rowell, G. (ed.), *The English Religious Tradition and the Genius of Anglicanism* (Ikon 1992)

Stenton, Frank, *Anglo-Saxon England 550–1087*, Oxford History of England (Clarendon Press 1971)

THE STORY OF CHRISTIANITY IN THE BRITISH ISLES

Primary Sources
(Chapters I – VI)

Adamnan, *Life of Columba* (Clarendon Press 1991)

Bede, *A History of the English Church and People*, trans. L. Sherley-Price (Penguin 1968)

Fawtier, R. (ed.), Life of St Samson of Dol, trans. T. Taylor (SPCK 1925)

Gildas, *The Ruin of Britain*, trans. and ed. M. Winterbottom (Phillimore 1978)

Hood, A.B.E. (trans. and ed.), *St Patrick, His Writings and Muirchu's Life* (Phillimore 1978)

Nennius, *British History and Welsh Annals*, trans. and ed. J. Morris (Phillimore 1980)

Webb, J.F. (trans.), *Lives of the Saints* (Penguin 1981)

Secondary Sources
(Chapters I – VI)

Barley M.W. & Hanson R.P.C. (eds.), *Papers on Christianity in Britain 300–700* (Leicester University Press 1968)

Blair, P.H., *An Introduction to Anglo-Saxon England* (Cambridge University Press 1977)

Bowen, E.G., *Seaways and Settlements in the Celtic Lands* (Cardiff University Press 1977)

Bulloch, J., *The Life of the Celtic Church* (St Andrew Press 1963)

Chadwick, N., *The Age of the Saints in the Early Celtic Church* (OUP 1961)

Chadwick, N., *Studies in the Early British Church* (Cambridge University Press 1958)

Deanesley, M., The Pre-Conquest Church in England (A & C Black 1961)

Deanesley, M., Augustine of Canterbury (A & C Black 1964)

Dodd, E. & Heritage, T.C., *The Early Christians in Britain* (Longman 1966)

Ellis, P.B., *Celtic Inheritance* (Muller 1985)

Ellis, P.B., *The Cornish Saints* (Redruth: Tor Mark Press 1998)

Fisher, D.J.V., The Anglo-Saxon Age (Longman 1976)

Gallyon, M., The Early Church in East England (Dalton 1973)

Gallyon, M., The Early Church in Wessex and Mercia (Dalton 1980)

Kirby, D.P., The Making of Early England (Batsford 1967)

Kylie, E. (ed. and trans.), *English Correspondence of Boniface* (A & C Black 1966)

Leatham, D., *Celtic Sunrise: An Outline of Celtic Christianity* (Hodder & Stoughton 1951)

Mayr-Harting, H., *The Coming of Christianity to Anglo-Saxon England* (Batsford 1972)

McNeill, J.T., *The Celtic Churches: A History AD 200–1200* (University of Chicago Press 1974)

Rees, B.R., *Pelagius: a Reluctant Heretic* (Woodbridge 1988)

Richards, J.D., *Viking Age England* (English Heritage 1991)

Thomas, Charles, *Christianity in Roman Britain to AD 500* (Batsford 1981)

Warren, F.E., *The Liturgy and Ritual of the Celtic Church* (Clarendon Press 1881)

Chapter VII

Barlow, F., *The English Church 1000–1066* (Longman 1963)

Barlow, F., *The English Church 1066–1154* (Longman 1979)

Clover, H. & Gibson M. (eds. and trans.), *Letters of Lanfranc* (Clarendon Press 1979)

Eadmer, *History of Recent Events in England* (Cresset Press 1964)

Gibson, M., *Lanfranc of Bec* (Clarendon Press 1978)

Knowles, D., *Religious Orders in England Vol 1* (CUP 1948)

Loyn, H.R., *Anglo-Saxon England and the Norman Conquest* (Longman 1962)

Moorman, J.R.H., *Church Life in England in the Thirteenth Century* (CUP 1945)

Southern, R.W., *Western Society and the Church in the Middle Ages* (Penguin 1970)

Thorpe, L. (trans. and ed.) *Gerald of Wales, the Journey through Wales* (Penguin 1978)

Chapter VIII

Aston, Margaret, *Lollards and Reformers* (Hambledon Press 1984)

Chaucer, Geoffrey, *Prologue to the Canterbury Tales* (Dent 1958)

Julian, Fr J. (ed. and trans.), *Revelations of Julian of Norwich* (Darton Longman & Todd 1988)

Kenny, A., *Wyclif* (Oxford University Press 1985)

Langland, W., *Piers the Plowman*, trans. J.F. Goodridge (Penguin 1980 reprint)

Manning, B.L., *The People's Faith in the Time of Wyclif* (Harvester Press 2nd ed. 1975)

Underhill, E., *The Mystics of the Church* (J. Clarke & Co 1925)

Upjohn, S., *In Search of Julian of Norwich* (Darton Longman & Todd 1989)

Chapter IX

Assoc. W. Allen, Three Centuries of an English Presence at Douai [*Trois Siecles de Presence Anglaise a Douai*]

(Archives Municipales de Douai)

Boehmer, H., *Luther and the Reformation* (Bell 1930)

Bouyer, L., *Spirit and Forms of Protestantism*, trans. A.V. Littledale (Collins 1963)

Chadwick, O., *The Reformation* (Penguin 1990)

Dickens, A.G., *The English Reformation* (Batsford 1989ed.)

Duffy, E., *The Stripping of the Altars* (Yale University Press 1992)

Duffy, E., *The Voices of Morebath* (Yale University Press 2001)

MacCulloch, D., *Tudor Church Militant* (Penguin 1999)

McNeill, J.T., *The History and Character of Calvinism* (OUP 1954)

Wendel, F., *Calvin* (Collins 1963)

Chapter X

Cragg, G.R., *The Church and the Age of Reason 1648–1789* (Penguin 1990 ed.)

Hutton, W.H., *John Bunyan* (Hodder & Stoughton 1927)

Houghton, E., *Christian Hymnwriters* (Evang. Press of Wales 1982)

Nicolson, A., *Power and Glory (Jacobean England and the Making of the King James Bible)* (Harper Collins 2003)

Chapter XI

Balleine, G.R., *History of the Evangelical Party in the Church of England* (Longman 1933)

Bebbington, D., *Victorian Nonconformity* (Bangor: Headstart History 1992)

Church, R.W., *The Oxford Movement* (Macmillan 1909)

Cragg, G.R., *The Church and the Age of Reason 1648–1789* (Penguin 1990 ed.)

Crowther, M.A., *Church Embattled* (Archon USA 1970)

Gilbert, A.D., *Religion and Society in Industrial England 1740–1914* (Longman 1976)

Howse, E.M., *Saints in Politics* (Allen & Unwin 1953)

Norman, E., *The English Catholic Church in the Nineteenth Century* (Clarendon Press 1984)

Reardon, B.M.G., *Religious Thought in the Victorian Age* (Longman 1980)

Rowell, G., ed., *Tradition Renewed: The Oxford Movement Conference Papers* (Pickwick Publications US 1986)

Sellers, I., *Nineteenth-Century Nonconformity* (Edward Arnold 1977)

Vidler, A., *The Church in an Age of Revolution* (Penguin 1974 ed.)

Watts, M., *The Dissenters* (Clarendon Press 1928)

Chapter XII

Hastings, A., *A History of English Christianity 1920–1990* (SCM Press 1991)

Jenkins, D., *The Calling of a Cuckoo* (Continuum 2002)

Kloosterman, A.M.J., *Contemporary Catholicism* (Collins 1972)

Rosman, D., *The Evolution of English Churches* (CUP 2003)

Ramsey, M., *Image Old and New* (SPCK 1963)

Robinson, J.A.T., *Honest to God* (SCM Press 1963)

Vidler, A., *The Church in an Age of Revolution* (Penguin 1974 ed.)

Wales

Hughes, T.J., *Wales's Best 100 Churches* (Seren 2006)

Victory, S., *The Celtic Church in Wales* (SPCK 1977)

Walker, D. (ed.), *A History of the Church in Wales* (Church in Wales Publications 1976)

Williams, G., *The Welsh Church from the Conquest to the*

Reformation (University of Wales Press 1976)

Williams, G., *The Welsh and their Religion* (University of Wales Press 1991)

Scotland

Burleigh, J.H.S., *A Church History of Scotland* (OUP 1960)

Donaldson, G., *Scotland: Church and Nation through Sixteen Centuries* (SCM 1960)

Fawcett, R., *Scottish Abbeys and Priories* (Batsford 1994)

Killeen, R., *A Short History of Scotland* (Gill & MacMillan 1998)

Knox, J., *A Quatercentenary Reappraisal: Lectures,* ed. D. Shaw (Saint Andrew Press 1975)

MacLean, C., *Going to Church* (National Museum of Scotland 1997)

Torvill, E.S., *The Saints of Scotland* (St Andrew Press 1983)

Watson, F., *Scotland A History 800 BC – AD 2000* (Tempus 2001)

Ireland

Corish, P., *The Irish Catholic Experience* (Gill & Macmillan 1985)

Hughes, K., *Church and Society in Ireland AD 400–1200* (Variorum, London 1987)

Hughes, K. & Hamlin, A., *The Modern Traveller to the Early Irish Church* (SPCK 1977)

de Paor, M. & de Paor, L., *Early Christian Ireland* (Thames & Hudson 1958)

Architecture

Brook, C. & Andrews, S. (eds.), *The Victorian Church* (Manchester University Press 1995)

Clapham, A. W., *English Romanesque Architecture*

(Clarendon Press 1930)

Hutton, G. & Cook, O., *English Parish Churches* (Thames and Hudson 1989)

Jenkins, S., *England's 1000 Best Churches* (Penguin Press 1999)

Kerr, N. & M., *A Guide to Anglo-Saxon Sites* (Granada Publishing Ltd 1982)

Scotland's Churches Scheme, *1,000 Churches to Visit in Scotland* (National Museums of Scotland 2005)

Poetry

Bradley, S.A.J. (ed. and trans.), *Anglo-Saxon Poetry* (Dent 1982)

Davies, O. & Bowie, F., *Celtic Christian Spirituality* (SPCK 1995)

Hamer, R., *Choice of Anglo-Saxon Verse* (Faber & Faber 1970)

Watts, Murray (compiler), *The Wisdom of Saint Columba of Iona* (Lion Publishing 1997)